GERMANY'S OSTPOLITIK

The Royal Institute of International Affairs is an unofficial body which promotes the scientific study of international questions and does not express opinions of its own. The opinions expressed in this publication are the responsibility of the author.

The Institute gratefully acknowledges the comments and suggestions of the following who read the manuscript on behalf of the Research Committee: Geoffrey Stern and Dr W. E. Paterson.

GERMANY'S OSTPOLITIK

Relations between the Federal Republic and
the Warsaw Pact Countries

Lawrence L. Whetten

Published for

THE ROYAL INSTITUTE OF
INTERNATIONAL AFFAIRS

by

OXFORD UNIVERSITY PRESS
LONDON OXFORD NEW YORK

1971

Oxford University Press

LONDON   OXFORD   NEW YORK

GLASGOW   TORONTO   MELBOURNE   WELLINGTON

CAPE TOWN   IBADAN   NAIROBI   DAR ES SALAAM   LUSAKA   ADDIS ABABA

DELHI   BOMBAY   CALCUTTA   MADRAS   KARACHI   LAHORE   DACCA

KUALA LUMPUR   SINGAPORE   HONG KONG   TOKYO

ISBN 0 19 285051 2

© Royal Institute of International Affairs 1971

First published as an Oxford University Press paperback
by Oxford University Press, London, 1971

Printed in Great Britain by
The Eastern Press Limited, London and Reading

To my parents

CONTENTS

ACKNOWLEDGEMENT

MATERIALS for this book have been collected during the author's seven-year residence in Germany. Publication of this book, however, is in large part due to the encouragement and assistance provided by the staff and facilities of Chatham House. The author is particularly indebted to Hermia Oliver and Katharine Duff for invaluable editorial assistance, to Margaret Cornell for patient counselling and to Dr Roger Morgan for perceptive and instructive insight.

April 1971

ABBREVIATIONS

ADN	East German News Service
Bull.	Federal Republic, Press Information Agency, *Bulletin.**
CDSP	*Current Digest of the Soviet Press*
CDU	Christlich-Demokratische Union (Christian Democrats)
Comecon	Council for Mutual Economic Assistance
CSU	Christlich-Soziale Union (Bavarian wing of CDU)
DPA	Deutsche Presse-Agentur
DSB	*Department of State Bulletin*
E-A	*Europa-Archiv*
Euratom	European Atomic Energy Community
FAZ	*Frankfurter Allgemeine Zeitung*
FDP	Freie Demokratische Partei (Liberals)
GDR	German Democratic Republic
IAEA	International Atomic Energy Authority
ICBM	Intercontinental ballistic missile
MLF	Multilateral Nuclear Force
ND	*Neues Deutschland*
NPD	Nazionaldemokratische Partei Deutschlands (National Democrats—extreme right)
NPT	Non-Proliferation Treaty
PCC	Political Consultative Committee (Warsaw Pact)
RFE	Radio Free Europe
Rom.	*Documents, Articles and Information in Romania* (Agerpres)
SALT	Strategic arms limitation talks
SED	Sozialistische Einheitspartei Deutschlands (Communist Party, GDR)
SPD	Sozialdemokratische Partei Deutschlands (Social Democrats)
SWB	*Summary of World Broadcasts* (BBC)
SZ	*Süddeutsche Zeitung*

* References are to the English version unless otherwise indicated.

1
INTRODUCTION

THE German problem remains after two decades of attempted reconciliation the most controversial international problem in Europe and the principal source of regional tensions. The German issue can be defined as the proper geographical location for the German peoples in the established world order, the types of social institutions they should adopt, their relations with external powers, the dimensions of their international political aspirations, and the degree of influence they should exercise over the course of European developments. During the 1950s the several interested parties viewed a solution in terms which included the following elements: self-determination, free elections, mutual recognition of prerogatives and spheres of influence, and German neutrality. The prospects for accommodation were dim because of the degree of divergence between East–West policy positions on these proposals.

Only minor progress was registered in 1955 when the Austrian State Treaty was signed and Bonn and Moscow exchanged ambassadors after Chancellor Adenauer's visit to the Soviet Union. After this timid initial opening, however, each side reverted to a policy of strength through integration and consolidation of its position within its respective military alliance. The unrest in Eastern Europe during the late 1950s forced Moscow to focus increasingly on internal Pact problems, rather than on the basis for a durable solution to the region's main source of tension. Indeed, Moscow viewed the German and Berlin issues at that time as a major source of provocative actions. The November 1958 ultimatum, demanding Western endorsement of Soviet terms for a German settlement, was intended to eliminate this irritation by securing West German recognition of the Soviet presence on the Elbe as the essential precondition for a permanent settlement of the German problem. Both the Soviet terms and presence, however, were objectionable to West Germany and her allies. After the cautious opening in 1955, then, Soviet assertive moves in 1958 introduced the final stages of the cold war in West German–East European relations; a climate that persisted for nearly a decade.

In the mid-1960s minuscule progress was noted in the loosening of the intransigent positions of both sides, gradually followed by more substantial policy modifications. Between 1968 and 1971 the most significant changes in relations between the states in Central Europe in the past quarter-century marked the beginning of a possible normalization process. A number of factors and influences contributed to these developments; events that startled a world accustomed to view Central European affairs through polarized cold-war spectacles. Probably the most important single influence was the achievement of strategic parity between the two super-powers. The eradication of the final vestiges of American assured deterrence destroyed the quarter-century-old precedents and policy framework of East–West relations and provided no mutually acceptable alternative guidelines. American strategic resources have been firmly confined to use in only the most ' unthinkable ' circumstances and, accordingly, regional forces have been allotted an importance for the defence of local interests unprecedented in the atomic age. By neutralizing strategic resources, a new power asymmetry has developed in Central Europe strongly favouring the Soviet Union. Thus not only have relations between the two super-powers been affected in an unpredictable manner, but the modality and context of future relationships between great and small states have also been drastically altered. For these reasons West German–East European relations at the beginning of the 1970s may provide valuable keys for assessing the role of Europe in world affairs over the next decade and its function in the broader international *détente*.

With the value of hindsight, it is apparent that the Soviet Union launched her programme for achieving parity and calculated its impact several years before her decision was perceived in the West. In the light of this anticipated position of unprecedented strength, Moscow's German policy and relations with its allies during 1965 and 1968 take on a new perspective. But in order to exploit fully both the expected advantages and uncertainties in this unique power relationship, Moscow needed the political solidarity of its allies. Its objective of consensus, viewed by many East Europeans as an instrument for Soviet policy centralization, became a major contentious point within Warsaw Pact councils. The alleged West German ' threat ' and appropriate regional security measures were the chief points of dispute. The ' northern tier ' countries—the GDR, Poland, Czechoslovakia, and the Soviet Union—regarded security as a function of West German renunciation of territorial claims and recognition of the inviolability of the borders in Eastern Europe. The Soviet Union, in particular, tended to view security in terms of regional political stability. Accordingly, Moscow made a series of important concessions to its partners' interests in security matters; it first acceded to the idea of an all-European security conference and then agreed to a greater priority for bilateral negotiations on national grievances against the Federal Republic. The adjustments within the Pact were prerequisites for the gradual accommodation with West Germany noted in 1969 and 1970.

Rumania played a highly provocative role in this transition, not only for her own national advantages but also for the advancement of her views of regional normalization. Rumania led the dissident elements with demands for greater representation in regional matters and autonomy in national policies that soon polarized the East Europeans. Rumania chose the issue of Soviet-sponsored schemes for economic integration as the first target in her campaign to counter Soviet hegemony. Because arguments were advanced which aligned the more industrial against the largely agrarian Pact members, a virtual ' cold war ' developed between East Germany and Rumania which chilled relations throughout the decade. After ' winning ' the round on economic integration, Rumania concentrated her assertive policies on the Sino-Soviet dispute and inter-party affairs, gaining reluctant acceptance by Moscow of her stature as a spokesman for smaller nations. By 1966, however, Bucharest felt compelled to focus its attention sharply on European developments. Moscow revealed to its allies the plan for nuclear parity and the expected political profits. Rumania foresaw that this programme would seriously imbalance the existing power relationships in Europe and launched an intensive campaign against military blocs and proposals for force modernization. Unable to block or delay the scheduled missile construction programme, Rumania succeeded in postponing major improvements within the Pact itself and shifted attention from military preparedness to the nature of the alleged external threat. In 1967 she created a major breach in socialist solidarity and Pact discipline by adopting a two-Germanies policy and establishing diplomatic relations with West Germany. By recognizing the Federal Republic as a friendly state, Rumania seriously deflated her allies' charges that Bonn's ' revanchist ' claims against Eastern Europe were the ' main threat ' to European security, and raised serious reservations for them about her reliability in the event of increased East–West tensions or hostilities. Rumania's unswerving defence of her two-Germanies policy as a demonstration of her autonomy and the urgent need for acceptance of mutually agreed principles for proper socialist behaviour eventually forced her allies to adjust their policies along lines advocated by Bucharest. Due in large part to this Rumanian defiance on the German issue and the subsequent acquiescence of Pact members, Eastern Europe will not be the same phenomenon in the next decade that it has been in the last two; its cohesion has been weakened, its external interests have been magnified, and its inner relationships have been compounded.

The role of West Germany in the transition in Central European affairs is more difficult to plot. German-Soviet relations must be viewed from the perspective of the centuries-old love-hate relationship that has characterized views in both countries. Russia's traditional xenophobic anxieties about the outside world or about alien ideologies that allegedly threatened her perspective of the established order are well known. After the collapse of nineteenth-century Europe the stature of Russia as a European power was not immediately enhanced by the sentiments associated with world revolution. The harsh terms imposed by Germany on the revolutionary regime and its confinement in 1919 by a hostile coalition to the perimeters of Muscovy left the indelible impression on successive Soviet leaders that the Soviet Union had survived by the smallest margin and that future security required ' 300 per cent ' assurance of co-operation or subjugation of the chief Western threat—Germany. At the outset, the Bolsheviks viewed the durability of their revolution as a function of a successful socialist revolution in industrialized Germany and later as a product of mutual economic co-operation. Thanks to the Soviet purges, Germany gained substantially more from the secret military collaboration conducted between the two countries from approximately 1920 to 1933, yet she destroyed the ' Rapallo spirit ' and later abrogated the 1939 non-aggression pact. The Soviet Union emerged from the Great Patriotic War convinced that Germany must never again rise to the position of a dominant power. While she has often manipulated the reportedly persisting ' German menace ' to advance other national objectives, Soviet anxieties have been sufficiently deep-seated for her to insist upon recognition of the division of Germany as the precondition for *détente*.[1]

During the inter-war years, Germany adopted a policy of securing acceptance and respectability with her Western neighbours, while pursuing a policy of manipulation and pressure in Eastern Europe. The chief threat to her at the time was in the West, but the means for enhancing her stature as a world power was in the East. In the immediate post-World War II era, Bonn again stressed Western integration and national reconstruction, while opposing the partition of Germany. Its tactics for challenging the division, however, resulted in the confirmation of the *status quo*. Germany's claims in Eastern Europe were actively maintained, subject to the Potsdam Agreement and a final peace treaty. The defence of these claims was to be assured by establishing a position of strength from which the eventual negotiation could be favourably resolved. At that time Bonn regarded the normalization of relations as a consequence of solving the German problem on its terms.

In December 1967 the Grand Coalition inaugurated a new policy position. Normalization was no longer considered a function of, but a precondition for, durable *détente*. In revising its former hard line, Bonn still calculated that Moscow

[1] See for example Walter Laqueur, *Russia and Germany: a Century of Conflict* (1969); Gerhard L. Weinberg, *Germany and the Soviet Union* (1954); F. R. Allemann, *Bonn ist nicht Weimar* (1959); W. Hubatsch, ed., *Die deutsche Frage* (1961); Elizabeth Wiskemann, *Germany's Eastern Neighbours* (1956); Walter Ulbricht, *Zur Geschichte der deutschen Arbeiterbewegung* (1954).

was the principal obstacle to relaxing tensions. Accordingly, the Federal Republic opened a campaign of adjustment with the East Europeans, initially Rumania. In concert with French and later American ' bridge-building' programmes, Bonn estimated that economic and political inroads into Eastern Europe would induce a more pliable Soviet position, especially if they were accompanied by lucrative incentives. The Czechoslovak crisis, however, demonstrated the limits of this approach. No important modifications could be expected in Eastern Europe until fundamental changes were first introduced in Moscow. Further, the Soviet Union would not tolerate concessions by the East Europeans at the expense of her strategic interests. While states like Rumania and later East Germany could introduce provocative new concepts into Pact deliberations, the pace and direction of East European accommodation with the West was still firmly controlled by the Soviet Union. Accordingly, any attempt to influence these changes by West Germany would have to be directed first at the Soviet Union and then at the East Europeans.

West Germany conducted her sixth national election in the autumn of 1969, primarily on the issues of *Ostpolitik* and *Deutschlandpolitik* (policies towards Eastern Europe and all Germany). The results provided a thin parliamentary margin for an SDP–FDP coalition, which interpreted the election as a strong mandate to seek new terms for an adjustment with the East. Accordingly, Chancellor Willy Brandt opened discussions with Eastern Europe on an unprecedented range of issues, and eventually modified Bonn's traditional position to such an extent that formal negotiations with the Soviet Union and Poland resulted in treaties resolving outstanding differences. In the process, the East Europeans made important concessions, but Brandt renounced Germany's position towards the East (maintained since Stresemann) by abandoning territorial claims east of the Oder–Neisse line and forgoing the expectation of gaining stature at Eastern Europe's expense. This represented a policy change of historic importance whose favourable impact on East–West relations has been only partly compromised by the growing intransigence of East Germany. With each West German concession to East European terms,

the questions of East Germany and Berlin loomed proportionally larger as the overriding obstacles to genuine accord. Bonn's
adjustment with the East Europeans only diminished tensions
and contributed little to the solution of the German problem.
Thus the limited success of the *Ostpolitik* has been diluted by
the continuing failure of Bonn's *Deutschlandpolitik*.

Bonn's *Ostpolitik*, then, resulted in an acknowledged reduction in tensions with Eastern Europe that unintentionally increased the danger and tensions with East Germany. This
paradoxical development in European developments places the
German problem back in the larger context of the East–West
global perspective. The roots of the changing power relations
within Eastern Europe that allowed both adjustments and
checks can be traced to the Cuban missile crisis, the Sino-
Soviet rift, the rise of polycentrism, the contraction of Soviet
interest in far-flung national-liberation movements and the
concentration of Soviet diplomacy in nearer regions, the
achievement of strategic parity, American preoccupation with
Asian affairs, and the creeping malaise in NATO solidarity.
The cumulative effect of these factors on both Soviet and American leadership has been to curtail their international authority
and to open new areas of competition, such as the Middle East,
lacking historical precedents and guidelines. The Soviet Union
may have foreseen the implications of these developments before the United States or other Western states. She apparently
formulated a programme whereby her partners could bilaterally
pursue their respective national grievances against West
Germany, within the confines of mutual consultations, in
return for unfettered latitude in the conduct of policy relating
primarily to great-power problems such as the SALT talks
(which began in November 1969) and the Middle East. It is
not clear whether the premises of the plan were the Brezhnev
Doctrine of limited socialist sovereignty or an adaptation of
Western coalition politics. (As only partial evidence, no East
European group or government has voiced even guarded
criticism of the unprecedentedly active Soviet participation in
the defence of the UAR. In contrast, East European reactions
to Soviet involvement in the 1967 Middle East crisis started a
public debate that eventually overthrew the Czechoslovak

leadership, precipitated a major purge of Poland's hierarchy, added fuel for Rumania's defiant stand, and even prompted Tito to make his first official visit to Moscow.) The result of this new tacit relationship among Pact members is that within mutually defined limits or on specifically designated issues, such as the Oder–Neisse border, a much greater degree of autonomy is now exercised by the respective national authorities. Thus it is now possible for East Germany to act virtually as independently as has Rumania for the last ten years. It is on this basis, then, that some East European states can accommodate Bonn's overtures and East Germany can confidently repel them, a phenomenon that is only slowly being recognized in West Germany.

It is too early to predict accurately the long-term implications of the changing nature of power relations in Central Europe. The purpose of this book is not to establish guidelines or models for predicting behaviour. Rather it is to trace the transition in West German relations with the Warsaw Pact countries by examining the positions of the principal states on the key divisive issues of the previous two decades: the ' German threat ', regional stability, collective security, and political accommodation. Its scope will be confined to those factors that exercised the greatest influence over the gradual evolution of the respective parties' policies. It is recognized at the outset that a basic asymmetry exists in the sources of policy among the various parties. For example, a stronger link exists between West German public expectations and the formation and conduct of Bonn's foreign policy than is present in the Soviet Union. Yet Moscow's German policy is shaped in no small manner by the attitudes of its allies, while Bonn's *Ostpolitik* reflects only partial NATO influence. It is hoped that the reconstruction of recent events in Central Europe will contribute to generalizations relevant to the broader aspects of *détente* policy.

2

THE GERMAN THREAT IN
HISTORICAL PERSPECTIVE

SINCE World War II, Germany has traditionally been the principal link between the NATO and Warsaw Pact countries, sometimes a barrier, sometimes the bond between them. The national aspirations of both Germanies have been profound and complex examples of the correlation between public aspirations and foreign policy. These aims have been at once key cohesive and divisive factors in both halves of Europe, since the Germans on both sides of the Elbe still regarded partition as temporary.

The unity of the wartime allies split irreparably over the issue of Germany, with France seeking dismemberment for defensive purposes and the Soviet Union demanding a unitary government as an implement for her expansionist policy. The chill of the cold war forced the Western allies to close ranks and, for their own protection, to create a West German political entity in a Western likeness, while preserving the ultimate goals of reunification and self-determination. The tentative nature of these arrangements is the main reason why ' the German problem ' has been a repeated source of international tensions and crises for Germany's neighbours and defenders. In no other instance during the past quarter-century have local interests had such a decisive impact on international developments and national priorities of other nations—a rare distinction for the German people.

When Soviet expansion beyond Central Europe was blocked, Moscow concentrated on the consolidation and the sovietization of Eastern Europe, using deep-seated fears of German territorial claims, and centuries of political domination, as an important inducement for accepting Soviet protection. Since both East and West held opposing objectives in trans-Elbian affairs, it is essential at the outset of an analysis of recent Central European diplomacy to assess the Eastern Europeans' estimate of the historical German threat to their present national interests, and its manipulation as a policy instrument. In other words,

9

whether the menace of a divided nation is contrived or real, or to what degree persisting German territorial claims have served as a bond among Eastern Europeans. To what extent were the history of German domination and the existing territorial claims to the ' lost ' territories a justifiable foundation for East European security arrangements and Soviet priorities on regional stability? If an adjustment in West German demands were conceivable, would the Eastern Europeans respond with sincere attempts to normalize relations with Bonn? Thus the contribution of the German threat to the East–West barrier is an appropriate point of departure in an examination of the German role as a common bond in Central Europe.

East European apprehensions of Germany are based on a long history of expansionism at their expense. Although German concern with East European affairs dates back many centuries, the most consistent policies emerged after the national state was founded. This era was opened when Bismarck sought to stabilize Central Europe by defeating first Austria and then France, and consolidating German unity under the security of an alliance with England and Russia. Many West German scholars now concede, however, that this policy was ultimately unsuccessful, primarily because no major political party at that time could conceive of security and peace without decisive influence in Alsace-Lorraine and Belgium in the West, and also annexations or hegemony in Eastern Europe.[1] The pursuit of these goals contributed to the formation of the encircling world coalition that defeated Germany in 1918 but failed to divert her Eastern aspirations or solve the German problem to the satisfaction of her neighbours.

After World War I the leading German statesman, Gustav Stresemann, established the framework for German foreign policy that prevailed for over forty years. He stressed reconciliation, respectability, and security systems with the West but left the Eastern policy intentionally ambiguous. It was characterized by vague statements renouncing the use of force, as well as by broad irredentist claims and hostile propaganda about national self-determination. Stresemann secured Ger-

[1] Fritz Fischer, *Germany's Aims in the First World War* (1969).

many's western flank with the Locarno Pact of 1925 and then prepared diplomatic démarches against Poland and Czechoslovakia. Hitler later implemented a similar strategy with more vigorous diplomatic and military campaigns which again resulted in defeat and failure to provide a universally approved formula for Germany's future.

West Germany's Eastern policy after World War II bore certain similarities to these earlier patterns. Faced with the realities of the permanent Soviet presence in the heart of Europe and the urgency for reconstruction, Konrad Adenauer placed a higher priority on gaining respectability and integration into Western institutions than on the reunification of Germany. These policies proved so successful that West Germany became the strongest European industrial nation and a bulwark of Western Europe's military, economic, and political organizations, but the very degree of success became a source of apprehension and tension.

The Soviet Union realized that such close German identification with the West could restrict Soviet influence to the east bank of the Elbe and accordingly sought to entice West Germany back into her traditional central position between Eastern and Western Europe. Reunification under some form of guaranteed arms limitation was apparently regarded as an acceptable price for blocking West German rearmament and permanent integration into the Western alliance. Moscow made qualified concessions to Bonn's demands for self-determination during the early 1950s, but soon retracted them. West Germany's subsequent entry into NATO and the 1956 upheavals in Eastern Europe forced the Kremlin to entrench along the entire length of the iron curtain.

Correspondingly, Adenauer adopted an even harder, more hostile policy towards the Warsaw Pact countries than Stresemann. While German policy planners in the inter-war period regarded Eastern Europe as the most lucrative region for enhancing Berlin's international status, post-World War II Germany maintained important claims to territory administered by communist regimes. One-quarter, or 40,000 square miles, of the former Reich was awarded by the Potsdam Agreement to Poland pending final settlement in a peace treaty. The Soviet

Union received important sections of East Prussia and the key Baltic port of Königsberg. The Federal Republic maintained large indemnity claims against Prague resulting from the expulsion of 3.25 m. Sudeten Germans. Finally, Bonn refused to recognize the legitimacy of the communist rule in East Germany, insisting on its claims to represent all Germans. The cumulative impact of these claims was that the Federal Republic had far larger grievances against the East Europeans than had the Reich under Stresemann.

To reinforce these claims, Adenauer insisted that any move towards relaxing tensions in Central Europe must be matched by a complementary move towards reunification on the basis of self-determination. Normalization of relations was equated with free elections. This theory of ' maintained tensions ' was reinforced by the Hallstein Doctrine, which prohibited diplomatic relations with states which recognize the GDR.

The doctrine was designed to isolate the GDR and to demonstrate that Soviet advantages held there were also diplomatic liabilities that could profitably be relinquished.

This was a policy of strength, fully endorsed by Bonn's allies. It was argued that only a firmly held position of superiority could induce the Soviet Union to relax her stand. Accordingly, no modifications could be accepted to the formula of establishing a unitary state through German self-determination. And integration with, and consolidation in, the West were viewed as instruments for strengthening Bonn's leverage against Moscow and East Berlin. This inflexible policy was reinforced by the moral certitude of the ' free world ' and American assured strategic deterrence.

The Soviet Union responded to this tough line by maintaining that the foriegn-policy objectives of the Federal Republic under Adenauer were fundamentally the same as those of Germany before World War I and during the interwar period, and that Germany had pursued a concerted expansionist policy towards the East for over a century. Moscow seized upon an alleged proclamation by Adenauer to liberate the lost territories to emphasize the first axiom of Soviet policy on Germany: ' It has always been the objective of Bonn's foreign policy to annul the results of the Second World War and to change the post-war territorial *status quo* in Europe ', and it was their aim to prevent such alterations.[2]

Moscow identified seven key elements in Adenauer's ' liberation campaign ' which it feared could inject instability into Eastern Europe through ' political and ideological subversion '. First, according to this argument, the Germans would advance by small steps towards their goals: reunification on Bonn's terms, i.e. annexation of the GDR, restoration of Germany's 1937 frontiers, and the return of Germans expelled from Czechoslovakia. ' These aims are allegedly based on international law and the right of self-determination.' Secondly, they would steadily reinforce military power as the principal instrument of foreign policy, including the acquisition of nuclear weapons. Thirdly, Bonn would reinforce the military-political alliance with the United States while strengthening its own relative weight and leading position. Fourthly, it would seek to extend its position in Western Europe through more intensive integration in West European organizations until it would be strong enough, by virtue of its economic superiority, openly to proclaim its supremacy. Fifthly, the Federal Republic would expand all alliance systems in order to gain increased security, while seeking greater unilateral freedom of action. This might be demonstrated periodically by provoking a military venture intended to involve foreign forces. Sixthly, to placate Eastern fears, the Germans would proclaim that their intentions to alter the *status quo* were confined to ' peaceful means ', through ' renunciation of force ', and by ' peaceful accommodation '. Finally, the Germans would vigorously resist every measure designed to relieve tensions and speed disarmament (such as the NPT) and would continue to wave the ' bloody red flag ' of Soviet danger.[3]

Under the threat of this ' liberation campaign ', the Soviet Union accelerated her programme to stabilize political life in Central Europe and to consolidate her position east of the Elbe. She proposed in 1958 that a general German peace treaty be signed by all belligerents, guaranteeing the *status quo* and the existence of the three German political entities: the Federal

---

[2] Josef Schleifstein, ' Bonn Foreign Policy—Legend and Reality ', *World Marxist R.*, May 1967, p. 11.   [3] Ibid., pp. 11–14.

Republic, the GDR, and West Berlin. Implicit in this proposal was either the continued presence of Soviet troops in the GDR or the right to intervene unilaterally at Moscow's discretion. This proposition was unanimously rejected by the West, because of both its strategic and political implications. Accordingly, the Soviet Union threatened to legalize the existing situation by negotiating a separate peace treaty with the GDR. She subsequently dropped this demand, but the construction of the Berlin Wall in August 1961 recorded the determination of the Soviet Union and the GDR to preserve the *status quo* and contain Western influence.[4]

The construction of the Wall indicated the gravity of the Soviet commitment to two separate Germanies. Moscow probably abandoned any hope of securing dominant influence in a unitary state after the June 1953 revolt in East Germany. This demonstration of the insecurity of the East German Communist Party (the SED) forced the Soviet Union to forgo her ultimate strategic aspirations in West Germany and to consolidate her holdings in the GDR. The construction of the Wall was a crucial step in her consolidation efforts; it physically divided Germany and confirmed that both the United States and the Soviet Union had a vital interest in preserving the viability of their respective spheres, but not in the liberation of the other sphere. The US response of strengthening her conventional forces in Europe rather than employing nuclear coercion was widely regarded by the West Europeans as an irrelevant reaction and a clear indication of the value she attached to reunification.

At the 1963 SED Congress Khrushchev underlined the change in emphasis, when he stated that by adopting ' defensive measures ' in Berlin the problem of a general German peace treaty had lost its importance. This reasoning opened wider tactical options in pursuit of Soviet objectives west of the Elbe, i.e. to reverse the integration of the Federal Republic into the West and through a policy of limited accommodation to encourage her return to the historical central position formerly held by Germany. The Soviet Union hoped thereby to make West Germany more susceptible to Eastern influence without

[4] J. M. Schick, in *Orbis*, viii/4, Winter 1965, pp. 816–31.

upsetting the existing European power equation, whereby each bloc held hostage the opponent's forces across the Elbe. Accordingly, the Soviet Union entered into negotiations with the Western powers on major accords related to global security, including the Moscow–Washington hot line and the nuclear test ban, and explored the utility of opening a direct dialogue with Bonn through Khrushchev's personal envoy, Alexei Adzhubei.

Coincidental with the Soviet endorsement of accommodation was a growing awareness in West Germany that a prerequisite for regaining the initiative on the German problem was the abandonment of the policy of 'maintained tensions'. The philosopher Karl Jaspers was the first to perceive that the Wall had forced Bonn to alter the priorities of its German policy. In a book criticizing the entire structure of this policy he called for the abandonment of the programme for reunification through the establishment of common institutions. He proposed instead that greater stress should be placed on the welfare of the German people in the GDR.[5] His arguments started a major public debate. Leading West German newspapers were already calling for a reconsideration of Bonn's Eastern policy: 'Today when Germany wants to overcome her division, she needs an opening to the East more urgently than in Stresemann's time.' Initially all three West German political parties rejected Jaspers's reversal of strategies, but with FDP participation in the government in October 1963 a gradual adjustment became noticeable.

Growing disenchantment was due to the gradual realization that: (1) the Wall demonstrated the inability of the policy of 'maintained tensions' favourably to alter developments in the East; (2) the slowdown in Western integration compromised Bonn's hopes to use its enhanced stature within consolidated organizations to exert pressure against the East; (3) the resurgence of nationalism within the Warsaw Pact provided opportunities for the extension of West German influence at East German expense; (4) the Cuban missile crisis demonstrated Moscow's strategic limitations which might be exploited by a progressive rather than a negative policy; and (5)

[5] *Lebensfragen der deutschen Politik* (1963).

Washington's bridge-building and de Gaulle's rapprochement with Eastern Europe raised the spectre of a political accommodation at West Germany's expense if she persisted in her intransigence.

When traditional German fears of estrangement and isolation crystallized, what were formerly editorial proposals and admonitions were converted into concrete measures. Cultural exchanges were given a new impetus. Permanent West German trade delegations were established in all East European capitals except Prague, and the Federal Republic became a leading Western trading partner for East European countries. These contacts were broadened by exchanges at semi-official levels. In October 1965 the Evangelical Church of Germany published an important statement criticizing the government's position on the Oder–Neisse line and encouraging a formal renunciation of territorial claims in Poland. This formal break with the official line had a sharp impact on German public opinion, especially in Socialist circles. In the spring and summer of 1966, the SPD proposed to the SED that the two parties exchange speakers for their respective political rallies (the SED initially accepted but then rejected the offer).

Such activities were not indicative of new popular support for an accommodation with Eastern Europe but were a symptom of growing disillusionment with the tactics formerly employed. They reflected a mood that tangible rapprochement with the communists was becoming more important than the manner in which it was accomplished. Both old and new methods could be used as long as progress towards *détente* was made, though without weakening Germany's ultimate bargaining position in a peace settlement.

These gradual developments contributed to the changing atmosphere that was acknowledged by Adenauer in his farewell speech before the Party Congress of his CDU on 21 March 1966, when he put an end to his system of ' maintained tensions '. He stated that the Soviet Union had now ' entered the ranks of those countries that want peace in the world '. Although this volte-face created indignation in conservative German circles and widespread scepticism in the Warsaw Pact countries, Adenauer's successor, Ludwig Erhard, tried to

capitalize on this changing mood. On 25 March he launched a
' peace offensive ' in a diplomatic note delivered to 115 states
(including those of Eastern Europe) proposing a reduction of
nuclear weapons in Europe, an agreement prohibiting the transfer of nuclear weapons to non-nuclear powers and the renunciation of their production by nuclear powers, and finally, that
agreement should be reached with the East European governments prohibiting the use of force in international disputes.[6]

Eastern Europe branded the effort as cynical and pointed to
Erhard's insistence that Germany continues in international
law within the frontier of 31 December 1937, as long as a freely
elected all-German government does not recognize other
frontiers. From the Polish viewpoint, this begged the question
of his offer to negotiate with Warsaw on the boundaries
problem. Further, Erhard's note concluded that Hitler's
aggression negated the Munich Agreement of 1938 and, therefore, the Federal Republic had no territorial claims against
Czechoslovakia. This fell short of Prague's demand that Bonn
should formally renounce its part in the agreement. (Unofficially Bonn's position was that the Munich Agreement was
a freely negotiated multilateral document whose abrogation
would require the consent of the other signatory powers. But
Prague insisted that because of the immensity of German
claims to personal property and historic German ambitions in
the Sudetenland, Bonn must demonstrate its peaceful intentions
through the gesture of formally revoking its signature to the
Munich Agreement, allegedly promulgated for the protection
of ' German ' citizens.)

In October 1965 the Foreign Minister Gerhard Schröder
amplified the position of the Erhard government when he
stated: ' No German government, constitutionally sworn as it
is to act on behalf of all Germans and to restore German unity,
could abandon the policy of reunification '. To do so ' would
help to consolidate the unnatural and unjust partition of our
country without bringing peace and security to Europe; and
would perpetuate a dangerous source of tension in Central
Europe indefinitely '. Therefore ' our policy must be not to

---

[6] Federal Republic, Auswärtiges Amt, *Die Bemühungen der deutschen Regierung und
ihrer Verbündeten um die Einheit Deutschlands 1955–66* (1966).

arouse false hopes, but to establish relations between East and West based on mutual trust and thus enable us to remove, first of all, the minor sources of tension, but subsequently the major ones as well.'[7]

Viewed from Moscow, this position could only heighten the German danger, since Bonn appeared determined to secure concessions ' collectively if possible, individually if necessary ', without making the slightest move towards accommodating the strategic interests of the Warsaw Pact countries. The Soviet Union reacted in April 1966 by launching a major campaign in both Eastern and Western Europe to promote a variety of all-European security schemes. This move culminated in the Warsaw Pact PCC meeting in Bucharest in July and the Conference of European Communist and Workers' Parties at Karlovy Vary in April 1967. The Bucharest meeting was important as the high-water mark in Eastern Europe's efforts to establish a common anti-German policy, while the Karlovy Vary conference was interpreted as an attempt to propagate its security campaign in the West.

Soviet motives behind this new drive apparently stemmed from an awareness of the possible implications of the following changes believed to be occurring in Western policies: (1) French policy towards NATO provided opportunities to encourage the further disintegration of the Alliance; (2) Britain was again knocking on the Common Market's door, and if it opened, this would integrate West Germany into broader Western institutions; (3) Bonn was toying with some form of nuclear sharing, such as the multilateral nuclear force (MLF) which raised the danger of its gaining a dominant voice in nuclear policies; (4) the 1963 Paris–Bonn axis had become problematical; its dormancy meant it could not restrain Federal ambitions in the East, yet it could still serve as a vehicle for expression of German Gaullist sentiments in domestic politics; and (5) the failure of Erhard's diplomatic ' new look ' to produce explicit results had stimulated extreme right-wing political agitation in West Germany.

The Soviet pressure on Bonn was, however, blunted by the fall of Erhard's administration and the formation in December

[7] ' Germany looks at Eastern Europe ', *Foreign Affairs*, Oct. 1965.

1966 of the CDU–SPD Grand Coalition. The Socialist terms for entering the coalition dealt primarily with the *Ostpolitik*, i.e. promotion of international *détente*, renunciation of nuclear ambitions; modification of the Hallstein Doctrine to include establishing diplomatic relations with communist countries, and a more flexible policy towards East Germany, short of formal recognition.

The first clues of a pragmatic adjustment between the two partners were revealed in the new Chancellor's initial speech before the Bundestag on 13 December 1966. Kurt Georg Kiesinger promised to promote *détente* as the foundation of his *Ostpolitik* and as a goodwill gesture he officially dropped the onerous terms of ' Middle Germany ' and the ' Soviet Occupied Zone ' for the GDR. He suggested extended contacts in the economic, cultural, and technical fields, and proposed to explore ways to reduce differences with the East. But in specific problem areas, he qualified a statement denouncing the Munich Agreement by asserting Bonn's responsibility to protect the interests of Sudeten Germans. He expressed a keen wish for a reconciliation with Poland, whose ' claim to live finally in a state with assured boundaries ' Germany understood, but said that it could be expected only within the context of reunited Germany; yet he unequivocally refused to recognize East Germany.[8]

In a more realistic vein, Kiesinger put forward fifteen proposals [9] designed to increase contacts with East Germany, including greater freedom of travel, broader trade and credit facilities, joint economic projects, and cultural and educational exchanges. He also made an important step towards *de facto* recognition by formally recommending that both sides should appoint commissioners to discuss these and other possible ways for easing the lives of all Germans. In a further step towards *de facto* acceptance, Bonn offered to include East Germany in its proposed accords for renouncing the use of force. Finally, the Foreign Minister Willy Brandt registered the high-water

[8] Government Declaration of 13 December, *Bull.*, 14 Dec. 1966; also J. Korbel, in *Orbis*, Summer 1970.
[9] Federal Republic, Bundesministerium für gesamtdeutsche Frage, *Texte zur Deutschlandpolitik, 19 Dez. 1966–5 Okt. 1967* (1967).

mark of official German leniency towards Poland before the Czechoslovak crisis when he advocated ' respect ', in lieu of recognition, of the Oder–Neisse border.

In another important move, the Kiesinger government reversed the policy of ostracism and adopted a programme of official contacts with East Berlin. In April 1967 both the Chancellor and the SPD transmitted messages to the SED Party Congress, outlining specific proposals for expanding inter-German relations. Further, during the spring and summer Kiesinger and Premier Willi Stoph exchanged a series of notes which further established Bonn's *de facto* acceptance of the GDR. Indeed, Kiesinger offered, in his State of the Nation speech in March 1968, to negotiate on German problems directly with Stoph, if sufficient progress could be made in preliminary discussions to assure success.

The ' new opening to the East ' was promptly and widely denounced by the communist governments. It was feared that no significant concessions would be made and that any opening was intended to be on Bonn's traditional terms. The Socialists' presence in the coalition would probably not exert significant influence on a governmental bureaucracy that for decades had been consistently right wing. Eastern observers estimated that the new tactic was a stratagem to jeopardize Warsaw Pact cohesion and encourage further economic inroads in traditional German markets.

In particular, the GDR used the unique opportunity of the Federal policy of contacts only to establish a precedent, but then suspended further exchanges. Like the inter-party contacts, East Berlin apparently viewed these exchanges as a device to gain recognition and was apprehensive lest they should give rise to serious domestic pressures. A dramatic comparison of the internal policies of the two regimes was an implicit motive in the Kiesinger ' opening to the East', but the GDR's precautions apparently blunted the impact of the demonstrated Federal Republic's openness.

In reality, the importance of Kiesinger's new policy was that it abandoned the concept of 'maintained tensions' and the policy of strength, without requiring a *quid pro quo* or sacrificing basic aims. His position was that each move towards normalization must be matched reciprocally, and that normalization of relations could be a valid intermediate goal to the final solution of the German question. This had the tactical advantage of forcing the GDR and Poland themselves into the embarrassing position of pursuing a policy of ' maintained tensions '.

Barely one month after Kiesinger's initial policy statement, lengthy negotiations between West Germany and Rumania culminated in the establishment of full diplomatic relations, a move repeated one year later (in January 1968) by Yugoslavia and contemplated by Hungary, Bulgaria, and Czechoslovakia as well. The accord apparently surprised the Soviet Union and precipitated a major crisis throughout Eastern Europe. On the one hand, Poland and East Germany viewed the agreement as a dangerous attempt to undermine their basic foreign policy that had been maintained for over twenty years. Yet the Soviet Union could not take a firm public stand against Rumania's pre-emptive action without accepting the risk of further alienating the unruly Rumanians.

Poland and East Germany called for the negotiation of bilateral treaties of friendship, co-operation, and mutual military assistance with other Pact members specifically directed against German aggression, thus augmenting commitments provided in the Warsaw Treaty. The majority of the Pact members accepted these demands, and a series of bilateral agreements was signed declaring unqualified endorsement of the territorial integrity and the sovereign rights of the states involved. Only Rumania persistently held out against making any bilateral commitments with the northern-tier countries which were directed against the Federal Republic. Hungary and Bulgaria belatedly and reluctantly renegotiated the accords, and Czechoslovakia balanced her pledge to East Germany by an agreement with West Germany to establish permanent trade delegations.

The Warsaw Pact countries' response to West Germany's most serious challenge to date was clearly defensive and produced wide gaps in Eastern solidarity. Moscow sought to create firm regional guarantees against the ' German menace ' similar to the security system negotiated in the 1930s. This effort, however, only solidified the northern tier's own policy of ' maintained tensions ' and prompted Rumania to abandon the Pact's common foreign policy against its ' main threat ' and to refuse participation in the new regional security arrangement.

In 1967–8 the German issue in Soviet policy became partially neglected through preoccupation with events in the Middle East and Czechoslovakia. Claims that West Germany was intensifying her revanchist campaign against the East and the inability of Czechoslovakia to defend herself from this subversion were held by the five Pact members as the justification of their intervention. The Soviet Union intensified her charges by restating her claims to the right of intervention in West Germany under Articles 53 and 107 of the UN Charter if she judged Bonn's policies detrimental to international peace.[10]

The Prague crisis was clearly one of the most serious challenges Soviet rule had ever encountered. The Hungarian revolt in 1956 broke with both communism and the Soviet security system by proclaiming a multi-party neutral state. The Czechoslovaks merely questioned the applicability of the Soviet models for advancing social and economic progress while remaining dedicated to their Warsaw Pact commitments. While less immediate than the Hungarian challenge, the more subtle Czechoslovak reforms embodied in the Action Programme undermined the utility of the Soviet formula for progress. Indeed, the sanctity of the entire socialist experience propounded by the socialist fatherland would inevitably be attacked if such wholesale revisions were allowed. Accordingly the fundamentalists within the Pact felt compelled to strike. In justifying their harsh action, however, they could obviously not allude to the real source of their anxiety—Prague's questioning of socialist orthodoxy. A scapegoat was sought outside the framework of revisionism, thereby removing the entire episode from its true context. In selecting West German ' revanchism ' as the antagonist, the fundamentalists could interweave fantasy and fact to produce a plausible rationale.

The persistence of West German claims against the Eastern Europeans was common knowledge. Likewise it was well

[10] *Pravda*, 18 Sept. 1969.

known that Bonn had attempted to undermine Pact solidarity and establish inroads in Eastern Europe in order to induce greater acceptance of its terms for German reunification. Thus it was plausible to argue that Bonn was openly encouraging liberalization of a socialist regime not only to enhance Western influence among Pact countries but to isolate the GDR and weaken socialist resistance to its solution of the German problem. Fantasy was introduced by the deliberate confusion of public sentiments and official West German policies, and the allegation that Bonn was prepared to use force to assert its aims. Precisely the opposite occurred. Bonn restricted the scope and pace of its contacts with Prague almost in proportion with the growing intensity of Dubcek's revisionism. The determined efforts of the Rumanian and Yugoslav governments and the world news media to analyse and explain the true motives for the invasion created sufficient suspicion among East Europeans about the official explanation that the spectre of West German aggression could no longer be plausibly employed to induce popular support. On its side, Bonn realized that the degree of influence it could assert on Moscow via inroads in Eastern Europe was limited. It could no longer avoid seeking a solution to the German problem without speaking to the Soviet Union.

The continuation of the Czechoslovak 'renaissance' and the inability of the Soviet Union to cultivate an acceptable native leadership until eight months after the invasion led to further observations about the veracity of 'the German threat'. (1) The failure of the German danger to materialize intensified the existing rift among Warsaw Pact members. (2) As tensions mounted during the Prague Spring, Bonn's prudent suspension of diplomacy with Czechoslovakia increased the onus of the conservative Pact nations for their abrasive actions. (3) The persistence of the communist renaissance in Czechoslovakia after the installation of a permanent Soviet garrison and the suspension of Bonn's diplomatic offensive forced acknowledgement that 'the German threat' was not the only source of tension or challenge to Soviet interest in Eastern Europe. (4) The use of force over the German issue was a firm indication of the growing apprehensions of the conservative Pact members, mainly the GDR, about the rise of West German influence in Eastern Europe. Probably most important, the limited utility of ' the German threat ' as an instrument of public coercion and the challenge to Soviet models for progress forced Moscow to revise its former analyses of security and stability in the Warsaw Pact. Earlier measures for achieving both aims had finally lost their value; new schemes and strategies were now required. Chapters 3 and 4 develop the evolution of Soviet and East European policies regarding stability and security, especially after the Prague emergency foreclosed the use of traditional means.

To minimize the adverse impact of the invasion of Czecho-slovakia the Soviet Union sought to reopen a dialogue with the West after she had secured Prague's signature on the treaty governing the ' temporary ' garrisoning of Soviet troops in Czechoslovakia. During talks between the Foreign Ministers Gromyko and Brandt in New York on 8 October 1968, both sides agreed to suspend polemics on intervention rights and to seek areas of mutual interest instead. When the Soviet ambas-sador Semyon Tsarapkin returned to his post in January 1969, he expressed his government's willingness to expand talks on general political matters and practical problems of co-opera-tion. Chancellor Kiesinger replied, in a probing remark, that before Moscow could expect Bonn's collaboration on important issues, such as the pending NPT, it must clarify its claimed right of intervention in the Federal Republic. On 7 February the Soviet Union responded by offering West Germany positive concessions on the NPT, in the form of strong assurances that the Soviet intervention claims had no practical meaning at the present time. (The Soviet Union had repeatedly asserted her right to use force against the non-communist part of Germany.) At a time when the East German press was labelling as a sharp provocation Bonn's decision to hold its presidential election in Berlin, the Soviet Union took the unusual step of briefing Kiesinger on the details of Sino-Soviet Ussuri river clashes, implying that she was affording Bonn preferential treatment in security matters. Further, conducting top-level Soviet-West German discussion of security questions relating exclusively to the communist world indicated to Walter Ulbricht that Russia had closed his option employed in 1964 of siding with the Chinese to exert pressure on Moscow.[11] These developments were firm signs of a change in the Kremlin's German policy, but additional evidence was required to determine more accurately the extent of this modification and its implications for Bonn. As the pace of West German-Soviet contacts accelerated, further signals were made. Unlike the 1966 Bucharest PCC meeting, the Warsaw summit meeting in Budapest on 17 March 1969 dropped its vindictive denunciation of West German ' militaristic ' policy and called for an all-European security conference that would have to deal in part with the German issue. Although the Federal Republic rejected the proposal (primarily over the status of Berlin), the Soviet Union subsequently indicated that the terms were subject to revision. The West German press observed that the primary gain over earlier Pact proposals for any multilateral gathering was its failure to demand Bonn's legal recognition of the GDR, requiring only *de facto* acceptance. These conditions were within the purview of Bonn's new leniency towards East Germany.

In a more tangible gesture, Tsarapkin requested Kiesinger to send a personal envoy to Moscow for preliminary discussions on broader topics of mutual interest. Rudolf Heizler, an important CDU functionary, conducted exploratory talks with Soviet officials in March on the terms for conducting formal discussions. He reported that his visit was highly successful and that the Soviet Union ' . . . is seeking a dialogue with the Federal Republic; it is clearly interested in a reconciliation and understanding with Bonn '.[12] (The significance of the visit was heightened by Ulbricht's sudden arrival in Moscow at the same time.)

New developments also occurred in the economic field. During this period talks started on reciprocal commercial air rights: Aeroflot flying to Frankfurt via Schönefeld (East Berlin) and Lufthansa flying to Moscow via Tegel (West

[11] *FAZ*, 12 Mar., *Der Spiegel*, 17 Mar., & *Frankfurter Rundschau*, 26 Mar. 1969. For a different viewpoint see M. Croan, in *Problems of Communism*, Jan.–Feb. 1969, pp. 1–7.
[12] *Bonner Rundschau*, 26 Mar. 1969.

Berlin). By August the Western allies had approved the use of Tegel, and Lufthansa sought onward rights to Japan via Siberia. Even more significant, Moscow opened an unprecedented commercial transaction with Bonn. It proposed to supply 5,000 m. cubic metres of natural gas in exchange for 1 m. tons of large-diameter steel pipe. The final agreement was financed by a West German consortium and is expected ultimately to exceed $350 m. Yet, even before this transaction was concluded, West Germany had become the Soviet Union's most important Western trading partner. In 1968 their total trade amounted to $567 m., an increase of 38 per cent over 1967.

In the spring Moscow apparently sought to consolidate this favourable upswing in German-Soviet relations by strengthening the electoral prospects of the left-wing West German parties. Following the Rumanian argument, implied in the Karlovy Vary communique of April 1967, that there were both ' good and bad Germans ', Moscow adopted a policy of preferential treatment for the former. As early as 1965 the GDR leadership had sought some means of offsetting the adverse impact of the Wall that would at the same time strengthen its bargaining position with West Germany. After several visits to Moscow, Ulbricht and Honecker, his heir-apparent, publicly launched the idea that there was a need to form an alliance between the working classes of both parts of Germany. A united workers' front, it was argued, could provide an important tool for counteracting reactionary forces in West Germany and, thereby, improve the prospects for normalizing relations. The SED and the government returned to this theme in the exchange of letters in 1966 and 1967.

Moscow refloated this idea in March 1969 when an international communist gathering was convened to commemorate the 50th anniversary of the Comintern. In the presence of Ulbricht, the highest ranking non-Soviet participant, the Soviet Union formally condemned the Stalinist denunciation of the German SPD as the chief enemy of communism. The occasion was used to introduce a policy calling for co-operation with the SPD as the most plausible means of curbing German rightist tendencies. East European representatives were admonished to explore ways to support the SPD without damaging its election prospects—Ulbricht demonstrated his displeasure by a premature departure. Since the initial GDR opening to the SPD in 1965, the Socialists' strength in Bonn had increased to the point that they could control the next government. From Ulbricht's viewpoint, reactionary Christian Democrats were preferred opponents to liberal Socialists.

Poland quickly accepted the Soviet proposal. Gomulka delivered a major speech on 17 May 1969 dealing with the declining German threat and the need to re-examine Polish interests in an accommodation with Bonn. He acknowledged recent indications that Bonn's *Ostpolitik* was moving in a new direction.

I have in mind here, first of all, certain statements made by the leaders of the West German Social Democrats . . . particularly those made by the chairman of that party, Vice Chancellor of the Federal Republic, Willy Brandt. . . . One cannot fail to appreciate the fact that, from the political point of view, the SPD formula on the recognition by the Federal Republic of the frontier on the Oder and Neisse constitutes a step forward in comparison to the stand taken on this issue by all the previous Federal Republic governments.[13]

He concluded that it was now appropriate to explore ways to normalize relations. This was the frankest revelation to date by a Pact leader that a political adjustment with Bonn was now feasible and desirable.

Brandt responded at a press conference on 19 May calling Gomulka's offer for talks ' remarkable ' and stated (contrary to the traditional CDU preference for integration with the West): ' We regard the reconciliation with Poland as being just as important historically as the similar reconciliation with France.'[14] He skilfully enhanced the importance of Poland's opening gesture by contrasting it with East Berlin's recalcitrance. He called for discussions with East German officials on the basis of equality and repeated his party's formal denunciation of the GDR for refusing to conduct ministerial negotiations with Bonn. These goals have since then remained the fundamental tactical objectives for the SPD.

[13] *FAZ*, 24 May 1969; also *Życie Warszawy*, 1 Apr. 1969.
[14] *Die Welt*, 20 May 1969.

In June the Mayor of West Berlin, Klaus Schütz (SPD), visited Poland. On his return, he created a mild sensation by publicly urging a revision of the SPD formula for ' respecting ' the Oder–Neisse border. He claimed that normalization of relations with Poland required formal recognition of the border rather than verbal guarantees and declarations. While official West German spokesmen pointed out that Schütz was speaking as a private citizen and had no authority formally to commit Bonn, the independent and leftist press strongly supported his view.

It is significant that by July both sides had concluded that noticeable progress had been made. On 10 July the Foreign Minister Gromyko made a major policy declaration before the Supreme Soviet in which he said that a turning point in relations between the Soviet Union and the Federal Republic ' can occur ' if the Federal Republic ' follows the path of peace '.[15] On the same day, Brandt stated that relations with the Soviet Union were approaching normality for the first time since 1955.[16] After the traditional August holidays, diplomatic activity was resumed. On 12 September Moscow formally replied to a Federal note of 3 July proposing an agreement on the renunciation of the use of force. At a news conference on 16 September Brandt indicated that no specific reference to the status of East Berlin had been made in this reply and that Bonn was willing to exchange pledges on non-aggression with East German authorities that would be as binding as treaties concluded under international law.[17] The Soviet Union neither accepted nor rejected these proposed terms, suggesting that their chief aim was to indicate a desire to suspend the dialogue with Bonn during the national election campaign. The West German press commented that the general response to the Soviet note was guarded, but not negative, and the lack of polemics augured well for Moscow's willingness to elevate the talks to negotiations.

Such an increase in diplomatic activity and improvement in official contacts in a single year was unprecedented in West

[15] *Pravda*, 11 July 1969; *CDSP*, 6 Aug. 1969.
[16] *SZ*, 11 July 1969.
[17] *Bull.*, 23 Sept. 1969.

German-Soviet relations. The scope of the exchanges was as impressive as the weight of individual agenda items. The willingness of both sides to contribute additional issues for consideration indicated a desire to broaden and intensify the deliberations before accepting negotiations on any single item. These tactics demonstrated to both sides their respective sincerity in seeking areas of potential accommodation which might contribute to a general normalization in relations.

These developments were the product of fundamental policy changes in both Bonn and Moscow, particularly in the German position. The scale of Bonn's modifications and their implications are frequently underestimated in the West. With the formation of the Grand Coalition, the elements of compromise already existing in the Bonn government were strengthened. The Federal Republic subsequently abandoned her policy of strength, i.e. that reunification was the prerequisite for *détente*, and adopted the line that relaxation of tension was the precondition for normalizing relations and for improved inter-German co-operation. All other subordinate aspects of the policy of strength were also remodelled. The Federal Republic still claimed to be the only freely elected government entitled to represent all the German people, but modified her programme of ostracizing the GDR. She could not accept East Germany's claim to legitimacy, but in establishing diplomatic relations with Rumania and Yugoslavia she weakened her grounds for asserting exclusive authority. Unity was no longer viewed as the result of the eradication of communism in the Soviet zone and the resurrection of common German institutions. Indeed, a broad degree of *de facto* recognition was extended to the GDR that enhanced the prospects for closer contacts between the two hostile regimes. Finally, in abandoning the *détente*-through-reunification stand, Bonn lowered its aims to improving the living conditions of all Germans.

The implications of such a major reversal may not even now be fully perceived. Many West Germans experienced a severe shock as they witnessed their aspirations for reunification rapidly receding without a *quid pro quo* or significant concessions from the East. Likewise, many saw their position in the West constrained as their principal allies declined to press for reunification on Bonn's terms. Indeed, as a result of Bonn's leniency towards Eastern Europe, it had lost leverage in the West. It could no longer pose as the chief governor for Western policy on the German question, a fact that its friends had begun to exploit through various ' bridge-building ' schemes. The West Germans were acutely aware of the ramifications of these developments which, when coupled with the ' encircle-ment neurosis ' that has so frequently plunged German policy into rash actions, could result in serious internal disturbances.

There were positive effects, however, that tended to balance these pessimistic assessments. First, Bonn had re-entered Eastern Europe at the official level at the price of greater flexibility and the prospects of further concessions. This opening held out as many potential advantages as drawbacks for the injection of German influence in its traditional sphere of manoeuvre. As earlier, the measure of the international stature of West Germany was still in part determined by her standing in Eastern Europe. Greater latitude in her *Ostpolitik* could, therefore, earn political profits by a substantially larger factor than the mere immediate gain. Likewise in the West, Bonn's position had been significantly improved in the tangible area of political prestige. The West had offered the Federal Republic international rehabilitation, economic recovery, a return of self-respect, and a sense of purpose unrelated to Eastern developments. But the durability of these rewards remained questionable as long as West Germany regarded her-self as the stronghold for Western orthodoxy. The abandon-ment of a victory aim in the Soviet zone through a policy of strength and the break-out from her protective mental defences greatly enhanced her respectability and stature among her allies.

What were the main factors causing the reversal of Bonn's foreign policy? Karl Kaiser, in an analysis of German policy, identifies three major influences: (1) the construction of the Wall, raising the danger that the partition of Germany could become permanent; (2) the *détente* policy of the Kennedy administration, posing the threat that the division of Europe could be overcome without solving the German problem; (3) de Gaulle's overtures to the Soviet Union, indicating the value

of new policy options.[18] Determined maintenance of the hard-
line position was clearly obstructing Washington's endeavours
to relax East–West tensions and could be rationally defended
only as long as Soviet policy on reunification appeared uncertain and the East German regime seemed on the verge of
collapse. But the construction of the Wall clarified these uncertainties; Moscow was prepared to defend the *status quo* east
of the Elbe. De Gaulle was the first of the Western statesmen
to acknowledge these new realities. He argued that the fate of
Germany could best be solved by Germany's neighbours
through overcoming the division of Europe. Whenever necessary, he firmly resisted Soviet pressure against Bonn, but he
also demonstrated that the price for normalization of relations
with the East Europeans was to enhance their security by
recognizing their borders. Accordingly, France was the first
Western power to recognize the Oder–Neisse boundary, bearing
the fruits of political inroads into Eastern Europe. By 1966
France's opening to the East had culminated in a way that was
warmly applauded by many Germans.

Roger Morgan has also pointed out that the pace of change
in Bonn's *Deutschlandpolitik* and *Ostpolitik* was largely checked
by the right wing of the CDU, not by the opposition.[19] The
SPD and the FDP had already done important pioneer work in
establishing a new approach towards Eastern Europe. In
March 1965 Erich Mende, then leader of the FDP and Vice-
Chancellor, injected a note of flexibility in the coalition government's hard line by calling for a more active German policy to
preclude the two entities from drifting further apart. But there
was insufficient interest in a revision of the German policy for
it to become a campaign issue in the 1965 national elections.

In June 1966, however, both the FDP and SPD introduced
major modifications in the party positions. Helmut Schmidt,
then SPD deputy parliamentary leader, told the Party Congress
that the policy of strength had definitively and unequivocally
failed.[20] The congress concluded that since the four Allied

[18] *German Foreign Policy in Transition* (1968).

[19] ' The Scope of German Foreign Policy ', *Yb. of World Affairs, 1966* (1966),
pp. 78–105.

[20] Speech at annual SPD conference, 3 June 1966, *Tatsachen-Argumente*, 205
(1966), p. 10.

powers were deadlocked on all important aspects of the German problem, the Federal Republic would have to pursue a more active role. It called for a shift in emphasis from reunification to the welfare of the East Germans and for a reversal of the Hallstein Doctrine in Eastern Europe. The SPD adopted the line that greater security should be extended to Eastern Europe through abrogating the Munich Agreement and a compromise formula on the Oder–Neisse border. While official recognition was withheld, peaceful coexistence and a reduction of the burdens of partition were encouraged through pursuing contacts with the GDR at all levels.[21]

This new policy platform was the basis for the SPD-initiated exchange of correspondence with the SED in 1966 and 1967. The momentum of the SPD's revisionism was maintained at the 1968 Party Congress when it encouraged Bonn to ' respect and recognize ', pending a final peace treaty, the existing frontiers of Eastern Europe. Early next year two SPD *Länder* Party organizations called for full recognition of the GDR, and the Party Chairman, Willy Brandt, pledged ' full co-operation with East Berlin at all levels below recognition under international law '. Revisionism still prevailed at the April 1969 Party Congress, when the SPD delegates adopted by 344 to 10 votes a key plank in their election platform accepting the ' state-like existence ' of East Germany. The weight of this new trend in German politics had been indicated by the election in March 1969 with FPD support of a liberal Socialist, Gustav Heinemann, as the Federal President.

While the pace of revision and reconciliation was being set by the left-wing West German parties, it was being partially checked in Eastern Europe. Moscow's German policy had shifted from advocating a unitary government to encouraging neutralization, and finally to consolidation. However, Moscow had to balance between several perilous obstacles. It had to encourage sufficient co-operation among the two German states to preclude hostile competition for supremacy, yet preserve enough mutual suspicion to prevent the two from uniting. On the other hand, if it failed to respect the GDR's legitimate

---

[21] *Parteitag der Sozialdemokratischen Partei Deutschlands 1966: Protokoll der Verhandlungen* (1966).

interests, East Germany might be likely to compete with the Kremlin as the guardian of orthodoxy and for leadership of the Pact, as had occurred during the Czechoslovak emergency. Yet if those interests included an autonomous, but ultra-conservative, communist Prussia, it would be as potentially dangerous to Soviet interests as a liberal Czechoslovakia.

The gradual relaxation in Federal policy led to a corresponding hardening of the GDR position, and ultimately to the adoption of her own policy of strength. The exchange of correspondence illustrated this trend. Reflecting her growing political power, the GDR increased her demands for cooperation to unqualified Federal recognition. Indeed, in the last Stoph letter, the GDR included a draft state treaty confirming her legitimacy.

By the end of the Grand Coalition, relations between the two German states had reached an impasse. West Germany had attempted to accelerate her policy of reconciliation through a series of small steps for agreement on pragmatic issues, while the GDR had insisted upon agreement on the larger issue of her legitimacy as the precondition for accommodation on lesser matters. West Germany was now squarely confronted with several hard questions. What should be the proper relationship between reunification and *détente* and what should be the desirable level between normalization and reconciliation? Answers to such questions were becoming increasingly dependent upon East Germany. The division of Europe had become a function of East Germany's existence, and European unity was becoming linked to a future role of the GDR that was acceptable to both the Soviet Union and West Germany.

Despite the failure of Bonn's *Deutschlandpolitik* under the Grand Coalition to improve the atmosphere with the GDR, the initial success in relations with Poland and the Soviet Union strongly suggests that Moscow had revalued its estimation of the German threat. The new Soviet attitude towards ' the German menace ' was still sufficiently rooted in traditional fears of the potential dangers posed by a unified Germany for Moscow to insist upon the permanency of the partition. Concrete signs of Bonn's acceptance of the unalterable character of this policy were the preconditions for normalization. But when Bonn extended positive indications of its acquiescence, Moscow recognized that its claims about ' the German menace ' would have to be modified. It would have been counterproductive to participate in major diplomatic encounters with the ' main threat ' to international peace. Yet East Germany could not accept this reasoning and Pact policy tended to split along lines of national interest on this crucial issue, the Soviet Union advising that the German threat was potentially dangerous but manageable and East Germany demanding positive concessions to her own legitimacy as evidence of Bonn's peaceful intentions. Thus the changing interpretation of the German challenge becomes the touchstone both for expanded diplomacy in Central Europe and a major reappraisal among East Europeans of their respective interests in an accommodation and the impact any adjustment would have on intra-Pact relations. A growing awareness in West Germany of this changing atmosphere stimulated probings in the Soviet Union and Eastern Europe to explore other aspects of an adjustment and the limits of accommodation. The Soviet price was stability in its sphere, the Eastern European one was security.

3
THE BUCHAREST-BONN-MOSCOW TRIANGLE:
GERMAN POLICY AND EAST EUROPEAN STABILITY

MOVEMENT towards a limited reconciliation in West German–Warsaw Pact relations, first observed under the Grand Coalition, suggested that Moscow had reassessed its estimate of ' the German menace ' and concluded that it was still serious but controllable. Moreover, the prime challenge was not to the Soviet Union proper, but to her immediate security system in Eastern Europe. The consolidation of her position in this region is a vital Soviet interest; the Soviet Union has forcefully demonstrated that she is prepared to use whatever pressure may be necessary to achieve this aim. But the Prague Spring provided convincing evidence of the precarious nature of the Soviet hold, even after nearly a quarter of a century. While there were many reasons for social unrest during this period, the German question was the most unsettling foreign policy issue in Eastern Europe. The Soviet Union consistently followed a policy of exaggerating the nature of the German threat and containing Bonn's influence, until the Federal Republic adopted a more flexible posture. Moscow was then forced to reappraise its attitude towards both West Germany and Eastern Europe. Rumania played a key role in reinterpreting the socialist definition of the German threat and in probing the limits of Soviet tolerance on the German question. An analysis of the interaction between these three states may provide insight into the degree of regional stability that can be expected and the extent of Soviet willingness to accommodate German policy aims.

The question of relations with both Germany and the Soviet Union produces traditional reactions among Eastern Europeans. Zbigniew Brzezinski has observed that the Eastern Europeans have maintained historically a separation between territorial adjustments and German reunification. West German recognition of existing boundaries is regarded as absolutely essential for their national security and the normalization of relations. They see reunification as a product of, but border recognition as a precondition for, *détente*. Bonn's insistence on pursuing its terms for reunification and maintaining claims to its ' lost ' territories reinforced the East European stake in keeping Germany divided.[1] When the SPD formulated a policy of an interim recognition and began to press for its formal adoption by the Grand Coalition, several East European countries reconsidered their hard anti-West German position.

Adjustments on this scale should not be underestimated. Most Eastern Europeans accept Soviet protection as the lesser of two evils. There is little genuine admiration for the Soviet Union or for Russian culture, except possibly in Czechoslovakia and Bulgaria. The more prevalent view is that the smaller countries remain pinioned between the traditionally dominant powers in Eastern Europe—the Russians and the Germans— and that only through prudent manoeuvring can their political options against either or both be expanded. Rumania enjoys a privileged position for employing this strategy: she has only minor outstanding grievances with the Federal Republic and no history of Germanic domination, she places a high priority on regional stability and reconciliation, has a popular regime that is not dependent economically on the Soviet Union, and yet has a long contiguous frontier with the preponderant regional power, providing the latter reasonable assurances that it retains sufficient leverage to block Rumanian actions detrimental to its vital interests, and, unlike Czechoslovakia, has preserved a highly authoritarian form of government. Thus Bucharest has had fewer restraints than the other East European states as it sought to establish its respective stand between the two larger powers. Through the skilful manipulation of the German issue—seen in Bucharest only from the viewpoint of its relationship to regional tensions—Rumania has pursued a policy that has gradually reduced Soviet hegemony in Eastern Europe, and has in part been responsible for Moscow's revision of its own German policy.

Initially hegemonic rule was the most vulnerable Soviet target for Rumanian manoeuvre. Soviet high-handedness

[1] *Alternatives to Partition* (1965), p. 91.

within the world communist movement and inter-party affairs became a major trouble-spot in relations between the two countries. After 1962 state relations were also affected by Gheorghe Gheorghiu-Dej's successful counter-moves against Moscow's attempt to integrate the East European economies along lines of comparative advantage, regarded as detrimental to Rumania's industrialization and as a manifestation of Soviet aims to centralize decision-making. In April 1964 Gheorghiu-Dej announced Rumania's ' declaration of independence ' by asserting her right to national autonomy and equality within the communist world. Rumania's dedication to socialism and allegiance to the Warsaw Pact were reaffirmed as axioms of national policy. But a new age of manoeuvre was inaugurated that soon included virtually all aspects of foreign policy.

Bucharest seized upon the Sino-Soviet dispute as the means of asserting its new leverage. As self-appointed mediators, Rumanian officials frequented Peking and Moscow, contributing little to the relaxation of tensions but earning reluctant acceptance of Rumanian leadership as a minor power. Rumania vigorously attempted to prevent the expulsion of China from the communist movement, since her presence would perpetuate the dispute with Moscow and serve to legitimize the conflict of interests among sovereign states and ruling communist parties.

The tempo of Soviet-Rumanian relations was accelerated as the scope of the disputes was extended from economic and party matters to include security and foreign-policy issues. When Gromyko launched the Soviet programme for an all-European security conference in April 1966, the Rumanian party chief Ceausescu responded in a celebrated speech on 7 May emphatically restating his country's policy of actively asserting its national sovereignty.[2] Viewing the Soviet plan as a means of extending its authority, Ceausescu concluded that military blocs were ' an anachronism ' and incompatible with national sovereignty and normal relations among states. He called for the simultaneous disintegration of the opposing military alliances. Three days later the Soviet party First Secretary

---

[2] *Scînteia* (Bucharest), 8 May 1966; *The Romanian CP: continuer of the Romanian people's revolt and democratic struggle* (Bucharest, 1966).

Leonid Brezhnev made an unexpected visit to Bucharest, purportedly to discuss Bucharest's attitude towards its Pact obligations and solidarity against the common danger.

Rumania was not persuaded to moderate her obdurate stand during Brezhnev's visit. Two unprecedented ministerial-level Warsaw Pact meetings, lasting nearly the entire month of June, were subsequently convened in Moscow to deal with the general problems of military strategy and East–West relations. The Soviet Union was reported to have reiterated her earlier pro- posals for institutional improvements, such as the creation of 'a permanent operating facility', or an enlarged permanent secretariat, and an accelerated arms-modernization programme. It now seems certain that the Soviet Union also briefed her allies on her new ICBM programme and the impact that strategic parity with the United States was expected to have on East– West relations. The implementation of the Soviet proposals would allow the Pact to negotiate from a position of enhanced political strength when parity was reached and serious negotia- tions began on Europe's future.

Rumania reportedly argued that attempts to improve sub- stantially the Pact's military capabilities would undoubtedly be observed by the West and would provoke counter-measures that would not reduce tensions. She called for a greater voice for the smaller states in decision-making in the Warsaw Pact, as a guarantee that their interests would be respected, and for a reduction of Soviet troops stationed abroad, as a gesture of dis- armament by mutual example. To emphasize her point, on 16 May it had been reported from Moscow that Rumania had sent a note to other members of the alliance suggesting that the cost of maintaining Soviet troops in other Pact nations should be borne by the Soviet Union and maintaining that Soviet troops and bases were no longer needed.[3] Thus she contested the legality of the implied Warsaw Treaty provisions for stationing Soviet troops in Eastern Europe.

The more serious dispute, however, centred on the denuncia- tion of the Federal Republic. Rumania sought only a moderate

[3] This was denied by the Rumanian Foreign Ministry, but, according to Le Monde, this was 'a more or less organized leakage' (Keesing's Contemporary Archives, 1965–6, p. 21651).

condemnation that would allow continued probing for an opening in the West. East Germany insisted upon unqualified condemnation and accused Rumania of disloyalty to the collective cause. To check the mounting recriminations, Moscow granted an important and far-reaching concession whereby further disagreements would be discussed bilaterally between Rumania and her allies, denying her opponents the advantage of numbers. On these grounds, Rumania has refused to participate in any Pact meeting that might be directed against her independent foreign-policy interests, e.g. against China, West Germany, Israel, or Czechoslovakia. (This was also the precedent for Dubcek's insistence on dealing bilaterally with his accusers in July 1968.) The Rumanian arguments had sufficient appeal among the other members for a compromise to be reached. Later it became apparent that no institutional changes were made, the pace of modernization was left largely to the respective state's discretion, and several concessions were made to the Rumanian stand. Upon his return to Bucharest, the Rumanian Foreign Minister Corneliu Manescu told reporters he was pleased with his two weeks of hard bargaining and Rumania's efforts towards ' bridge-building ' with the West.[4]

The strength of the Rumanian position became apparent when the Pact's highest policy body—the Political Consultative Committee—issued on 8 July 1966 the historic ' Declaration on Strengthening Peace and Security in Europe ',[5] known as the Bucharest Declaration. This Declaration was heralded in the communist press as the definitive position of all Warsaw Pact countries on European security and foreign-policy issues. The key points of the document were directed mainly against the Federal Republic, the United States, and NATO, whose policies were identified as the chief sources of international tensions. The Declaration demanded that the preconditions for a lasting peace in Europe were Bonn's recognition of the inviolability of the existing frontiers between European states and its renunciation of all territorial claims and interest in acquiring nuclear weapons. The principles of independence

---

[4] *New York Times*, 3, 10, & 22 May, 1, 12, & 16 June 1966.
[5] *Pravda*, 9 July 1966 (*Survival*, Sept. 1966).

and non-intervention were emphasized. The strong denunciation of the Federal Republic was qualified by a provision
stressing the importance of strengthening relations between
states regardless of their political systems. The Declaration also
called for the abolition of military blocs and for other measures
of military disengagement.

The challenge of the American-promoted *détente* and the
barely preceptible loosening in the West German position had
been regarded by Moscow as a threat to the entire cohesive
fabric in its security zone. The stability of Eastern Europe
seemed in greater jeopardy than when Western policy was more
pacific. This new danger forced Moscow to formulate a stand
reminiscent of Adenauer's 'maintained tensions'. The
marginality of the compromise embodied in the Declaration,
after the extremely hard bargaining in Moscow the previous
month, suggests that Moscow opted for a common hard line
on the external threat and an imprecise formula for forward
movement. This decision was probably made in partial deference to the diverging poles in East European opinion and the
necessity to produce a common united position that would deter
further inroads.

But it would be inaccurate to portray the Bucharest formulation as purely defensive. The concerted attack on the West
provided a common framework for a rough division of labour
among the Pact members, allowing each to cite this joint
authorization as justification to pursue more vigorously its
respective national grievances against the West. For example,
the GDR won incorporation of the idea that the pan-European
security system envisaged in the Declaration would require
formal state relations between West and East Germany, and
pressed this line consistently after the meeting. The Declaration
demanded recognition of all borders, allowing Poland to argue
that the border issue was the threshold to European security.
Hungary pursued the security conference theme, and the
Soviet Union directed her attention to Bonn's policies in
general, following her classical strategy of consolidation through
expansion.

The Bucharest Declaration was the high-water mark of Pact
agreement on a common German position. Yet it contained

noticeable reservations and loopholes, and appropriate counter-measures were imprecise and ambiguous. The northern-tier countries had outstanding complaints against the Federal Republic but no positive plan of concerted action. The vague division of labour implied in the Declaration pertained mainly to propaganda, not to concrete proposals designed to induce greater West German flexibility. The lack of a more dynamic plan of action was undoubtedly due to the growing polarization within the Pact along lines of national interest. This tendency may be due in part to the Pact's confidence that Soviet erosion of America's assured deterrence and the deterioration of US international leadership would eventually compel West German acceptance of the Pact's terms, and that only interim measures to meet East European demands and to ensure stability were required.

The exception to the Pact's common policy was again Rumania. She saw East European chorusing on ' the German threat ' as a dangerous endorsement of Soviet authority that could jeopardize the degree of autonomy she had already won. She also apparently viewed the situation as an opportunity, by exploiting the inability of the Pact nations to formulate a more energetic programme, to assert her own minority stand. Accordingly, she accelerated negotiations with Bonn for the establishment of full diplomatic relations. Six months after the Bucharest Declaration was approved in January 1967, Rumania became the first Pact country, except the Soviet Union, to exchange ambassadors with the Federal Republic, a decision also contemplated by Hungary, Czechoslovakia, and Bulgaria.[6]

Rumania's decision was a major breach in Pact discipline which virtually refuted her adherence to the Bucharest Declaration and precipitated the worst crisis in Pact developments since

[6] The issue was initially broached when a Rumanian trade delegation to Bonn in February 1966 paved the way for a visit by the Foreign Trade Minister, Gheorghe Cisara, in May. The Federal Economics Minister, Kurt Schmücker, returned the visit in September and invited the Foreign Minister Manescu to Bonn for the signing ceremonies. The fall of the Erhard government in October delayed the schedule; nonetheless the Grand Coalition government informed Moscow in mid-December 1966 that it intended to send delegations to Hungary and Czechoslovakia to explore diplomatic relations (' Interview with Foreign Minister Brandt ', *Münchener Merkur*, 25 July 1969).

1956. The Bucharest Declaration was intended to be a new demonstration of solidarity that could serve to counter Bonn's ' opening to the East ' and Washington's peaceful engagement. But Rumanian defiance denied the Pact the consensus upon which effective implementation depended.

In her defence Rumania argued that her decision advanced both the general Pact policy of promoting a regional security system through relaxing tensions and the erosion of Bonn's intransigence. By accepting unqualified relations with a socialist state and an ally of East Germany, Bonn had compromised its claims to exclusive representation of the German nation.[7] And gestures towards normalcy, if followed up by tangible mutual benefits, might induce a greater understanding in West German circles of the Eastern Europeans' views on a regional settlement—security through border stabilization as the basis of durable *détente*. Finally, the Rumanians argued by implication that there were ' good and bad Germans ' and that the most appropriate means of alleviating the German menace was to encourage the ' constructive forces ' within the Federal Republic, such as the SPD and FDP, which were already switching their priorities from reunification to normalization.

This rationale was not convincing to Rumania's allies. Within one month of her ' defection ' from the common line, on 8–10 February 1967, the Pact Foreign Ministers met in Warsaw to devise a joint stand against both Bonn and Bucharest. Rather than a sign of moderation, Bonn's tactics were denounced as schemes to undermine the Pact's united front. Poland and Czechoslovakia now sided firmly with East Germany's demands for a tough line to counteract Rumania's alleged encouragement of West German ambitions.[8] At this

[7] In an apparent gesture of affirmation, Brandt commented, on his visit to Bucharest in August 1967, that the problem of creating a European security arrangement applied equally to the two political systems that exist on German soil. This was his first step away from the policy of exclusive authority (cited in Kaiser, p. 118). See also Ceausescu's speech before the Grand National Assembly, Radio Bucharest, 25 July 1967; joint communiqué on Brandt's visit (*Rom.*, 21 Aug. 1967).

[8] For the polemics on Rumania's move, see *ND*, 25 Jan., 3 Feb., 11 May, 12 June, 6 & 10 Aug. 1967; Rumania's reply *Scînteia*, 4 Feb. & Radio Bucharest, 25 July 1967; and for the gradual shift in the Soviet position Tass, 8 Feb., Radio Moscow, 13 Apr. & 8 Aug. 1967.

and subsequent sessions three measures were apparently approved. A polemical campaign was launched to expose the dangers of Rumania's position and explain the correct inter-pretation of the Bucharest Declaration. Secondly, East Germany won endorsement of her own policy of selective diplomacy, or an inverted Hallstein Doctrine, whereby full recognition by Bonn of East Berlin became the condition for diplomatic relations between any other Pact member and the Federal Republic. [9] Finally, to reinsure their territorial integrity and to demonstrate the permanency of the existing borders in Eastern Europe, it was agreed to negotiate a series of bilateral mutual defence treaties, supplementing the obligations provided in the Warsaw Treaty.

The bilateral security treaties were intended originally by their sponsoring states as concrete demonstrations of solidarity against German and imperialist reaction. But they became important disruptive factors themselves in Pact solidarity as a common German policy became increasingly difficult to define and the unifying factor of a mutual threat regressed. The original series of accords was negotiated in the immediate post-war era, and the Warsaw Treaty was concluded specifically to supersede this set of individual agreements. It was regarded as an artifice, therefore, when they were resurrected and submitted for renewal to counter the alleged Bucharest–Bonn subterfuge. But they symbolized the growing fears of the northern-tier members about expanding West German influence and the mounting frustration over their inability to rectify their claims. However, the inability of the Pact to achieve a consensus on a German policy was only emphasized by the reinstitution of archaic anti-Bonn devices.

East Germany had signed a bilateral defence treaty only with the Soviet Union, concluded in 1964 mainly as a face-saving device for Moscow's refusal to negotiate a separate peace treaty. The GDR concluded similar accords between March and September 1967 with her other allies and, in turn, they renewed their own treaties with each Pact member before the

<hr />

[9] The formal demand that this principle, the ' Ulbricht Doctrine ' should be applied was first expressed in Ulbricht's speech to the SED CC on 15 Dec. 1966 (*ND*, 16 Dec. 1966).

twenty-year termination deadline.[10] These pacts emphasized the existence of two German states, the inviolability of existing borders, the presence of West Berlin on East German territory, and mutual aid in the event of military aggression. The exception was again Rumania. She refused to accept such an agreement with East Germany because of the potential impact it would have on her relations with Bonn and declined to renegotiate existing treaties with her other allies. These agreements were allowed to lapse into their automatic five-year renewal provision, pending renegotiation, except for Rumania's treaty with Czechoslovakia, which was renewed barely two weeks before the August invasion and directed against any potential aggressor.

The Soviet-Rumanian treaty of 4 February 1948 was the key to other accords. The chief obstacles in this case were the ' consultations clause ' (Art. 4), the automatically binding nature of the commitments, and the agreement to take joint action to obviate ' any threat of renewed aggression by Germany or any other Power which might be associated with Germany '. The treaty stipulated that the two countries ' will consult one another on all important international questions touching on the interests of both countries '. Rumania maintained that Moscow violated this provision in the Cuban and Middle East crises, and apparently sought some formula whereby a greater degree of consultation could be assured when any issue affected Rumanian interests. Yet Bucharest probably objected to centralization schemes that would force co-ordination of all aspects of its foreign policy with the Kremlin. On her part, the Soviet Union probably proposed that non-obligatory consultations should be undertaken when both parties agreed on an *ad hoc* basis. A compromise that embodies portions of the Rumanian position would differ from the provisions in other bilateral treaties. The Soviet treaties with Bulgaria, Hungary, and Czechoslovakia include unqualified provisions for consultation. Soviet concessions on this point would be important

[10] The bilateral pacts were signed on the following dates: GDR–Poland, 15 Mar. 1967; GDR–Czechoslovakia, 17 Mar. 1967; GDR–Hungary, 18 May 1967; GDR–Bulgaria, 7 Sept. 1967. Text in Deutsches Institut für Zeitgeschichte, *Sicherheit und friedliche Zusammenarbeit in Europa; Dokumente 1954–1967* (East Berlin, 1968), pp. 366–75, 397–406.

deviations from Pact norms and would tend to ratify the independence Bucharest enjoys over her other allies in security
matters.[11]

The 1948 treaty also required both parties to extend assistance to each other in the event of hostilities ' immediately and
with all the means at their disposal '. The Rumanian constitution adopted in 1965, however, implicitly proscribed any
international obligation that automatically binds Rumania to
assist another state at war. Only the government of Rumania
can determine when a state of war exists and what international
defence commitments she will honour. In contrast, the renewed Soviet bilateral treaties with Hungary and Bulgaria
bind each country to the other's defence in any conflict, in other
words, in the event of Soviet-Chinese hostilities. Rumania
undoubtedly resisted Soviet pressure for conforming on this
issue.

Soviet-Rumanian negotiations were apparently opened in
October 1967. A deliberate Rumanian leak to the Western
press in December indicated that they had broken down. The
party chief Ceausescu then bitterly accused Moscow of employing economic blackmail against Rumania. Late in December
1967 Rumanian and Soviet leaders met in Moscow and agreed
to resume negotiations and a Soviet delegation promptly
departed for Bucharest, but soon returned empty-handed. It
was reported that a draft was initialled in July 1968, but then
shelved because of the Prague emergency.

Soviet motives in promoting this series of additional commitments for augmenting an existing operational multilateral
defence structure seem reasonably clear. First, the erection of
a separate security system based on bilateral accords could
allow the Soviet Union to abrogate the Warsaw Treaty as a
quid pro quo in a European security agreement while preserving
the legal basis for military intervention or joint defensive undertakings with selected East European countries. Secondly, the
series of agreements provided moral support for the northern-
tier nations at a time when there was growing uncertainty about
the future course of West German policy. Thirdly, these

---

[11] For the text of the Czechoslovak, Bulgarian, and Hungarian treaties see
Pravda, 7 & 14 May & 8 Sept. 1970 respectively.

separate commitments afforded additional legal grounds for organizing joint defensive operations with less than the full Pact membership, thereby minimizing the embarrassment caused by one partner exercising a quasi-veto or non-participation in a Pact military undertaking, e.g. a Rumanian refusal to support an East German operation against Berlin. Finally, a programme of this scale, conducted individually by all her partners, could demonstrate the degree of Rumania's isolation from the main stream of East European sentiment and could serve to coerce her, lower tensions with the Soviet Union, and restore Pact solidarity.

However prudent these motives might have been, Moscow misjudged Rumania's determination to preserve her hard-earned autonomy. This policy error allowed the Rumanian-Soviet accord to become the most significant test of Rumania's determination to formulate her own decisions since her April 1964 'declaration of independence' and breach of Pact solidarity on the German issue. Bucharest apparently viewed the treaty as a test case for registering Soviet recognition of her freedom of manoeuvre. If successful, it would represent an important foundation for establishing a new form of relationship among East European nations. Rumania's bargaining position was strong. She did not need to participate in the bilateral series, and the ostracism tactics were not persuasive. But Moscow had to obtain a Rumanian signature if it expected to prove the virtues of the whole scheme through its universal acceptance. Further, any significant variations from the series signed by the other Pact members would be as injurious to Soviet prestige as an outright Rumanian rejection of Moscow's line. Either move or the continued suspension of the negotiations would confirm Bucharest's special status and establish a precedence affecting future political relationships throughout Eastern Europe. By over-trumping the Soviet Union in exposing her attempted economic blackmail, Rumania demonstrated that she was prepared to undergo extensive pressure for her independent stand on the German problem. The bilateral negotiations became the most serious trouble-spot in Soviet-Rumanian relations that quickly spilled over into Bucharest's overall Pact policy.

Rising uncertainties about Bonn's *Ostpolitik* was an important agenda item at the Pact PCC March 1968 meeting in Sofia. The Federal Foreign Minister Brandt had made significant revisions in the coalition government's position which registered notable concessions to the East European arguments on security. Brandt, in his speech to the Council of Europe on 24 January 1967 and in subsequent statements, advanced his own concepts for a European security system reminiscent of his policy as Mayor of Berlin—a concept of rapprochement by small steps. Sensitive to the East European position, he distinguished between an *europäische Sicherheitssystem* (European security system) and an *europäische Friedensordnung* (European peace order). He regarded the security system as a prerequisite to a broader peace order that was to be based on military *détente*, the renunciation of the use of force, mutual force reductions, and other 'confidence-building' measures. Military disengagement, in Brandt's view, could be implemented through converting the respective military forces to a peace-stabilizing function—or by abolishing the function and structure of both military pacts, replacing them with some form of indigenous European arrangement. Brandt acknowledged that security could not be guaranteed by merely proscribing war and military threat. He emphasized that the continuing American presence and commitment to Western Europe was a vital means of providing stability in any East–West settlement, but the main requirement remained an adjustment with the Eastern Europeans.[12]

In 1967 the CDU still disagreed with the substance of the SPD position. The ultimate goal remained reunification based upon a unitary state with Germanic features. On this foundation a durable *détente* could be erected; until then the CDU regarded the East German regime as usurpers, to be tolerated, but never genuinely accepted, thus precluding sincere coexistence. (For example, because of the tenacity of the CDU 'hardliners', the entire year 1967 was devoted to

[12] *E-A*, yr 1967, *Dokumente*, p. D81; Willy Brandt, *Friedenspolitik in Europa* (1968), *Aussenpolitik, Deutschlandpolitik, Europapolitik* (1968), 'German policy towards the East', *Foreign Affairs* Apr. 1968, pp. 476–86, & 'Entspannungspolitik mitlangem Atem', *Aussenpolitik*, 18 Oct. 1967.

exhaustive probings of the respect of other governments for the Hallstein Doctrine in the wake of establishing ties with Bucharest and before diplomatic relations were initiated with Yugoslavia.)

Such divergent viewpoints were the main obstacles to a more active opening to the East. At the same time the extent of the differences itself was alarming to East Germany and Poland. In this ambivalent situation, the Grand Coalition could not only participate in a limited dialogue with Moscow and seek a *modus operandi* with the GDR, but it could explore some live-and-let-live formula with the remaining East European states. Brandt's distinction between security and stability and his emphasis on practical measures to ensure confidence must have appealed to many Eastern Europeans.

The Pact's Sofia PCC meeting on 6–7 March 1968 deliberated on the implications of these developments, the Federal Republic's attitude towards the NPT, and its impact on European security affairs, Pact cohesion in face of 'the German threat ', and institutional improvements in the Pact's command structure.[13] Rumania's hesitancy to conclude bilateral defence accords, coupled with her repeated statements about the obsolescence of military pacts, may have led to suspicions that she was fostering genuine reservations about her commitments to the Pact. And Rumania's refusal to endorse any public statement or to participate in any conference attacking West Germany strongly implied that she no longer shared the Pact's definition of the most probable opponent. Her rejection of the ' common threat ' had already had an impact upon defence spending, force modernization, and military training. Thus her partners may have held reservations about both Rumania's dedication and the quality of her contribution to the collective effort.

The gravity of the situation had become apparent a week earlier when the Rumanian delegation walked out of the consultative meeting held in Budapest from 26 February to 5 March to discuss an all-party conference. This was the first time a communist delegation of this importance had made such a dramatic break with the collective party will since Chou

[13] *CDSP*, 27 Mar. 1968.

En-lai's departure from the last world communist conference in 1960, and it was unmistakably intended to reassert a Rumanian prerogative to insist upon bilateral discussions of contentious issues.

Rumania won limited concessions at Budapest and Sofia. The Rumanians subsequently published their delegate's speech at Budapest,[14] in which he said that it would have been in the interest of good preparation for the conference if ' all communist parties and workers' parties with no exception ' had been invited, and ' we establish here that all communist and workers' parties will be invited ' and ' are equal '. At Sofia, Rumania's tactics forced the delegates to abandon earlier procedures of issuing a single definitive statement on the topics discussed. The meeting released a communiqué and a separate statement covering general proceedings and substantive issues. The communiqué, which Rumania accepted, was important for its omissions. It did not endorse an earlier statement on security matters and Germany released by the Committee at Warsaw in 1965, or the Bucharest Declaration. It also failed to list improvements in any of the disputed topics, implying both that Rumania had virtually repudiated the main provisions of the Bucharest Declaration and that intra-Pact differences were not narrowed at Sofia. It also registered Rumania's progress since the last session in establishing a bona fide special status within the Pact when Bucharest's actions forced the Committee for the first time to focus on ' that which divides rather than unites' the Pact.[15]

On the other hand Rumania refused to sign the separate statement which called for prompt ratification of the NPT as a major advance towards European security and world peace. The NPT was viewed by the Pact as a key element to a satisfactory solution to the German problem, but Rumania had consistently rejected the document as discriminatory against small states. Thus events in Sofia polarized the Pact on several vital questions, as witnessed by the refusal of the other members to invite Rumania to the Dresden summit meeting two weeks

[14] Speech by P. Niculescu-Mizil at Budapest Consultative Meeting, *Rom.*, Suppl., 29 Feb. 1968.
[15] *Rude Pravo* (Prague), 16 July 1968.

later (on 23 March) or to other conferences dealing with the Prague crisis.

Rumania's independent policy sharply reduced the manoeuvrability of the northern-tier countries on security and German matters. It demonstrated that Pact solidarity was more important to East Germany, Poland, and the Soviet Union than to Rumania. These states could no longer organize an anti-Bonn campaign that would win Rumanian support. Indeed, Pact moderates probably observed that attempts to formulate a common stand on security and Germany had only underlined disunity and increased Rumania's freedom of action. Before the Prague crisis it appeared that whatever gains the conservative Pact members might make against Bonn would not compensate for the loss of Rumanian support.

The phenomenon of the Bucharest–Bonn–Moscow triangle was an important contribution to the rise of national communism in Eastern Europe and a crucial integer in the conservative Pact members' estimation of dangers such as the Prague crisis. Again, the increasing flexibility in Bonn's *Ostpolitik* was regarded by Pact members both as a danger and as an opportunity to advance their national interests. Rumania's lead in this effort provided an important precedent and an indication of benefits to be expected from a moderate policy towards the West. The implication of this development was that a growing appreciation could emerge among other Pact members that the right to disagree is essential for the preservation of their expanding national interests. With the rising demands of national communism each member would be encouraged to cite the Rumanian precedent and increasingly assert its individual prerogatives in Pact deliberations. Moreover, the inclusion of a broader span of individual national interests in Pact affairs would probably divide proportionally the number of issues on which the Pact can find consensus or a common denominator. The gradual lack of uniformity could stimulate single nations, like East Germany, to pursue high-risk policies. This uncertainty could be amplified by Moscow's declining interest in endorsing political offensives against the West that did not reflect genuine Pact solidarity. Consequently, the Pact's German policy in 1968 was marked as much by the desire to prevent a further splintering of the Pact's political matrix as to achieve positive advantages. In this situation of declining options for the conservative members against their 'main threat', the emergence of Prague's liberalization programme multiplied apprehensions in the northern tier by a factor that is difficult to calculate in the West. The Bucharest–Bonn collusion was now compounded, not by active Czechoslovak encouragement, but by its introversion and lack of interest in the collective effort against the 'main threat'. Rumanian dissidence had provided the seedbed for a Czechoslovak challenge to Soviet authority on a much broader scale.

Ceausescu immediately grasped the gravity of the Rumanian predicament resulting from the invasion of Czechoslovakia. A Declaration adopted by an extraordinary session of the Rumanian National Assembly on 22 August stated: ' For no reason, in no case, and in no form, can the Warsaw Treaty organization be used in or invoked for military actions against a socialist country '.[16] It also called on the United Nations to carry out its obligation of ' taking the necessary steps when the independence and sovereignty of a member state have been violated, when a country becomes subject to a foreign armed intervention '. This Declaration stated that the invasion was a direct violation of the explicit provisions of the Warsaw Treaty and asserted that the National Assembly reserved the right of approving or disapproving ' all obligations of our people involving military collaboration and co-operation with other countries, and any clause concerning the stationing of any allied troops on Rumanian territory '. While registering her alarm, Rumania also publicly reiterated her absolute authority over all aspects of national security matters.

Ceausescu then requested a meeting with Tito, which took place on 24 August—both party leaders had been in Prague some two weeks before the invasion to bolster the Czechoslovaks' determination to resist external coercion. Tito asserted that the alleged grounds for the occupation, a threat from West Germany, were ' absurd '.[17] Both condemned the invasion and agreed to pursue parallel efforts to deter similar Soviet action

[16] *Rom.*, Suppl., 22 Aug. 1968, p. 16.
[17] *Tanjug*, 24 Aug. 1968.

in their respective countries, with the proviso that their co-operation be low-keyed to minimize the impression that Bucharest was collaborating with a non-Pact nation.[18]

By the time of another meeting between Tito and Ceausescu on 1–2 February 1969, a marked change had emerged. The immediate tactical danger of a Soviet invasion had receded and both leaders focused on the broader problems of ensuring continued latitude in their relations with Moscow. The concept of limited socialist sovereignty, or the so-called Brezhnev Doctrine, was denounced as incompatible with state authority. They reaffirmed their long-standing respect for the principles of national independence, sovereignty, full equality of rights, and non-intervention in internal affairs of other nations.[19] Yet it had become clear that a more activist policy was required to preserve their former policy options.

Tito adopted a cautious approach on the state level by welcoming Gromyko in September 1969 as the first Soviet leader to visit Yugoslavia in five years. But inter-party relations remained strained, cooling the atmosphere between the countries. Ceausescu, on the other hand, adopted a more aggressive programme, by increasing the scope and pace of Rumanian diplomacy. His new policy appeared to be intentionally ambivalent, providing sufficient points of mutual accord to deter Soviet retribution, but at the same time strengthening ties with the West to secure freedom of manoeuvre.

In security matters, for example, Rumania agreed to resume participation in joint Pact manoeuvres, albeit on a limited scale. The Pact exercise in 1964 was the last occasion when Rumania had provided major units, but she detailed smaller units to manoeuvres in the Soviet Union in May 1969 and in the GDR in October 1970.[20] These minor gestures were the minimum required to assure her allies of Rumania's ability and intention to engage in combined operations. At the same time Rumania consistently refused Soviet suggestions that Pact exercises be conducted on Rumanian territory. And on repeated

[18] See Soviet charges to this effect, *Izvestia*, 24 Aug. & *Pravda*, 25 Aug. 1968.

[19] Radio Bucharest, 2 Feb. 1969.

[20] Radio Moscow, 25 Oct. 1970. By November 1970 there had been thirty joint Pact field exercises, all conducted since 1961, and it is believed that Rumania has participated in only seven.

occasions, Bucharest proposed that the Geneva Disarmament Conference and the UN General Assembly should adopt a ban on military manoeuvres near international boundaries and on foreign soil.

In Pact affairs, Rumania has resumed participation in all gatherings. She undoubtedly concluded that her non-attendance—she was not invited—at the anti-Czechoslovak meetings had been detrimental to Rumanian interests and that a return to Pact councils was a crucial measure to defend her position. After revealing in November 1968 that Rumania had resisted Soviet proposals at the Sofia PCC meeting for improving the Pact's command and control structure,[21] she endorsed the most sweeping alterations in the Pact's organization since its inception, which were authorized at the March 1969 Budapest PCC meeting. This session established a Council of Defence Ministers and approved the appointment of senior East European officers to an expanded Pact international staff. References were later made to her approval of unpublished measures to ' integrate ' Pact forces. To soften this apparent increased centralization under Soviet authority, the concept of national armed forces remaining under national authorities was repeatedly stressed.[22]

Ceausescu returned to this theme in the wake of an international flurry because of an article published in January 1970 by the Pact Chief of Staff, S. M. Shtemenko, referring to the existence of an integrated command.[23] Ceausescu addressed the party cadre of the Defence Ministry on 5 February and bluntly denied that Pact forces had been integrated, stating: ' The development of collaboration between our armies (approved at Budapest), in conformity with the principles underlying the relations between the socialist countries and with the treaties in force, excludes any interference in the internal affairs of another country. . . .' ' The sole leader of our armed forces is the Party, the Government, the supreme

[21] See above, n. 13.

[22] *Nepszabadsag* (Budapest), 10 May 1969 (*Survival*, May 1969).

[23] BBC, *SWB*, 2nd ser., SU/3299, 7 Feb. 1970, reporting *Krasnaya Zvezda*, 24 Jan. 1970; later diluted by Marshal Ivan Yakubovsky, C. in C. Combined Armed Forces, *Smena*, 3 Feb. 1970; and by a commentary on Radio Moscow, 5 Feb. 1907.

national command . . .'[24] The achievement of an integrated command is an essential element in Moscow's consolidation programme, and events during the spring of 1970 indicate that a major behind-the-scenes struggle had developed in which this issue probably played a key role.[25]

In party matters Rumania returned to the Preparatory Committee for the all-party conference. She joined the minority opposition at a meeting of the Committee in February and pointed out the failure of the delegates to agree even on the basic purpose of the conference. The same difficulty remained unresolved at a session in March. In a final attempt to reach an understanding about the purpose of the conference and the contents of the documents to be approved, a session of all sixty-eight delegates was convened barely two weeks before the conference was scheduled to open. Over 450 amendments to the Soviet draft documents were proposed; Rumania alone was reported to have tabled over 100. The Committee, however, was unable to resolve its differences and was forced to leave final decisions to the conference itself.

Ceausescu's performance during the conference was noteworthy for its circumspection. When Brezhnev shifted the debate from the deliberation of the proposed documents to a condemnation of Chinese communist heresy, Ceausescu did not walk out but led the denunciations of the Soviet breach of socialist integrity. The Rumanian tactic weakened the relevance of the documents to the proceedings without gaining concurrence in the deliberations. Indeed, it afforded an opportunity for public disagreement without imposing the onus of censure for the dissidents. The former restraints on national party behaviour embodied in the concept of 'democratic centralism' were seriously eroded. A lapse in discipline was demonstrated by both the Soviet Union and the Rumanians, to the detriment of the Kremlin's authority.[26]

In political developments, Rumanian policy followed a

[24] *Rom.*, Suppl., 7 Feb. 1970, p. 11.
[25] Albania attempted to restart the war scare of 1968 by publishing reports of an imminent Soviet invasion of Rumania and Yugoslavia (*Zeri i Populitt*, 6 Mar. 1970).
[26] Kevin Devlin, ' Khrushchev's peak and Brezhnev's foothill ', *Osteuropäische Rundschau* (Munich), 1969, no. 6, pp. 7–8.

similar pattern. While she returned to Pact and party councils, she was the first East European state to act as host to a US President. In an unavoidable affront to the Soviet Union, President Nixon's visit in July 1970 coincided with the Soviet party-state visit by Brezhnev and Kosygin to sign the bilateral defence pact and attend the 10th Rumanian Party Congress. As the first such visit since 1965, it was to demonstrate a new era in Rumanian-Soviet relations. In these circumstances the Russians cancelled their visit and relations between the two capitals were less than cordial.

A second major development had led to a further deterioration in Rumanian-Soviet relations. Progress had been made in the bilateral relations between several East European states and West Germany, and some movement had been noted in the Soviet attitude towards a European security conference. The Pact PCC met on 3–4 December 1969 in Moscow to establish a co-ordinated position on both issues. It was agreed to place a higher priority on the bilateral negotiations with Bonn than on the multilateral approach to European problems. But the bilateral negotiations required closer co-ordination, and the delegates agreed to appropriate consultations.[27] While it strongly endorsed any Pact efforts to improve relations with Bonn as a means of vindicating its two-Germanies policy, Bucharest viewed the new demands for policy co-ordination on such vital issues as a renewed Soviet bid to intensify centralization.

Like the other party leaders, Ceausescu addressed the party Central Committee Plenum about the implications of the new approach. On 13 December he reaffirmed Rumania's independent stand on foreign-policy issues and resolutely defended his two-Germanies policy. He asserted that this policy was a bridge between East and West that served the interests of all East European peoples and called upon his allies to follow Rumania's example in this regard.[28] (This was in sharp contrast to the East German insistence that all Pact members had agreed to make the legal recognition of the GDR by Bonn a precondition for normalizing relations.[29])

[27] Communiqué, *E-A*, 25th yr, 25 Feb. 1970, p. D76.
[28] Ibid., 25 Apr. 1970, p. D186.
[29] *ND*, 17 Dec. 1969.

Ceausescu's statement was followed by a general intensification in polemics between Rumania and the Soviet Union. Radio Moscow broadcast daily commentaries in Rumanian stressing the importance of party unity, the leading role of the Soviet state, the need to subordinate national interests to international duties, and the dangers of national deviation. The Rumanian Central Committee's official organ, *Lupta de clasa*, answered by devoting its entire January 1970 issue to a restatement of Bucharest's independence on virtually all important points of contact with the Soviet Union. The doctrine of ' limited socialist sovereignty ' was condemned and efforts to integrate or centralize the policies and economies of Eastern Europe were denounced. ' Socialist nations as a whole represent an association in whose framework free individual development is the prerequisite for the free development of all.'[30]

The political manifestation of Ceausescu's new defiant stand became apparent in a major revision of Rumania's position on a European security conference. Traditionally Bucharest had maintained a lukewarm attitude on the issue, arguing that a conference or series of meetings would require a major improvement in East–West relations and exhaustive preparation. Other points of East–West contacts could be more beneficially exploited to normalize relations. In his 13 December speech, however, Ceausescu stated that ' conditions are favourable for the convening of a conference '. This was the opening of an intensive campaign to convene an East–West conference. Ceausescu stated in a major policy declaration on 6 March 1970 that the premises already exist for a phase of negotiations for the preparation of such a conference. In an interview with *Le Monde* on 16 June, during his first visit to France, he virtually demanded that a conference be convened in the shortest possible time. In an unprecedented move, the Foreign Minister Manescu wrote an article for the spring issue of the French quarterly *Preuves*, presenting Rumania's argument, and the Premier, Ion Gheorghe Maurer, stressed the issue at a press conference on 23 June in Bonn. The conference was reportedly also discussed during Ceausescu's visit to Austria in September

---

[30] Ion Mitran, ' The nation in the present world ', *Lumea*, 29 Jan. 1970.

and to the United States in October. The conference issue received such prominence that it had apparently become an important reason for Rumania's sudden spurt of international visits and diplomacy.

A policy shift of this dimension warrants an explanation. This issue may have been Rumania's allocated share of the Pact's concerted bilateral approach to the West, but it seems more likely that Rumania assumed a self-appointed role and that she was using the issue as a key instrument in her relations with both Moscow and Bonn. The deteriorating atmosphere with the Soviet Union probably increased the pressure on Rumania to seize an issue which would permit her to demonstrate her continuing independence and gain political advantages. In the past Rumania has often energetically pursued a single controversial topic primarily to show that she had the ability to act. The security conference presented another such opportunity. But more important, if successful it would provide important safeguards against Soviet intervention. The proposed conference would have to make some commitment, if no more than a joint communiqué, on the renunciation of the use of force or the threat of force and a ban on intervention in domestic affairs. Any measure that would tend to institutionalize these principles would inhibit the utility of the ' limited-sovereignty ' doctrine and reinforce Rumanian concepts of independence and national integrity. A collective commitment, especially if it included US guarantees, would be a significant instrument for countering Soviet hegemony.

On the other hand, progress in the Soviet and Polish bilateral negotiations with the Federal Republic held the promise of a successful conclusion, but the intransigence of the GDR raised uncertainties about the usefulness of these efforts, since they had only a marginal affect on the crucial questions of Berlin and the division of Germany. Hindsight now suggests that East Germany may have intentionally hardened her position in order to force her partners to abandon an individualist approach and return to the multilateral approach of confronting the Federal Republic. While this is purely conjectural, Bucharest may then have estimated that it was necessary to make more concessions to the GDR to break her growing stranglehold on the key pressure points of European tensions. At stake was the wisdom and veracity of Rumania's two-Germanies policy that had been the *raison d'être* for her dissidence against Moscow. Bucharest apparently saw the conference as a means of preserving the vitality of its most important démarche in foreign policy and its future options by breaking the growing deadlock. Convening even a preparatory gathering would force Bonn to extend *de facto* recognition of East Berlin beyond any levels hitherto suggested—both states would have to be represented as equal and sovereign entities. This is the most probable rationale that propelled Rumania to the forefront of the advocates of the immediate convening of a security conference; it is also an indication of the level to which the relations with the Soviet Union had declined.

The most outstanding question between the two countries was the shelved bilateral mutual defence treaty. A solution was arrived at in mid-May 1970. At the height of the worst floods in his nation's history, Ceausescu flew unexpectedly to Moscow and both sides compromised. First, the two parties agreed on a new five-year trade agreement (1971–5) that provided for a programmed 19 per cent increase in trade the first year to 1,000 m. rubles and a 30 per cent overall increase. To date, trade between the two has steadily declined. Rumania's share of total Soviet trade in 1968 was 4·4 per cent, while the share of the Soviet Union in Rumanian trade dropped from 51·5 per cent in 1958 to 28·7 per cent in 1968.[31] In an important new development, however, Rumania abandoned her traditional opposition to joint enterprises and agreed to contribute financially to the joint development of iron-ore deposits in the Soviet Union. This was a major advance in Moscow's dilemma over the high costs of supplying raw materials to the Eastern Europeans and followed a similar accord with Czechoslovakia on oil extraction.

A treaty of friendship, co-operation, and mutual assistance was signed on 7 July.[32] The Rumanian position had been complicated by the renegotiation of the Czechoslovak-Soviet bilateral defence a month before (on 6 May 1970). The

[31] Radio Moscow, 2, 7, 23 July & 9, 10, 17 Sept. 1970.
[32] *Rom.*, Suppl., 10 July 1970 (*Survival*, Sept. 1970).

Czechoslovak treaty was not due for renegotiation until 1983, and the premature signing of the new treaty emphasized the importance Moscow attached to its unprecedented provisions. The treaty justified the August invasion and any further intervention in Czechoslovakia the other party deemed warranted. On its side, Prague was committed to participate in any additional applications of the Brezhnev Doctrine against heretical Communist Parties and to aid the Soviet Union in the event of an attack by any state (including China). The latter provision was also included in the renegotiated treaties with Hungary and Bulgaria.

The Rumanian-Soviet treaty, however, contained several unique provisions and omitted many of the solidarity ingredients explicitly incorporated in the other renegotiated treaties. No mention was made of limited sovereignty, no commitment was cited to economic integration (Rumania had already refused to join the new Comecon Bank as an integrative institution), and no pledge was included to intervene against heretical regimes (on the contrary, specific provisions against interference were emphasized in Arts. 1 & 6). In exchange Rumania accepted the obligation to aid the Soviet Union if she was attacked by any other state—including (by implication) China. (Rumania's constitutional restraints, however, may limit the utility of this provision.) The principles incorporated as the guide to international behaviour were standard Rumanian fare and the clauses on consultation were milder in tone than in the other treaties (the aim of such consultations was to place in accord the positions of the two countries, while the other treaties provided that the two sides shall consult and act in accordance with a common standpoint). In a further compromise, the Soviet Union extracted an *unswerving* commitment to the treaty provisions, but Rumania won a time-limit to her obligation: ' during the period of the [Warsaw] Treaty '. The Soviet-Rumanian treaty, then, was an important step towards legalizing Bucharest's special status within the Warsaw Pact; it sanctioned Rumania's degree of autonomy and eliminated the more onerous obligations imposed on other Pact members—it stood as an important qualification on the application of the Brezhnev Doctrine. Moreover, to strengthen this qualification,

Rumania sent a note to the UN Secretary-General in July proposing a multilateral guarantee for a Balkan nuclear-free zone and despatched a high-level delegation to China to confide Rumania's interpretation of the treaty provisions.

This interpretation was reinforced by the Soviet Union's behaviour at the signing ceremonies in July. The treaty was labelled an important step towards 'normalizing' relations between the two countries and was to be signed by both Brezhnev and Kosygin, as was the Czechoslovak treaty. At the last minute Brezhnev cancelled his visit, and the ceremonies with Kosygin were remarkably cool. Brezhnev's cancellation was probably due to Soviet reluctance to conduct a full party-state visit that would seem to demonstrate full endorsement of the latest treaty and its unique provisions or of Rumania's independent stand. Moscow could not afford to repeat the mistake of appearing to support dissidence, as did Khrushchev in his 1955 visit to Yugoslavia.

The signing of the Soviet-Rumanian treaty arrested the deterioration in relations and opened the way for the prompt negotiation or renewal of bilateral treaties between Rumania and other Pact members. In their first official visits, the Polish party chief Wladislaw Gomulka and the Prime Minister Jozef Cyrankiewicz signed on 12 November 1970 a renewed bilateral treaty in Bucharest (the initial treaty had expired in January 1969). On 19 November a bilateral treaty with Bulgaria was signed in Sofia, and Radio Bucharest announced on 20 November that Ulbricht would come to Bucharest early in December to sign the defence treaty initialled on 1 October 1969. The renewed treaty with Czechoslovakia had been signed on 16 August 1968, and a defence accord with Hungary was to be signed in 1971.[33]

The conclusion of these treaties was widely regarded as a turning point in Rumania's strained relations with her allies over her German policy. The texts of the latest bilateral treaties were virtually identical. In concessions to Rumania, they include the same principles for international behaviour as were contained in the Rumanian-Soviet treaty. They are directed against imperialism in general and not exclusively

[33] *E-A*, 25th yr, 25 Apr. 1970, p. D186.

West Germany, and link European security specifically to the inviolability of existing borders. They do not provide for adjustment of viewpoints, but merely consultations on ' socialist construction '. And they aim at advancing European stability and *détente*, while pledging aid in the event of armed aggression. (As in the Soviet case, they were also accompanied by trade protocols covering the next five years which envisaged an 80 per cent increase in the case of Poland and 60 per cent increase in Bulgarian-Rumanian trade. The figures for projected trade with East Germany have not yet been released, but Rumania ranks the lowest among the Pact members in East German and Polish trade, and the projected increases are expected to relieve her growing deficit.)

The importance of Bucharest's opening negotiations with East Berlin should not be underestimated. Rumanian refusal to jeopardize her relations with the Federal Republic by accepting the GDR's definition of the threat was the chief obstacle in renewing her treaty with the Soviet Union, the corner-stone of the entire series. There were probably several factors that influenced Moscow, Bucharest, and East Berlin to alter their policies sufficiently to allow an accommodation on this scale. The Soviet Union probably concluded that as movement on the German problem and European security became visible, a higher priority should be placed on closing ranks with Rumania rather than attempting to discipline her through ostracism. In view of the uncertainties surrounding the scope of the change in Bonn's policies, it would seem essential to present the West with as solid a socialist front as possible. Further, Rumania's aloofness from the bilateral defence agreements tended to register her *de facto* special status within the Pact, a precedent that was dangerous for bloc solidarity. After three years of intense in-fighting over Bucharest's separatist German policy, drastic measures were required to reduce the polarization within the Pact. Accordingly, Moscow coupled favourable economic terms with provisions in the defence pact that met virtually all Rumania's key demands. The terms of the other bilateral treaties confirm that her allies had moved substantially towards Rumania's position on their basic differences.

On her side, Rumania probably estimated that the international atmosphere warranted a closer, but still guarded, identification with her East European allies. A climate both of growing uncertainty and stability was emerging in the Balkans that was a partial reflection of the general international uneasiness about the impact of great-power strategic parity and the growing prospects of a naval confrontation in the Mediterranean. In an era of parity the prerogatives of smaller states become less precise. The security of the smaller European states rests either on great-power protection or general durable *détente*. In a period of transition between these two, when future trends remain unpredictable, the smaller states have to seek additional options. In the Balkans this new barely distinguishable atmosphere became apparent as the Sino-Soviet dispute gradually subsided. A stabilization of the Soviet Far Eastern position was evident, affording greater potential latitude in her operations on other fronts (for example, it is noteworthy that China has refrained from any polemical attacks against Moscow's unprecedented participation in the active military defence of the UAR. On the other hand, she has refilled most of her formerly vacated ambassadorial posts, including all those in socialist countries. In a most unexpected development, she even agreed to reopen full diplomatic relations with her arch foe, Yugoslavia.) In the same vein, Albania sought to improve contacts with her socialist Balkan neighbours and extended diplomatic relations to four additional Western states (totalling ten). Pact members were also active. In September 1970 Bulgaria's party leader Todor Zhivkov was reported to have sent a personal note to Tito proposing a summit meeting and possibly signing a friendship treaty that would signal a solution to their most outstanding problem, the existence of a Macedonian nation. Zhivkov then embarked on an unprecedented tour of West European states, seeking support for a European security conference. These developments created an atmosphere of adjustment in the Balkans in which Rumania actively participated. Also in September Ceausescu visited Zhivkov in Sofia for their first bilateral discussion in over three and a half years. Thus began a new *rapport* and extensive exchanges between the two countries, reminiscent of their warm relations in 1965–6. In November, Ceausescu held his eighth and reportedly most comprehensive talks with Tito— both leaders had first-hand impressions of Nixon and US policy to exchange. Thus the regional atmosphere probably contributed to Bucharest's decisions to compromise with both the GDR and the Soviet Union.

The other international development affecting Rumania's external perspective, the great-power naval build-up in the Mediterranean, was also noteworthy for its unprecedented features. In less than four years, the Soviet Union established a permanent naval presence in waters formerly regarded as an 'American lake' and secured general recognition of her stature as a Mediterranean power. Moscow's commitment to Arab military parity with Israel indicated that she was prepared to pay a heavy price to expand Soviet influence in the Middle East. After 1964 Moscow launched a successful campaign to isolate Turkish and American interests and secure a reasonably reliable assurance of access through the Dardanelles under conditions less than general war. Equally important, stability in the Balkans was essential if the land flanks on the Soviet sea communications south and aerial overflight rights were to be secured. So far Soviet military power in the Middle East has only been employed to support Arab nations and will probably not be used to challenge a NATO country. It is conceivable, however, that the Soviet Union could employ her forces, as presently constituted, south of the Straits, to assert Soviet pressure among non-aligned nations, e.g. to influence a political-succession struggle in Yugoslavia, Albania, or North Africa. Thus the Soviet build-up in the Mediterranean has added an additional and immediate new dimension to the global great-power contest for the Balkan states.

In a more direct way, however, Rumania probably viewed the expanding dialogues between Bonn and Eastern Europe as an opportunity to advance her two-Germanies policy to its logical conclusion. After the partial reconciliation achieved with her allies at the March 1969 PCC meeting, Rumania was able to expand her contacts with Bonn (within five months four ministerial exchanges took place). But she maintained her former even-handedness towards both Germanies. In his speech on 13 December 1969 before the party Plenum, Ceausescu praised the growing contacts between Bonn and Poland and Moscow. He referred to the formation of the SPD–FDP government as evidence of growing strength of progressive forces in the Federal Republic. After pointing to Rumania's repeated demands that the Pact nations normalize relations with Bonn, he called on all states to recognize the GDR.[34]

Official impartiality towards both Germanies, however, had served its purpose. Rumania's successful defence for over three years of her two-Germanies policy had identified her stand on the German problem as vital to Rumanian interests, both for its intrinsic merits and for its value in inter-Pact relations. Her resistance had also polarized the Pact on an issue of vital interest to other states and had strengthened both Rumania's stature as a minority leader and her latitude within the Pact. At the opposite pole were East Germany's demands for universal recognition of her national sovereignty, with the Soviet Union's aim of consolidating her authority in Eastern Europe caught between these two extremes. Rumania undoubtedly concluded that the Soviet objective was the more dangerous of the two, especially since the merits of her German policy had now become generally accepted by her allies. But to preserve the initiative formerly associated with this policy and her freedom of action against Soviet hegemony it was necessary to shift the emphasis in her policy and give more active support to the GDP's claim to legitimacy and security. Thus, while no concessions were made to East Berlin's traditional charges against the Federal Republic, Rumania agreed to conclude a treaty with the GDR that called for universal recognition of her sovereignty, the inviolability of her borders, and the preservation of her territorial integrity. Both states profited: the GDR by gaining greater solidarity for her claims among her allies, and Rumania by promoting the legitimacy of both Germanies.

The GDR, the second polarizing force within the Pact, probably recognized her declining leverage against her allies as West Germany moved towards recognizing the permanency of her East European borders. Thus the border questions and

[34] *Rom.*, Suppl., 23 Nov. 1970; *Trybuna Ludu*, 12 Nov., Radio Bucharest & Radio Sofia, 16 Nov. 1970.

the German threat lost their cohesive effects, and East Germany's highest priority, the legitimization of her rule, had become seriously jeopardized. Moreover, the process of accommodation between the other East Europeans and West Germany heightened East Berlin's isolation from the only nations that could advance her major national objective. Therefore, as the East Europeans' anxieties over regional security diminished, the GDR gradually shifted her strategy to emphasize stability and regional endorsement of her claims. In these circumstances, the GDR tacitly accepted the cogency of Rumania's two-Germanies policy and implicitly compromised her own inverted Hallstein Doctrine by agreeing to Bucharest's terms for a bilateral defence accord. When she initialled a military pact with Rumania in October 1970, that did not specify West Germany as the chief danger to her existence; it implied recognition of West Germany's peaceful intentions and renunciation of her own claims to socialize the Federal Republic. German reunification on communist terms had been finally abandoned. Thus the partial adjustment between East Berlin and Bucharest was an important contribution to the reduction of the border issue and also to East European strategies for reunification. By the end of 1970 the crux of the German problem from the Eastern European viewpoint, then, had been largely refined down to the main issue of the legitimization of East German rule; a question that depended as much on popular endorsement of the GDR's domestic policies as on West German recognition or East European solidarity.

4

EUROPEAN SECURITY PROBLEMS:
THE MULTILATERAL APPROACH IN WEST
GERMAN–WARSAW PACT RELATIONS

ONE of the most contentious problems in West German–
Warsaw Pact relations has been regional security. From the
Soviet viewpoint, Bonn's ' revanchism ', or refusal to accept the
consequences of its defeat, has been the ' main threat ' to the
physical security of Eastern Europe. The Federal Republic's
rejection of the GDR claims to legitimacy and maintenance of
her own terms for reunification, her reluctance to accede to the
Czechoslovak demands for a formal abrogation of the Munich
Agreement, and her refusal to relinquish her eastern territories
by recognizing the inviolability of Poland's borders were cited
by Moscow as justification for establishing a collective-security
organization to protect Eastern Europe. These clarion calls
induced a visceral response among East European regimes who
have traditionally viewed their military threats as a product of
(*a*) US tactical and strategic nuclear superiority, (*b*) West
German rearmament, and (*c*) the confrontation between two
military blocs. The changing nature of these reference points
has corresponded with an evolution in the political aspects of
the East–West dispute and a modification in Moscow's attitude
towards its main European threat that have resulted in a
variety of communist proposals for the settlement of European
security matters in the broad context of regional accords. In
consequence, the Soviet position on European security in
general has become an important indicator of Moscow's
intentions to pursue an East–West *détente* and *rapport* with West
Germany.

On their side, the West Germans regard the entrenchment
of thirty-two Soviet divisions in Central Europe as a menacing
threat to their national survival. The solidarity of the Eastern
Europeans with the Soviet security arrangement is considered
far less ominous than the physical presence of Soviet troops
along all the eastern borders of the Federal Republic. These
garrisons guarantee a Soviet response to almost any outbreak
of hostilities along the Elbe, and they impart the risk of the

prompt delivery of tactical nuclear weapons if the conflict reaches major proportions.[1] Bonn's allies generally concur with this estimate and have responded by formulating a counter-vailing collective-security system and by seeking ways to alleviate the division of Germany. Thus Germany has been both the source of European insecurity and a key participant in various endeavours to reduce these anxieties and tensions.

When faced in 1954 with the realities of West German inte-gration into the NATO military structure, Moscow advanced its first scheme for general European security. Soviet proposals for universal disarmament, however, had been discussed and abandoned earlier, and the chill of the cold war eroded Western confidence in Soviet intentions. When these efforts proved unsuccessful, the Soviet Union established her own defensive pact. Accusing the West of initiating the division of Europe into hostile camps, Moscow's proposals for European security during the mid-1950s called for the dissolution of military blocs within the context of Article 11 of the Warsaw Treaty, which states that the treaty can be superseded only by a general European collective-security accord; in other words, after the abrogation of those Western institutions responsible for the Continent's division.

In the late 1950s and early 1960s the Soviet Union modified her position by proposing non-aggression accords between the two pacts that would have left the military organizations intact. She also sponsored a variety of plans to promote a military *détente*. As early as 1958, the Polish Foreign Minister Adam Rapacki called for a nuclear freeze in Poland, Czechoslovakia, and the two Germanies, followed by additional proposals for a nuclear-free zone in Central Europe. While unsuccessful, these schemes are now acclaimed by Warsaw as major contributions to inducing agreement and ratification of the NPT.

In December 1964, after Khrushchev's dismissal, the Pact announced a renewed interest in European security. Before the UN General Assembly, Poland called for a conference of European states to examine the problems of Continental

---

[1] Federal Republic, Bundesministerium für Verteidigung, *Weissbuch 1970*, *Zur Sicherheit der Bundesrepublik Deutschland und zur Lage der Bundeswehr* (Bonn, 1970), pp. 3–13.

security in their entirety. This initiative was promptly endorsed by the Pact's PCC, which met in Warsaw on 19–20 January 1965 to consider appropriate responses to the possibility of West Germany participating in NATO's MLF. The ensuing Pact communiqué urged the freezing of nuclear armaments and the creation of a nuclear-free zone in Central Europe, and proposed the convocation of a conference of European states ' to discuss measures ensuring collective security in Europe '.[2]

For the next fifteen months no formal Pact declarations on European security were issued. The propaganda apparatus actively pursued this theme, however, and a variety of bilateral discussions were opened, primarily between the smaller members of both alliances. Poland, Rumania, and Hungary were particularly active on the communist side and Belgium, the Netherlands, and Denmark showed the most interest within NATO. Initially these discussions focused largely on the complexity of the issue and the exploration of additional means for encouraging wider interest among their respective allies. Accordingly, a variety of international enterprises were organized. Non-governmental and unofficial groups in both East and West were encouraged to consider various aspects of collective security. Parliamentarians from ten European states were organized into a semi-official body to discuss the issue, and Yugoslavia became the prime mover in a campaign to convene an international conference on Mediterranean security which finally met in 1968. Budapest repeatedly sought Western support for its suggestion that a four-power preparatory committee (Hungary, Poland, Belgium, and the Netherlands) should be created to consider formally an agenda for a larger conference. At every opportunity Warsaw promoted this scheme, or alternatively a six-power preparatory committee. The configuration was less important than the need to commit the West to some kind of formal deliberation on European security at an early date.

Several features stand out in these initial East European endeavours. The smaller Pact nations displayed a keen sense of urgency in advancing the cause of European security and a

---

[2] *Pravda*, 22 Jan. 1965; *CDSP*, 10 Feb. 1965, pp. 14–15.

corresponding frustration at their lack of progress. The urgency reflected their assessment that only in the broader context of East–West *rapport* could they increase their freedom of manoeuvre in foreign policy. Their frustration was due in part to the variety of conflicting national priorities that were emerging in Eastern Europe and partly to a lack of high interest in the Kremlin.

The early Eastern European efforts projected the impression of being an integral part of the new Soviet leaders' policy of broadening rapprochement wherever feasible and advantageous. But they probably enjoyed only the Kremlin's acquiescence, not its active attention. Indeed, it was not until the Soviet Foreign Minister Gromyko's visit to Rome in April 1966 that Moscow officially restated its desire for an all-European security conference.

In view of her allies' active campaigning, the reticence of the Soviet Union is noteworthy. Several explanations may be offered for her seeming distraction and then renewed interest in the issue. First, the Sino-Soviet dispute had erupted again after Chou En-lai's visit and meeting with the new Soviet leaders, and preoccupation with China was paramount during the summer of 1965. It was not until the second Afro-Asian Conference in November 1965 that this trend was satisfactorily reversed. By the following spring, Chinese attentions were so introverted that Moscow's freedom of manoeuvre had been sufficiently restored to allow engagement on other fronts. Secondly, the new Soviet leaders quickly reversed the ' hairbrained ' schemes of their predecessor and attempted to place ' peaceful coexistence ' on a more credible basis, especially in vulnerable Afro-Asian states. While virtually all Khrushchev's former protégés in the third world, except Nasser and Castro, had been overthrown by their own people, ten heads of Afro-Asian countries, including all the Asian members of CENTO, paid official visits to Moscow within the first year of Brezhnev's administration. By the spring of 1966 a high degree of cordiality had been established with Moscow's southern neighbours, especially Turkey and Iran. Thirdly, the Cuban missile crisis had been a decisive demonstration of the precise limits of Moscow's strategic capabilities. On the rebound the Soviet

Union sought a highly circumspect *détente* with her chief adversary that would reduce the immediate danger to her in the confrontation. Accordingly, the hot-line accord and the limited Nuclear Test-Ban Treaty were signed. From the Soviet viewpoint, her relations with the United States had become less risky and more manageable, until she could offset her strategic inferiority by her massive ICBM construction programme launched during the same period. Fourthly, the heresy within the world communist movement had been temporarily quelled —serious disorder did not erupt again until the issue of the all-party conference was foisted on the non-ruling Communist Parties. With the erosion of Chinese pressure on Moscow, independent-minded Communist Parties recognized the limited leverage they could exercise in establishing mutually recognized autonomy within the movement.

Fifthly, Moscow viewed the West at that time as being in a state of acute crisis. Britain had been shut out of the Common Market and the MLF died under its own weight. The United States was becoming increasingly preoccupied with non-European affairs and antagonism was arising with individual partners, i.e. Turkey, France, then Greece. President de Gaulle was asserting France's ascendancy as the chief spokesman of Western Europe and his concept of a single European entity from the Atlantic to the Urals was basically compatible with communist ideas of a single European security unit. Further, after Gromyko's announcement in Rome, de Gaulle crowned his grievances against the Alliance and spurred his ambitions in Eastern Europe by withdrawing French forces from the military organization of the Alliance—marking what the Kremlin saw as a new low point in the erosion of US leadership. This ' Atlantic crisis ' was viewed by the Soviet Union as the inevitable development of natural demands for the restoration of national sovereignty from US hegemony. Radio Moscow on 23 March 1967 could thus claim that:

the national interests of individual NATO countries are gaining the upper hand. This process will inevitably continue as more people in the NATO countries grasp the senselessness of a military grouping directed against the socialist states which are no danger to European peoples.

Finally, the problems of the Erhard regime, partly because of offset-payment difficulties, were regarded as a propitious opportunity to increase pressure against Bonn and its policy of integration with the West.

The sum total of these events was that by mid-1966 the Soviet Union concluded that she was in a sufficiently secure diplomatic position to advance her interests in areas that appeared increasingly vulnerable to Soviet influence, primarily Western Europe. Gromyko's April 1966 programme for a European peace order called for all European states to work together to establish peaceful ties among peoples of East and West. This proposal was an important subject discussed at the July 1966 Pact summit meeting in Bucharest. The ensuing Bucharest Declaration identified West Germany, NATO, and the United States as the main dangers to European security and world peace. The gravity of the threat was the alleged reason why European nations must act promptly to erect a regional security order. This aim was to be achieved by mobilizing all ' anti-imperialist forces ' in Western Europe to promote the abolition of the two opposing military blocs. The abrogation of the Hallstein Doctrine and the establishment of full relations between the two German states was considered instrumental for these efforts. The vehicle for organizing this new order should be a European security conference, apparently without US participation since the United States had ' nothing in common with the vital interests of European peoples '.[3]

This was not a precise plan of action. The substantive issues related to military disengagement, such as mutual-force reductions, were not tackled. It was paradoxical that the Pact had originally promoted concepts of military disengagement, such as the nuclear-free zones, while the NATO countries were pressing for general disarmament; yet when the NATO countries sought a military sign of a *détente*, the Pact countries produced vague generalities. As a result of this imprecision in the Pact proposal, it received little formal attention in the West, but it did have a direct influence on Western initiatives towards Eastern Europe. President Johnson announced on 23 October his policy of ' bridge-building ' and Bonn opened the Kiesinger

[3] *Pravda*, 9 July 1966 (*Survival*, Sept. 1965).

administration by establishing diplomatic recognition with Rumania in January 1967. Thus the chief contribution of the Bucharest Declaration to East–West relations was the formulation of a new hard line against the Federal Republic, within the context of growing *détente*, that prompted positive, rather than negative, Western counteractions.

A modification in Moscow's estimate of the German threat became apparent at subsequent Pact conclaves. On 24–26 April 1967 a meeting of European Communist and Workers' Parties was held at Karlovy Vary. Unlike the Bucharest gathering, where states were represented, the Karlovy Vary meeting included leaders of both ruling and non-ruling Communist Parties. Its purpose was to expand the campaign for a European security conference. Accordingly, sweeping attacks were made on US, West German, and NATO policies in order to demonstrate that the political situation in Europe was rapidly deteriorating and to justify the conference's call for more energetic counter-measures. In its Declaration ' For Peace and Security in Europe ' it identified the German problem as the most disruptive factor in European stability. It called for the West's acceptance of Europe's existing boundaries; the GDR's claims to full diplomatic recognition; invalidation of the Munich Agreement (*diktat*); renunciation of the Hallstein Doctrine; acceptance of West Berlin as a separate political entity; ratification of the NPT; and renunciation of the use of force. A loosening on the stand on West Germany was registered, however, by the declaration's encouragement of co-operation with progressive elements there—without identifying them. The gathering concluded (by implication) that there were now both 'good and bad Germans'. [4]

The Karlovy Vary meeting endorsed the Bucharest Declaration and the earlier communist efforts to stimulate regional security, i.e. the nuclear-free zones, the Group of Ten parliamentarians, the cascade of bilateral approaches and, of course, the convening of an all-European security conference. The distinctive feature of the Karlovy Vary meeting was the inauguration of a campaign to gain broad popular support for the dissolution of NATO during the treaty's 20th anniversary

---

[4] *Survival*, July 1967; *E-A*, yr 1967, *Dokumente*, p. D259.

when members could legally withdraw. This was the most aggressive Soviet effort yet to promote security through the collapse of the opposing pact, but it was marred by Moscow's inability to induce all communist leaders to attend the conference and thereby assure full support for a concerted effort. (Rumania refused to participate because of the persisting anti-German tone. Yugoslavia did not attend, insisting that progress towards security could only be made at the governmental level, and several non-ruling parties were represented by lesser dignitaries because they had various reservations about Soviet intentions.) Moreover, the conference's new campaign was promptly sidetracked by the emerging Middle East crisis.

The NATO countries responded to the Eastern overtures on regional security matters with a sense of circumspection and caution. The first formal debate on the issue had been held during the 1964 NATO Ministerial Meeting in Paris, when Belgium, Luxembourg, and Denmark called for consideration of the Soviet proposal for a non-aggression treaty between the Pact and NATO. The Netherlands and Norway expressed qualified support for the suggestion and only Turkey and Greece voted against the proposal. For the next four years, however, the issue remained dormant in various NATO committees.

One of the first official unilateral Western responses to the East's position was made by Denmark. In April 1967 the Danish Minister for Disarmament, Helveg Peterson, opened a formal dialogue with his counterpart in the Polish Foreign Ministry that has since been maintained intermittently as an important bilateral channel for the exchange of views on security matters. Belgium and the Netherlands soon became active participants in similar exchanges, primarily with Hungary and Rumania. Bilateral contacts rapidly proliferated to the extent that the ' Harmel exercise ' was commissioned in part to examine and explore ways to co-ordinate NATO members' individual contacts with the East.

The bilateral discussions had also proved so rewarding that the entire question of European security was discussed at the June 1968 NATO Ministerial Meeting in Reykjavik.[5] This

[5] *DSB*, 15 July 1968, p. 77; *Survival*, Sept. 1968.

session established the general mood of the NATO members towards European security. The primary emphasis was to be placed on military *détente* rather than political *rapport*, unless the East agreed to discuss the key political reasons for the division of Germany and Europe. Accordingly, the NATO Defence Ministers offered to consider with Warsaw Pact members, proposals for a balanced mutual reduction of forces, and other practical steps in arms control. The introduction of this extremely complex issue into the East–West deliberations, as the official NATO position, had several effects: (1) it signified to the Pact that the West collectively viewed the settlement of European security problems primarily from the military viewpoint (while political differences may be the chief source of European tensions, the military confrontation not only substantiates tensions but is easier to regulate than the purely political factors); (2) the frank and candid tone registered the West's reluctance to engage in polemics or propaganda on issues of vital interest to NATO members; (3) it met the recommendations of the smaller, more optimistic members that a formal response was necessary to probe the East's intentions; and (4) it gained time for the less optimistic members in which they could explore more fully the extent of their individual interests at the bilateral level, primarily those of the Federal Republic in Kiesinger's opening to the East and of the United States in her preparations for the SALT talks.

The occupation of Czechoslovakia temporarily suspended further formal consideration of a military *détente*. The Pact needed time to consolidate its new position and to measure the impact of its actions on broader European issues, and the NATO countries sought time to appraise the motives behind the invasion and to assess its effect on the military confrontation. The initial estimate was that the Pact's posture had been significantly strengthened for the following reasons: (1) the creation of the Central Front with five Soviet divisions increased the Pact's weight directly against NATO's stoutest combat element—the US Seventh Army—and stiffened the backbone of Czechoslovakia's fourteen divisions; (2) the presence of Soviet troops could facilitate the rapid transfer of nuclear warheads from the Soviet Union to the Central Front and Czechoslovak units, thus enhancing the tactical readiness over the pre-August 1968 situation; (3) Prague's political reliability was guaranteed; (4) an important logistic supply line to the forward area was firmly in Soviet hands; and (5) the participation of Czechoslovak armed forces in Pact exercises was assured, reinforcing the prospects that national forces in this vital sector could maintain Pact standards for military efficiency—an important factor in the light of the present Soviet-Rumanian relations.[6]

Moscow proved sensitive to NATO reactions to the Prague crisis, and as soon as Czechoslovakia signed the treaty on 16 October 1968 legalizing Soviet troops to remain there ' temporarily ',[7] it sought to restore its former dialogue with West Germany. Contacts and issues were quickly expanded by both sides, leading to a general reassurance in the West that the Soviet Union was still prepared to explore a basis for *détente*. On 17 March 1969 Pact leaders met in Budapest to reopen the European security question. A statement was published, entitled ' Address to all European Countries '. It was noteworthy for its contrast with earlier declarations.[8] While portraying the European situation in sufficiently dark terms to warrant prompt international attention, it failed to blame the United States, NATO, or the Federal Republic for these circumstances. In a step backwards, the Address reaffirmed the validity of the 1966 Bucharest Declaration, but advanced three broad proposals for furthering European rapprochement: (1) strengthening general European political and economic co-operation; (2) acceptance of the *status quo* and pursuit of a solution to the German problem; and (3) convening a European security conference. The Pact nations thus expanded their efforts significantly. Emphasis was now placed on security and *rapport* with the West, including broader co-operation as well as a solution of outstanding problems, rather than promoting either a panacea for security matters or the erosion of the opponent's alliance.

The NATO Ministerial Meeting in Washington on 10–11

[6] For a more detailed appraisal, see my 'Military aspects of the invasion of Czechoslovakia ', *The World Today*, Feb. 1969.

[7] *Survival*, Jan. 1969.

[8] *Pravda*, 18 Mar. 1969 (*Survival*, May 1969).

April 1969 viewed the Budapest Address positively, referring to it as a favourable response to its earlier 'signal from Reykjavik', but adequate preparation was still necessary for a successful conference. NATO nations insisted that such questions as North American participation, the role of neutralized states, the precise purpose of the conference, and an appropriate agenda must be resolved before its convocation.

The members of West Germany's Grand Coalition reacted gingerly. The day after the Budapest meeting, Brandt called a press conference and noted with satisfaction that the Budapest Address contained 'a minimum of polemics', implying a new policy of relaxing tensions. The CDU parliamentary leader Rainer Barzel stated: 'We want a European arrangement, not only a security system.' [9] The larger question was the political solution to Europe's division. Finally, Chancellor Kiesinger stated on 11 April that the thrust of the Address was to gain Western endorsement of the *status quo* in Central Europe, which he rejected. He affirmed, however, that his government would study the document within the NATO context, if the Soviet Union were not making recognition of the GDR a precondition for the conference.[10]

Brandt sought an elaboration from Tsarapkin, and was assured that the Warsaw Pact nations would not object to American participation and did not regard Bonn's recognition of the GDR and territorial borders as a precondition for convocation. On 24 April Brandt presented four points to the Bundestag which the government regarded as essential for a successful conference: (1) no preconditions could be attached for its convocation; (2) the conference must be adequately prepared; (3) the North Americans must be allowed to participate at the outset; and (4) there must be reasonable prospects for progress.[11] Coinciding with the delivery of formal notes from Finland offering to act as host for a security conference, Brandt elaborated his terms for convening a security gathering in a major policy statement in Hamburg on 7 May. He said that the preparatory stages would require preliminary discussions

[9] *Bull.*, 19 Mar. 1969.
[10] DPA, 11 Apr. 1969.
[11] Ibid., 24 Apr. 1969.

between Bonn and East Berlin on the basis of equality to clarify East–West German differences.[12] This was a significant concession: Bonn dropped its refusal to attend any international gathering in which East Germany participated, thus broadening the extent of *de facto* recognition between the two Germanies. On the other hand, Bonn firmly tied its participation in a security conference to progress in resolving inter-German problems, a leverage that succeeded in launching the German summit talks in Erfurt and Kassel.

The Ministers' Committee of the Council of Europe met in May, stated its approval of the recent appeals for a conference and suggested that an intensive exploration of individual positions would advance its purpose. The six nations of the WEU, without France, met one month later and expressed their unanimous approval of a security conference by the summer of 1970, if satisfactory progress were made in establishing an agenda.

Following what was called a favourable response to the Budapest Address, the Pact Foreign Ministers met in Prague to appraise their stand. They issued a statement on 31 October 1969,[13] in which they said that particular attention had been paid to preparations for a European security conference and praised Finland's offer to help. A tentative agenda was proposed, consisting of two issues: European security matters and the renunciation of force, and the extension of co-operation among European states. The communiqué included the qualification that the agenda was merely suggested and that the Pact members were prepared to consider any suggestion that might contribute to the preparation and success of the gathering, thus underlining the high priority they gave to the convocation of a security conference. At the same time, the Soviet Union advanced her policy of increasing public pressure in the West. She sponsored the ' First Conference for Peace and Security ' in Vienna on 29 November that created a new international non-governmental organization for European security, and announced plans for a mini-Karlovy Vary type conference in January to organize a People's Congress ' to promote the

---

[12] *Bull.*, 13 May 1969.
[13] *Sov. News*, 4 Nov. 1969; *E-A*, 25th yr, 25 Feb. 1970, p. D89.

struggle for European security '. The timing of the Prague statement to the November NATO Council meeting which discussed European security matters further illustrated the Pact's sense of urgency.

NATO delegates voiced sharp disappointment at the Prague statement. Even the smaller Western nations which strongly supported the conference viewed the Pact's position as a setback. Pact members had again avoided the military aspects of a security arrangement. They formally refused to accept American and Canadian participation, and attempted to focus the conference on the non-military components of *détente*. Until at least the broad contours of a military disengagement are mutually accepted, the West would approach the conference table virtually empty-handed.

Accordingly, NATO prepared for its semi-annual Ministerial Meeting in Brussels on 4–5 December in greater detail than formerly. Smaller nations, e.g. Denmark and Belgium, were anxious that the conference idea be kept alive, and West Germany viewed the existing bilateral negotiations as a more rewarding approach to the East. Yet all realized the necessity of not allowing the initiative on this matter to pass to the Pact. For the first time, therefore, a ' reinforced ' NATO Council— attended by the respective ministries' no. 2 men—met in November to prepare for the December Ministerial Meeting.

The NATO Secretary-General Manlio Brosio set the tone for the Council session when he stated that there was no desire to convene a conference for a conference's sake. US Under-Secretary Elliott Lee Richardson projected a similar lack of enthusiasm. He gave warning against unilaterally giving away Western negotiating positions, pointing to the difference between serious negotiating positions and the mere creation of an atmosphere of *détente*. Richardson maintained that the Warsaw Pact's attitude towards the German problem, the status of Berlin, and the mutual reduction of forces should be regarded as a test of Soviet willingness to promote a genuine *détente*. The session concluded by adopting a list of twenty-six specific issues on which East–West discussions could contribute to European security and help to overcome the partition.

The December Ministerial Meeting was devoted mainly to

European security and registered significant progress in defining a common Western position that preserved the momentum of its earlier moves in this area. It adopted a code of conduct, and recommended its adoption by all states as a means of establishing standards that could serve as a basis for future collective security agreements. Paragraph 2 of the Declaration clearly states the traditional Western views on proper international behaviour.

Peace and security in Europe must rest upon universal respect for the principles of sovereign equality, political independence and the territorial integrity of each European state; the right of its peoples to shape their own destinies; the peaceful settlement of disputes; nonintervention in the internal affairs of any state by any other state, whatever their political or social system; and the renunciation of the use of the threat of force against any state. Past experience has shown that there is, as yet, no common interpretation of these principles. The fundamental problems in Europe can be solved only on the basis of these principles and any real and lasting improvement of East–West relations presupposes respect for them without any condition or reservations.[14]

Also the Ministers criticized the Pact's proposed agenda as vague and evasive: the real issues remained Germany, Berlin, and force postures. They said that no conference should be called that would merely confirm, rather than annul, the division of Europe. Three specific military issues were proposed on which East–West discussions could contribute to European security. Finally, the Ministers pressed this initiative a step further and charged the Secretary-General to develop appropriate models for the balanced reduction of forces, and common guidelines for conducting bilateral negotiations with the East.

The West's cool response may have been a key reason for the change in direction noted in the next Pact conclave. On 3–4 December the Pact PCC met in Moscow. A major communique was released touching on virtually all aspects of the Pact's European policy.[15] Initial efforts towards negotiating a settlement with the Federal Republic were favourably noted, but East Germany's claims for full recognition under international

[14] DSB, 29 Dec. 1969, p. 628; FAZ & Die Welt, 5 Nov. 1969.
[15] E-A, 25th yr, 25 Feb. 1970, p. D76 (NYT, 5 Dec. 1969).

law were upheld. Other problems were treated in a similar vein, revealing no deviation in the Pact's traditional line but indicating an awareness of the opponent's position. Most important, the meeting endorsed the bilateral East–West negotiations that had been under way for several months, and apparently established a division of labour among Pact members initially encouraged by the 1966 Bucharest Declaration. Accordingly, East Germany would concentrate on legal recognition, Poland on border problems, Hungary on a European security conference, Czechoslovakia on abrogation of the Munich Agreement, and the Soviet Union on a renunciation-of-force agreement with West Germany and on strategic questions with the United States.[16] But the communiqué emphasized the intentions of Pact members to continue mutual consultations and policy co-ordination on these matters, suggesting a greater acceptance of legitimate coalition politics than had hitherto existed.

In a notable omission, the communiqué failed to endorse earlier statements on the European security conference, particularly the Prague statement of October 1969. This gap in a major Pact policy statement suggests that a decision was reached to accept the West's reticence on the matter as momentarily insurmountable and to shift attention to the bilateral negotiations that were already in progress. The Hungarian Foreign Minister Janos Peter, a strong advocate of a security conference, admitted after the Moscow meeting that there was little enthusiasm for the idea outside the Pact and that its convocation would require extensive additional preparatory work.[17]

And in the West even the most optimistic supporters of the conference plan had acknowledged by 1970 that a general session of the all-European security conference could not be considered for the time being. The Dutch Foreign Minister Joseph Luns told the Rumanians: ' I cannot conceive of a useful conference on European security which could not previously reach agreement on its agenda.'[18]

None the less, the West preserved moderate interest in the

---

[16] Explained by Ignacy Krasicki, *Zycie literackie* (Cracow), 14 Dec. 1969.
[17] Cited by Charles Andras, RFE Research Memo, Mar. 1970, pp. 25–6.
[18] *Rumania News Service* (Agerpres), 10 Jan. 1970.

matter. The NATO Ministerial Meeting in Rome on 26–27 May endorsed proposals for mutual balanced force reductions and for joint East–West discussions on the possibilities for convening a European security conference.[19] The Warsaw Pact reacted in less than one month by calling a Foreign Ministers' meeting in Budapest on 21–22 June, and issuing a Memorandum [20] that responded specifically to points raised by NATO, representing new departures from earlier proposals. For the first time the Pact referred to the direct participation of the United States and Canada in an all-European conference, omissions that had formerly caused doubts in the West about the sincerity of the Pact in putting forward the conference idea. The Budapest Memorandum amplified references in the October 1969 Prague statement to areas for intra-European co-operation, including commercial, economic, technical, and scientific relations—an apparent follow-on gesture to the suggestion made in Rome that environmental problems should be considered in the general area of technical collaboration.

The Memorandum also called for the establishment of a permanent organ dealing with European security and co-operation. This too was apparently a response to a specific NATO suggestion that such a body could serve ' as one means of embarking upon multilateral negotiations in due course '. The NATO communiqué had stated that progress in the bilateral talks presently under way would help ensure the success of an eventual European security conference. The Pact replied in the Memorandum that progress already registered in these talks had brought their standpoints closer together, apparently to such a degree that some form of multilateral contact could be envisaged—although no exact date was mentioned. The Memorandum also diluted its formula for East German participation; it was to be regarded as on an equal footing with the Federal Republic, and the former insistence upon full diplomatic recognition under international law was dropped.

The most important feature of the Memorandum was its acceptance of the NATO proposal that military *détente* must be regarded as an essential ingredient for fostering European

[19] Communiqué in *Survival*, Aug. 1970.
[20] *Survival*, Sept. 1970.

security. For the first time, the Pact admitted publicly that the reduction of foreign troops would promote political *détente* and suggested that mutual reduction could be a topic for the proposed European security organ. This was a noteworthy shift in the Pact's position. By agreeing to place the issue of foreign troops on the agenda for multilateral talks or negotiations, Moscow must ultimately face the prospects of an adjustment of its forces in Central Europe.

This change was a partial surprise for the West, since barely two weeks before Gromyko had reaffirmed Moscow's traditional rejection of the NATO call for a mutually balanced reduction of forces during his vist to France. He endorsed the French refusal to support the NATO position on this issue and strongly implied that if these force reductions were the West's precondition for a European security conference, it would probably not be convened. The contrast between the Soviet stand on these two occasions suggests that only tactical alterations have been made, not strategic changes.

Were the general prospects for the conference improved by these developments? Earlier changes in Moscow's stand on the conference were made largely for intra-Pact reasons. The Budapest Memorandum was the first instance when Moscow responded seriously to the West on this issue, suggesting that it attached new weight to the conference. In a precautionary note, however, the Hungarian party daily, *Magyar Nemzet*, on 21 June issued a warning against too much optimism in expecting an early successful conference. While the rhythm of the European dialogue had been speeded up and the desire for a conference was generally accepted, it predicted that after some initial successes it would become increasingly difficult to convene a conference. The reason for this was allegedly the ' indisputable fact that the West is now moving to the right '. The *Länder* defeats for the CDU/CSU in West Germany, the Tory victory in Britain, and the shift towards conservatism in the Nixon administration were cited as indications of reaction. Regardless of the blame, the message was clear: party members should not expect any real progress in the near future; the road to European collective security is hazardous and even the first intersection was not yet visible.

This was an accurate harbinger of the Pact nations' attitudes for the remainder of the year, as confirmed by the Pact PCC meeting in East Berlin on 2 December 1970. At that time the NATO December Ministerial Meeting reviewed the Western position on multilateral security matters and issued a strong statement tying further consideration of a European security conference firmly to progress in solving the Berlin question.

They affirmed the readiness of their governments, as soon as the talks on Berlin have reached a satisfactory conclusion and in so far as the other on-going talks are proceeding favourably, to enter into multilateral contacts with all interested governments to explore when it would be possible to convene a conference, or a series of conferences, on security and co-operation in Europe. [21]

In the interim, the Council in permanent session was requested to continue studying the potential results of such a gathering and means for ensuring a desirable outcome.

This was the toughest stand yet taken by NATO. By reiterating its earlier offer in Rome to explore mutual-force reductions with the Warsaw Pact, but linking this invitation to progress on the Berlin issue, it firmly conveyed to Moscow that a simultaneous diminution of both the major outstanding military and political obstacles to normalization had to be made. The Western view of the link between the German problem and European security was clinched by the NATO communiqué. While this position is maintained, Moscow cannot expect further important positive results from its multilateral approach either to European security problems or to a German settlement.

The hardening in the American position on these and other East–West issues such as the Suez Canal cease-fire violations, autobahn harassments, and the suspected establishment of a nuclear submarine base in Cuba, was unquestionably conveyed to Gromyko during his visit to the United States in October 1970 and by subsequent US decisions. Moscow apparently wanted to use the opportunity of the Hungarian Party Congress in November to establish an appropriate counter-position before the December NATO Ministerial Meeting.

[21] *NATO* Press Communiqué, MD (70), 2–19, 4 Dec. 1970 & *NATO* Latest, no. 18, 4 Dec. 1970 (*Survival*, Feb. 1971).

But both Ceausescu and Ulbricht boycotted the Congress, denying Moscow the possibility of a consensus for any new initiative. The PCC had been convened on 2 December to coincide with the NATO Ministerial Meeting, providing a potential opportunity for propaganda advantages if a consensus could be achieved. The communiqué and subsequent official statements revealed, however, that immobilism had indeed set into the Pact's attitude towards a multilateral approach to a European settlement.[22] In a speech before the 14th Plenum of the SED Central Committee Ulbricht reported on 9 December that the Pact was not prepared to meet NATO's conditions for a security conference, and blamed the United States for obstructing the conference by raising irrelevant terms.[23] While he made minor concessions in the GDR's traditional policies towards Bonn and Berlin, there was insufficient flexibility to allow a consensus within the Pact on any new movement towards European security. In an unusual demonstration of coalition politics, a single Pact member was able to assert its national interests, and block Pact policy on matters regarded as important by its partners. But, more important, by December 1970 the peripheral issues in a European *détente* had been returned by both sides to rest squarely on the principal contentious issue—an appropriate solution to the German problem. Thus after years of skirting the German problem by promoting schemes for regional security, it emerged as the unquestioned key to European stability.

A comparison of the varying Eastern positions on European security reveals several notable shifts in emphasis, if not in direction. (1) Initially Eastern attention focused alternatively on the complexities of European security matters or panaceas that could eliminate the problem. Now greater stress is placed on the concrete procedures and conditions that will contribute to an eventual conference. (2) Soviet proposals in the mid-1950s called for the dissolution of military blocs within the context of Article 11 of the Warsaw Treaty. In the early 1960s Moscow proposed non-aggression agreements between the two pacts that would probably have left the military organizations

---

[22] *Pravda*, 3 Dec., *ND*, 4 Dec. 1970 (*Survival*, Feb. 1971).
[23] *ND*, 10 Dec. 1970.

intact. Under Rumanian pressure Moscow accepted in 1966 both the dissolution of alliances and the withdrawal of foreign-based troops as a guarantee of the abolition of military pacts. While this reversal was primarily for intra-Pact political reasons, all members apparently now concur that NATO is unlikely to disintegrate further in the near future. (3) Before Rumania's defection from the common line, a consensus existed in the Pact countries about the common threat and the aggressive intentions of the United States, West Germany, and NATO. The documents released in 1968 and 1969 reveal a marked reduction in communist bombast against these traditional targets. The present division of Europe is currently accredited only to ' certain reactionary forces '. (4) Accompanying the loosening of the East's position noted since the Karlovy Vary meeting, has been a greater accreditation of the influence of neutralists in European security matters—Helsinki and Vienna were both asked to sponsor the proposed conference; and, since 1967, formulas for preparing the conference have also included neutral participation. (5) Before 1969 Pact proposals centred on some form of military *détente* or disengagement. With the proposed inclusion of neutral states and in the light of military advantages accruing from the invasion of Czechoslovakia, the 1969-vintage Pact documents stressed non-military co-operation with the West and relegated military disengagement to the field of general disarmament. Until the June 1970 Budapest Memorandum, the military aspects of regional security matters were obscured.

Nine plausible suggestions may be sketched of the influences that may have produced these oscillating policy positions.

1. The rise of polycentrism within the communist world, and especially within the Pact countries, tended to polarize opinion on important issues to the point that parties between the two poles often supported the minority position solely in order to assert the right of dissent. Accordingly, Moscow was forced to make substantive concessions to achieve solidarity.

2. Soviet aims before the Prague crisis were to settle regional problems on Soviet terms, thereby extending Soviet influence to Western Europe. After the crisis, Moscow concentrated more on consolidating its holdings in Eastern Europe and securing

recognition of the *status quo* based on the continuing existence of the present alliances. This retrenchment was accompanied by agreement to allow Pact members more latitude in pursuing their individual grievances against West Germany. The momentum of these bilateral negotiations has partly relieved pressure for a multilateral approach to European problems.

3. Rumania's return to Pact councils on security matters was in part an acknowledgement of the risks in her exposed position after the invasion of Czechoslovakia. But, more important, it was a response to the shifts on key issues by other members toward the Rumanian position. The 1969 documents more closely reflect Bucharest's position than do those of the 1966-8 period. The notable exception is Rumania's continuing insistence upon the mutual definition and fulfilment of the military prerequisites for regional security.

4. Moscow was caught between the conflicting national interests of its allies. East Germany wanted a conference that would confirm her international stature. Poland and Hungary viewed a conference as a means of extending their contacts with the West in a form acceptable to the Kremlin. And Rumania saw a conference as a means of reducing the discredit her allies imposed on her two-Germanies policy. In her own interests, the Soviet Union would reportedly prefer an inter-pact conclave in which delegates would participate as members of a military alliance and discuss only broad topics. Accordingly, the compromises embodied in the Budapest Address and the Prague statement were ambiguous formulas which only the East Germans could support over the bilateral approach (even the creation of a Preparatory Commission would expand *de facto* acceptance of the GDR without requiring reciprocal concessions).

5. A persisting handicap for the Pact members was their inability to concur on the purpose of an all-European collective-security arrangement. Was such a plan to increase East–West understanding, stimulate *rapport* and co-operation, facilitate closing the technological gap, sponsor political *détente*, consolidate the *status quo*, expand the appeal of neutrality, ensure international recognition of vital interests, outline military disengagement, encourage NATO's dissolution, curtail American

leadership, or disarm and incapacitate the Federal Republic? All of the above have been cited by various Pact members as a just cause for an international conference; together, however, they are self-defeating. Pursuing their varying national interests, the Eastern regimes have also been unable to agree on appropriate tactics. Should a conference inaugurate or lead to security negotiations; should the North Americans be included in the negotiations, if so, when; what weight should be allotted to neutral opinion; would a conference be desirable if West Germany afforded only *de facto* recognition of East Germany; if one pact will not be dismantled without concrete evidence that the other is doing likewise, what credence and verification procedures are compatible with security requirements; are unilateral steps towards disengagement feasible or prudent; what institutional and legal structures should replace existing ones; is the return to the Potsdam Agreement and all its anachronisms, as some advocate, either feasible or desirable; what is the future of the small states in a europeanized Europe; will a europeanized Europe be inherently more or less stable than the existing division with its established checks; if not, what improvisations are possible before Europe is europeanized, either through settlement or American lack of interest? From the Western viewpoint the inability of the East to establish a common position on such fundamental concepts and tactics has undermined the credibility of the East's proposals, which, in turn, has prompted additional modifications or has further postponed decisions.

6. President de Gaulle's September 1967 visit to Poland and his call for the assertion of Polish independence, *à la* France, marked the end of the Soviet-French honeymoon and the curtailment of French overtures to Eastern Europe. The Soviet Union apparently recognized the limited opportunities and potential risks in attempting to solve Europe's problems with a government that had such limited control over them. While the de Gaulle episode was an important stimulant for the expansion of bilateral contacts, the treks of President Pompidou to the Soviet Union in October and of the Prime Minister Jacques Chaban Delmas to Poland in November 1970 were indications of French sensitivity to and determination to offset

Bonn's increasing influence in Eastern Europe. But the relative futility of both excursions revealed that relations have cooled and the issues are being more squarely faced.

7. NATO's recovery from malaise caused by de Gaulle indicated that Moscow's earlier analysis of an ' Atlantic crisis ' was not entirely accurate and that the crippled but still operational organization provided uncertain opportunities for Soviet inroads. Accordingly, the later Pact statements on security entirely avoid the issue of NATO's durability.

8. On the other hand, the attainment of strategic parity with its chief adversary has undoubtedly strengthened Moscow's confidence in its ability to deal with lesser opponents without the risks of their making undue demands for Washington's unqualified protection. The concepts behind the SALT deliberations imply that Moscow will eventually enjoy greater options in formulating its regional security plans.

9. Moscow's inability to achieve its European aims without speaking to the Germans about the German problems has led to a major policy change. The entry of the Social Democrats into the government provided the opportunity for a cautious, muted dialogue with Bonn. The issues under deliberation have been expanded in depth and multiplied in number to the point that important substantive matters are being negotiated. The grievances of the smaller Pact states are also being negotiated with Bonn. West German co-operativeness in these bilateral undertakings has been instrumental in weakening the East's momentum for a pan-European security movement. The bilateral approach is likely to continue to be given priority over the multilateral approach, unless and until significant obstacles arise.

These factors were the most probable influences shaping the evolving Soviet multilateral approach to European and German problems. In contrast to this vacillating Soviet policy, the Western position has remained remarkably consistent, despite differences on tactics and timing. For example, France hesitantly supports the conference idea on the grounds that if successful it would circumscribe the utility of her strategic independence and could reduce her authority in Berlin, without providing alternative institutions within which she could assert influence over both Eastern Europe and Germany. On the other hand, the Federal Republic remains rather cool to the idea because a conference could not produce significant results unless it tackled the German problem, and a multilateral approach at this time would resemble a premature peace conference. Even the smaller countries that have shown the most enthusiasm have not weakened their insistence that a conference must contribute to a solution of Europe's political problems.

The US position reflects the general reservations of most Western nations. In December 1969 US Secretary William Rogers stated in Brussels:

. . . while NATO has identified issues on which East and West might negotiate to achieve an increase in security and a reduction in tensions, what has been the Warsaw Pact's response? It has proposed a European security conference based on what appears to be a nebulous and imprecise agenda. What does the Soviet Union want to achieve by proposing such a conference? Does it want to deal realistically with the issues which divide Europe, or does it seek to ratify the existing division of Europe? Does it intend to draw a veil over its subjugation of Czechoslovakia? Does it wish to use a conference to strengthen its control over the trade policies of other members of the Warsaw Pact? Does it wish to seek to retain the right to intervene in Eastern Europe?

. . . the Warsaw Pact proposals do not deal with these fundamental questions. What is proposed cannot properly be described as a security conference at all. The Warsaw Pact countries have suggested merely (1) that a conference discuss an East–West agreement on the principle of non-use of force—which has been a basic principle of the United Nations Charter for over 20 years, so that another pronouncement of the non-use of force would have no meaning—and (2) increased trade and technical exchanges, for which regular diplomatic channels are always available.[24]

Washington has maintained that a general conference is only one means among many for reducing European tensions. The main effort at this point should be to continue probing to identify issues where serious negotiations are possible—e.g. access to Berlin, the East–West German dialogue, specific

[24] William Rogers, ' Our continuing commitment to Western Europe ', *DSB*, 29 Dec. 1969, p. 624.

ingredients in a military *détente*—before the broader issues can be effectively approached. In Rogers's words: ' We would favor a negotiation that holds out realistic hope for a reduction of tensions in Europe. But we will not participate in a conference which has the effect of ratifying or acquiescing in the Brezhnev doctrine.'

The NATO countries have been sensitive to public pressures for reductions in military expenditures and troop withdrawals, and have encouraged a cautious circumspect approach to all facets of *détente*, lest unwarranted public clamour erode Western morale and resoluteness before a military disengagement is achieved. Should various Western states be pressured into excessive unilateral military reductions, a general loss of confidence among the Europeans could develop, creating a mood of increased deference towards Soviet interests. Secretary Rogers underscored these general Western fears: ' we must be careful not to confuse the progress toward agreements, and we must not lull ourselves into a false sense of detente '.[25] Accordingly, the May 1970 NATO Ministerial Meeting adopted common guidelines for the pursuit of bilateral negotiations that stressed prior consultations and the need to avoid arousing excessive public expectations about immediate normalization of relations, thus contributing to the relative stability and firmness of the Western position.

In summary, the Warsaw Pact position on European security arrangements has been subjected to a variety of unforeseen international circumstances and has become the victim of competing national priorities among sponsoring states. The Soviet motive behind a European security convention has been to consolidate her position in Eastern Europe and extend her influence west of the Elbe. Her promotion of an open agenda would allow her to spur deliberations that would further this aim and regulate those that do not. The mere convocation would provide an opportunity for the Soviet Union to demonstrate her reasonableness, to pose as the spokesman for European interests, and to induce acceptance of the *status quo* in Eastern Europe. If accompanied by further distractions within NATO over unilateral force cuts and equitable burden-sharing,

[25] Ibid., p. 623.

Moscow's demonstrated conciliation could foster a more complacent Western attitude towards Soviet interests.

While the West has refused to negotiate multilaterally on such disadvantageous terms, it should be noted that virtually all the demands raised in the Bucharest and Karlovy Vary documents as preconditions for permanent European security since then have been negotiated bilaterally in some form. Further progress on the bilateral basis will have an importance transcending immediate agenda items: it will promote acceptance of the Warsaw Pact's growing interest in Western cooperation and avoid the troublesome task of establishing a common line on all aspects of the confrontation with the West. Bilateral advancement will also accommodate the Western powers' insistence that accord on substantive matters must precede a general conference and agreement.

West Germany has been the chief benefactor in the evolution of the Pact position on European security matters and the firmness of the NATO terms for military disengagement and political *détente*. This stand has strengthened West German confidence in NATO's commitment to her security. On the other hand, the Pact policy changes have relieved Bonn of the onerous charge of ' revanchism ' and of constituting ' the main threat ' to European stability. Moscow's apparent conclusion that the policies of the Grand Coalition reduced the traditional ' German menace ' to a manageable scale was the primary reason for the new leniency in the former Soviet hard line. Accordingly, Bonn has been afforded a respectability among the socialist states formerly extended to other capitalist powers, such as France and Britain. Bonn's co-operation in the various bilateral negotiations was in large part responsible for Moscow's modified stand, and the Soviet Union is currently committed to this line. She can no longer facilely invoke her former allegations of ' revanchism ' without risking an eruption of cold-war tensions and endangering broader Soviet global interests. Furthermore, this commitment to German respectability has had the direct effect of increasing Bonn's stature both in NATO and in Eastern Europe, without providing commensurate Soviet leverage against either her allies, the West, or Bonn. Moscow's influence has not been seriously eroded, but it has not been proportionally enhanced. The realization that the Germans and Eastern Europeans gained more flexibility through Moscow's gradual shift on security matters may be an important reason for the subsequent hardening of the Soviet position on other aspects of her relations with Germany.

5

THE HISTORICAL PERSPECTIVE
OF BRANDT'S OSTPOLITIK

THE sixth national election in September 1969 was one of the most important in the history of the Federal Republic. At issue for the first time was the fundamental question of the proper place of the German people in the established international order. The political systems in both Germanies were a direct product of the larger East–West struggle; indeed, foreign-policy aims of other nations had served as the origins of both regimes. Previous elections had centred mainly on reconstruction policy, with the three major parties agreeing that reunification was a prerequisite for an ultimate *détente*. This similarity of views allowed for differences in tone and nuances but prohibited bold new approaches to the German problem.

Before the sixth national election, Bonn's policy of dealing with the communist East from a position of strength had resulted in the paradox of the Federal Republic becoming the economic giant and the political dwarf of contemporary Europe. The principal reason for this anomaly was that Bonn's German policy was the chief constraint on her other political options. The myopic characteristic of Bonn's German policy resulted from its defensive outlook and its obsessive concern with East Germany's response to each policy decision. Even the Federal Republic's integration into Western Europe was envisaged by Adenauer as a strategic move to strengthen his bargaining position on reunification. Erhard's and Kiesinger's ' opening to the East ' were both intended to foster favourable opportunities to enhance Bonn's influence east of the Elbe at Moscow's expense. Each concession extended was firmly linked to the fundamentally unchanged objectives behind Bonn's *Ostpolitik*.

East Germany suffered from the same restraints. Like the Federal Republic, she was in the front-line position of the East–West confrontation and used her strategic position to extract concessions from her allies regarded as important to her vital interests. And like the Federal Republic, the GDR remained the junior partner in her alliance because of her hypersensitivity

93

to the rival German state's policies and her inability to gain recognition legitimizing her rule independently of her allies' support. To a greater extent than West Germany, however, the GDR had been the cause, not the source, of alliance policy. And unlike the Federal Republic, she was continually faced with the problem of securing popular support, as well as international recognition.

International events, such as Rumania's recognition of the Federal Republic and the decline in West European integration, demonstrated the growing unproductiveness of both Germanies' policies. A gradually more assertive position against both their respective allies and each other emerged in the mid-1960s. While neither state could afford to act independently of its allies, domestic and international attention was being refocused on the basic ingredients of the German problem with greater intensity than at any time since the construction of the Wall. By 1969 West Germany was dealing with various socialist states on a wider variety of issues than at any time since the postwar era. These developments cultivated an atmosphere of soul-searching in the Federal Republic not witnessed since the reconstruction period. The election campaign focused public attention as never before on basic issues, such as the viability of East Germany, the implications of recognizing her existence, even the desirability of physical reunification, or alternative schemes like accommodation through the modernizing process in both Germanies (the 'convergence thesis').

The shifts in West German public opinion were noted in polls taken in 1967 and two years later. In June 1967 19 per cent of those interviewed favoured recognition of the Oder–Neisse line and 51 per cent were opposed.[1] Yet 50 per cent favoured recognition if unity was achieved as against 25 per cent who did not. By the end of 1969, however, 74 per cent of the West Germans polled favoured official talks with the GDR and over 50 per cent favoured formal recognition of the GDR and renunciation of the 'lost territories'.[2] The latter

[1] Cited by Kaiser, *German Foreign Policy*, p. 45.
[2] Polls conducted by the semi-official Inst. for Applied Social Science (Bad Godesberg), cited in *Bull.*, 2 Dec. 1969.

figures were unprecedented in the history of the Federal
Republic and reflected the profundity of the public examinations of German policy conducted in the news media and
bierstuben. West Germans were asking: is Germany (before its
division) merely a memory? What do youth and foreigners
envisage when referring to Germany? Should unity be a policy
aim or merely be kept in mind? Would acceptance of our
actual borders in 1970 automatically negate debate on our 1937
borders which the Potsdam Agreement still presupposes? Do
we then have a right or a duty to negotiate on the Oder–Neisse
line? Can we still seek a peace treaty for Germany if the German state no longer exists, not even on paper, and if only what
remains is a German nation? What is the position of the
Western allies; they have not had to face the question of
reunification since 1955, do they now agree that the Federal
Republic has sufficient sovereignty to negotiate and sign a
peace treaty? Does the apparent Allied legal stand on the
validity of the Potsdam Agreement and their status in West
Berlin induce or inhibit German unity or normalization?
What will be Bonn's stand on GDR participation in multilateral organizations now that it has acquiesced in her sitting
in the European security conference? Will the two Germanies
be petitioning for UN membership in the autumn of 1971?
Can West German participation on the IAEA's Board of
Governors (the assurance of appropriate nuclear safeguards
under Euratom and the Federal Republic's price for ratification of the NPT) be traded for GDR membership in
other UN agencies? Is there not grave danger inherent in
allowing normalization in international affairs to proceed
ahead of the humanization of inter-German relations? Has
not the momentum itself of Brandt's *Ostpolitik* induced a greater
cohesiveness within the Warsaw Pact that is likely to benefit
only Moscow and East Berlin? How would Bonn respond to
the accreditation of an East German ambassador with Stock-
holm, Vienna, Geneva, or Paris?[3]

The three major West German parties entered the 1969
election campaign in virtual agreement about the basic tenets

[3] *Stuttgart Zeitung, FAZ, Frankfurter Neue Presse*, 15 Jan. 1970; *Handelsblatt,
Münchner Merkur, Die Welt, SZ*, & *General-Anzeiger*, 16 Jan. 1970.

of European and Alliance policies, but in growing disagreement about solutions to such questions as *Deutschlandpolitik* and *Ostpolitik*. It is obviously over-simplistic to present West German public opinion as polarized between only two political positions. Each of the three major political parties (SPD, FDP, and CDU/CSU) was divided by deep ideological fissures and polarizations around leading personalities. The CDU and its Bavarian sister party, the CSU, displayed the greatest factional disarray. Gerhard Schröder and Helmut Kohl advocated unreserved reliance on American deterrence and active engagement in Eastern Europe. Rainer Barzel and Gerhard Stoltenberg called for hard-line negotiations with NATO for increases in individual commitments and strict reciprocity in dealings with Eastern Europe, and Franz Josef Strauss and Baron von Guttenburg of the CSU pressed for a reduced US military presence and creation of a European nuclear deterrent and no concessions to Eastern Europe. For the sake of clarity, however, it is convenient to typify the basic argumentation of the two major political orientations as a means of demonstrating both the range and limits of West German policy in 1969.

The April 1969 SPD Party Congress decided to wage the campaign primarily on the *Ostpolitik* and opened a ' now or never ' drive to offset voter apathy on the issue. Unprecedented prosperity and the declining influence of the refugee groups had increased German passivity on reunification. Of a population that was formerly composed of over one-fifth refugees, over one-half of the present populace had never seen the Eastern territories or had first-hand recollections of the war. Thus the 1969 elections were probably the last time when reunification or reconciliation could be an election issue.

In focusing the election on the Eastern problem, the SPD gained a natural ally in the FDP, who sought full reconciliation with the GDR. The possibility of a left-liberal coalition forced the CDU into a difficult corner. To draw sufficient votes from the SPD to gain nine seats needed for an absolute majority, the CDU would have had to moderate its Eastern stand and risk alienating its own extreme right-wing. The NDP forced the CDU's hand by adopting an ultra-nationalistic platform at its

May Party Congress: 'No recognition of territorial adjust-ments or acceptance of the stolen territories.' In response, the CDU adopted a 'national conservative' position to preclude 'being passed on the right by the NPD'. But to avoid being drawn to the left by the SPD initiative towards the East, the CDU focused its campaign largely on domestic issues: war crimes, student unrest, revaluation of the mark, worker protests, and integration with the West.

The Eastern Europeans viewed these tactics as confirmation of the CDU's determination to preserve its historic policy of non-commitment and manipulation rather than settlement in the East. Accordingly the progress made under the Grand Coalition was accredited to the SPD, and the socialist countries formally adopted in March a programme designed to encour-age the SPD's electoral prospects. The East later noted with self-satisfaction the paradox of SPD and FDP leaders conduct-ing extensive interviews during the campaign in Moscow rather than in Washington, suggesting that times had changed.

The CDU tactics left the foreign-policy field open to the Socialists, who initiated a nation-wide reappraisal of the Eastern question. The fundamental issue from the Socialist viewpoint was not reunification (the CDU's cross), but the viability of East Germany and the appropriate relationship that should be developed with its regime. In the light of the SPD/FDP victory, the rationale most frequently heard in Socialist and liberal circles warrants detailed examination.[4]

The Socialists argued first of all that political developments in Western Europe over the past year had introduced basic changes in the Federal Republic's overall international position. De Gaulle's replacement allowed Europe to reassess France's true position in Continental affairs and, for the first time since World War II, Bonn could speak with the authority of Western Europe—the Federal Republic could assert the political initiative in solving European tensions formerly com-manded by de Gaulle. Because of this new image, movement to-wards solving Bonn's grievances would enhance its political influence, possibly to the level of its economic stature as the

---

[4] The following observations are taken in part from my own notes made during seven years' residence in the Federal Republic.

world's third industrial power. The SPD argued that from this position of strength, the adoption of positive guidelines could minimize the former debilitating impact its confrontatioe with the GDR had had upon Bonn's international political standing.

Further, the clashes along the Ussuri river that spring, the Soviet adoption of a more liberal attitude towards its allies and its defensive posture in the Middle East, all suggested that Moscow was again experiencing the fears of its traditional encirclement neurosis on a scale that might make it more susceptible to important new overtures from the West. On the other hand, the occupation of Czechoslovakia demon- strated that there could be no basic changes in European Europe until there were fundamental revisions in Soviet policy. Moreover, the Prague crisis indicated that Bonn would have to deal directly with Moscow (not at its expense) to achieve any strategic modifications in Eastern Europe.

On the explicit details of the former German policy, the Social Democrats argued that the CDU position of upholding a *deutscher Rechtsanspruch* (German legal claim) and *Recht auf Heimat* (right to the homeland) to the territories east of the Oder–Neisse implied that a reunited Germany would demand territories beyond the present Polish boundaries. The Eastern Europeans also feared that a repatriation of the expellees would follow earlier patterns, where militants would press for a territorial return to Greater Germany. This policy had proved counterproductive and the entire strategy of strength must be abandoned as a symbol of the sincerity of a new border policy: the German signature of the Munich Agreement should no longer be regarded as sacred and the Oder–Neisse line should be recognized pending a final peace settlement. As Helmut Schmidt had argued earlier, ' an unrestricted claim to our former eastern borders would give Eastern Europe . . . an insurmountable reason to reject not only reunification but also a normalization of relations with the Federal Republic '.[5] This rationale demonstrated that the SPD had acknowledged

[5] Speech at the SPD party Congress on 3 June 1966 (see ch. 2, n. 19). See also G. Mann, *Verzicht oder Forderung?* (1964); and Hans A. Stöcker, ' Völkerrechtliche Implikationen des Heimatrechts ', *E-A*, Aug. 1966, pp. 547–54.

the Eastern European priorities, that normalization depended upon security achieved through a solution of the border question.

The SPD charged that the government position of recognition of the GDR had been only marginally successful. Until Iraq recognized East Germany in May 1969, no other non-communist country had established full diplomatic relations with her. But the lack of representation in the world's capitals and councils had not weakened East Germany's viability; it had merely reinforced Moscow's indispensability in transmitting foreign requirements to East Berlin and defending East German interests abroad. Therefore, the SPD urged acceptance of a formula for equal partnership between the two state-like entities, short of full recognition under international law.

Many SPD intellectuals argued that reunification on CDU lines through establishing common German institutions was neither attainable nor desirable. In 1967 reunited Germany would have ranked fourth among the industrialized nations in population and steel production, third in GNP, and second in total exports—double the volume of the next European competitor.[6] An increase in international stature of this scale would clearly be viewed with alarm by the Federal Republic's Western allies and the Eastern Europeans and could give rise to both recriminations and the revival of German nationalism. Moreover, the tacit abandonment of formal reunification would remove the strictures imposed on both Germanies by their division and free their international policies from their present countervailing inhibitions. It would also encourage both sides to seek a mutually accepted form of accommodation, short of confederation or institutionalized association.

This stand struck at the core of the CDU position, that the GDR was an artificial state. (It was, however, easier to refute the Christian Democrats' priorities and tactics in normalizing relations with Eastern Europe than to formulate a publicly accepted rationale that a communist German state was a viable entity which did not pose a threat to West Germany and, therefore, permitted fraternal co-operation.) The Christian Democrats maintained that the chief source of Central

[6] Kaiser, *German Foreign Policy*, p. 54.

European tensions was the artificiality of the GDR. The CDU argued that, if given a free choice, most East Germans would probably hope for some modification in East Berlin's existing institutions along Western lines, if not for outright integration with West Germany. Further, after twenty-five years in power, the SED had not been able to establish an authentic national character and genuine roots of sovereignty independent of either Soviet or West German influence. Finally, without direct, massive, and determined Soviet military support, the survivability of Ulbricht's apparatus would be questionable.

These assertions were traditionally regarded by the CDU as self-evident. But the Social Democrats argued that they are not a conclusive proof of the state's artificiality. Soviet troop strengths reflected more estimates of the NATO threat than domestic dangers (twenty crack Soviet divisions were not necessary to maintain order). Whether East Germany had developed a unique, peculiar way of life was the subject of partisan judgements, but the synthesis of Prussian character and Marxist ideology was probably more easily identifiable than, say, Canadian traits developed after many more years of existence. Moreover sovereign rights nowadays depend less on bona fide national character and free choice than upon legitimacy in the transfer of power and the effectiveness of governmental administration. East Germany was the most efficiently managed communist country and the succession of power had not yet been adequately tested.

Thus the arguments supporting charges of artificiality were subject to question. Yet how was the viability of the new entity to be measured? Leftist intellectuals argued that the responsibility of the government in fulfilling its international obligations contributed to the respectability and the degree of permanency other nations attached to its rule. The continuity that leaders and social institutions provide in achieving traditional and historic patterns and goals also fostered legitimacy in the eyes of other nations. (In the case of communist regimes, this is usually translated into the degree to which national communist practices operate in domestic politics.) The pursuit of independent foreign-policy aims indicated that a capability of legitimate decision-making exists, based upon valid criteria for assessing national interests. Finally, the provisions of the basic material necessities of the people, as well as civil rights and elements of justice, were pragmatic gauges of the regime's durability. Judged by these standards, the East German performance stands and falls on several accounts.

Economically, the GDR had achieved a miraculous recovery, second only to that of the Federal Republic. While this region of the former Reich had achieved a relatively high level of industrialization before World War II, employing more industrial workers than did the regions of the present Federal Republic, the impact of the war was more severe. The Federal recovery effort was aided by approximately $10,000 m. in foreign assistance, but the GDR paid at least the same amount in reparations to the Soviet Union and experienced a similar level of industrial losses through the Soviet demolition of Nazi properties. Due to both war damage and demolitions, the electrical, steel-processing, machine-tools, precision-instruments, optical, and electronics industries and overall vehicular inventories lost between 75 and 85 per cent of their total equipment.[7] The restitution of these losses was complicated, moreover, by a near-total lack of local raw materials; the bulk of the industry (machinery and skilled labour) was confined to consumer products, textiles, and appliances; and the northern provinces of Mecklenburg, Brandenburg, and parts of Sachsen were almost exclusively agrarian and could contribute to reconstruction little in skills of materials. The very scale of the losses, however, was a major factor in the rapid growth rates, since the restored plants were more modern and efficient than the older equipment in other socialist countries. And the GDR also benefited from the talents of over 3 m. expellees from the east who contributed to the most skilled labour force east of the Elbe.[8] Thus, with one-third of the Federal Republic's population, the GDR became Europe's fifth industrial power and the second trading nation in the East, contributing

[7] Bremer Ausschuss für Wirtschaftsforschung, *Am Abend der Demontage* (Bremen, 1951), pp. 59–113; and Ernst Rickert, *Das zweite Deutschland* (1964), pp. 242–5.

[8] Karl C. Thalheim, ' Wachstumsprobleme in den osteuropäischen Volkswirtschaften', *Schriften des Vereins für Socialpolitik* (Berlin, 50/ii, 1970), pp. 1–40. See Ulbricht's speech on the 20th anniversary of the GDR for figures on growth-rates, *ND*, 10 Oct. 1969; and *Statistisches Jahrbuch der DDR*, 1968.

one-fifth of the Soviet Union's total import requirements. The GDR is now exporting more than one complete factory weekly and has become the second most important source of producer goods for Comecon members. The Social Democrats emphasized that this astonishing economic recovery had earned the GDR the highest living standards in the East, double that of the Soviet Union, and sufficient power and prestige to define and defend her own national interests in economic matters.

Indeed, the GDR was able to devise a highly original national communist model for transition to the post-industrial era. To offset the dislocations caused by forced collectivization in 1960 and stabilize the impact of the Wall, and to reactivate the economy in the post-reconstruction period, in 1963 she introduced the most far-reaching economic reforms by then implemented in any communist state. The reforms were threefold: a decentralization of decision-making authority from the national economic agencies to new associations of enterprises (*Vereinigungen Volkseigener Betriebe*, or VVBs) and the individual firms; the rationalization of economic planning in the central and regional bureaucracies; and the improvement in technical training for managerial personnel. In a remarkably short time, these efforts produced a more flexible and efficient economic structure and a new ' institutionalized counter-elite ' that compensated for the older party cadres' inability to grasp the requirements of technological specialization, data processing, cost accounting, profitability, automation, and cybernetic rationale. These reforms led to further local improvisations, such as the institutionalization of local *ad hoc* investigative committees, which allowed the GDR, rather than the Soviet Union, to respond promptly to the economic crisis in Czechoslovakia in the wake of the occupation with massive deliveries of capital goods. The resulting economic boom has reached proportions unprecedented in the history of the communist movement.[9]

The GDR's achievement in constructing the most modern and efficient economic machine in the East has lent credence to the ' convergence thesis ' espoused by intellectuals such as Ralf

---

[9] E. Fortsch & H.-J. Müller, *Parteielite im Wandel, Marginalien zu Peter Christian Ludz' Buch* (Cologne, 1968); P. C. Ludz, ' The SED leadership in transition ', *Problems of Communism*, May–June 1970, pp. 23–31.

Dahrendorf, Arnold Gehlen, and Karl Jaspers. Indeed, many West Germans now view the ultimate course of reunification as an accommodation of the two entities through the attraction of their mutually compatible technologies, or adjustment and conversion through the demands of modernity. As the two most industrialized countries in their respective halves of Europe, they will inevitably be drawn closer together to meet the increasingly urgent needs of modernization, and this will tend gradually to obviate political and ideological differences. Members of this school called in 1969 for a reduction of the artificial political barriers to this natural process, such as a genuine renunciation of the policy of strength. Such measures they argued, would stimulate the social reformism already evident in East Germany, as witnessed in the programmes of men like Professors Wolfgang Harich and Robert Havemann, which antedated the Czechoslovak Action Programme by at least ten years. Finally, they argued that the desired liberalization of the East German regime could not be achieved through West German coercion; it could only be secured by a genuinely domestic process. Federal pressure merely forced the reformist communists to support the SED's dogma, since to do otherwise would be both treasonable and would lead to the weakening of their own institutions. These forces could not, therefore, effectively combat the Stalinist elements in the GDR, when to do so would appear to strengthen West German influence and jeopardize their own sovereign interests and even their individual positions.[10]

As final evidence to support the correctness of these theses, the Social Democrats pointed to the increasing independence of the GDR in formulating her own foreign-policy objectives and tactics. It was argued that the foreign-policy criterion was the most bona fide standard for measuring East Germany's artificiality. Until the mid-1960s East Germany was the object, not the source, of policy, and became the cause of some of the most serious crises in the cold war. Her actions reflected complete dependence on the Soviet Union and lack of original initiative. Two events in the early 1960s altered this pattern:

[10] Heinz Lippmann, ' East Germany today ', *Problems of Communism*, May–June 1970, pp. 15–22.

the construction of the Berlin Wall, which relieved the most aggravating East German problems and allowed the regime to consolidate its domestic position, and the Cuban missile crisis, which demonstrated the limits of Soviet strategic manoeuvrability. In the wake of these crises the Soviet Union modified her former hostility towards the West, and this prompted East Germany to protect her own interests.

During the 1964–8 period the GDR feared that the developing dialogue between Moscow and Washington might result in an accommodation over the German problem. To preclude an adjustment with the West at her expense, she adopted a more active, but largely negative, foreign policy. For example, when Khrushchev explored a rapprochement with Bonn through his intermediary, Alexei Adzhubei, East Germany protested and sided with Peking in the Sino-Soviet dispute. For an extended period, the question remained open whether this negative policy could be converted into positive, dynamic actions.

The weight of East German opinion in Moscow, however, gradually increased during this period. This was due in part to the failure of the Kremlin to convert the Warsaw Pact into an effective instrument of foreign policy in which a consensus on all major issues could inhibit independent action. Also the Sino-Soviet dispute and the rise of polycentrism reduced membership of the Soviet camp, but increased the importance of the European members, especially those who contributed to Soviet security. This increasing lack of communist unanimity permitted East Germany to extract political concessions in compensation for her exposed strategic position.

The requirement to devise appropriate reactions to the Federal Republic's ' aggressive ' overtures forced the GDR increasingly to assert originality and creativity to the point that her foreign policy was no longer completely responsive to the static Soviet policy. Indeed, with each subsequent inroad West Germany made into Eastern Europe, the GDR, rather than Moscow, goaded the Pact nations into counteractions.

The reality of the GDR's independent foreign policy was demonstrated by her determination to polarize the Warsaw Pact over Rumania's economic and two-Germanies policies, by her role as the prime mover in the anti-Prague coalition, her open rivalry as the guardian of orthodoxy, and her repeated confrontations with Moscow over the status of Berlin and the access routes. In the latter case, communist powers hold opposing views on the legal status of West Berlin: the Soviet Union maintains that it is an autonomous political entity within GDR territory and the East Germans insist that it is an independent entity on her territory. The Soviet Union sees Berlin as her most important means of leverage against both the GDR and the Federal Republic, and East Germany regards West Berlin's ties with Bonn as a flagrant affront to her prestige and a manifestation of the precarious nature of her claims to sovereign statehood. Such divergent views have led to repeated clashes of interest.

One of the most serious events occurred only six months before the September elections. The GDR concerted with the Soviet Union to approach Bonn to seek concessions for a new Wall pass agreement in exchange for transferring the election of the Federal President from West Berlin to another site. After initially agreeing, East Berlin retracted its commitments, forcing Moscow into the difficult position of having to side with an adversary against its ally. In the end, Moscow had to endorse East Berlin's terms for an agreement and the negotiations broke down. At the same time the GDR took the unprecedented step of formally incorporating the parliamentary deputies from East Berlin into the Volksrat, in direct violation of four-power agreements, as a means of signifying to the Soviet Union the seriousness of her demands for unqualified sovereign rights. By 1969 East Germany was certainly no puppet and was probably exercising as much diplomatic initiative as the more quiescent of the East European states. Thus many West German voters concluded by that date that East Germany was a viable ' state-like ' entity, equal in virtually every respect to the Federal Republic, and that the improvement of the lot of the Germans east of the Elbe, through encouraging liberalization without coercion, should be the highest national priority.

If again, for the sake of simplicity, it can be argued that one orientation that tended to crystallize during the 1969 elections was acceptance of two German entities and a more activist programme to relieve the welfare of the other half (supported mainly by the traditional left-leaning segments), the opposing orientation adhered to the historic Bismarckian model for German unity, based on a unitarian *kleindeutsche Lösung* (solution) formula (drawing strength largely from the conservative segment of the electorate). Supporters of the latter position gravitated towards the CDU, which campaigned on a neo-Bismarckian platform. They were far more circumspect in the tactical moves towards an adjustment with the GDR, fearing that the SPD's policy of accommodation would jeopardize the prospect of the final solution of a unitary state. While the focus of the SPD tended to be the immediate, the CDU policy was projected into the future. Yet it was clearly recognized that Bonn could not profitably reverse the trends established by the Grand Coalition; it could not return to a policy of isolation and hostility towards the East; it could not abandon the policy of *détente* and resume its posture of a bastion Germany. The differences, then, between the polls were often subtle and complex.

While the CDU insisted that unity remained the country's major foreign-policy aim, it was more difficult to define the degree of emphasis Bonn itself should place on advancing this goal. Traditionally the CDU had preferred to rely heavily on Allied support to promote this objective, but the Allies had adopted a defensive stand—designed to preserve existing prerogatives without solving the dilemma. The prospects of the *détente* by-passing a German solution loomed large in the 1969 elections, and the Allies' seeming inability to equate their *détente* objectives with their long-term interests in a German settlement and durable European accord forced the CDU to accept the fact that a settlement would only be possible within the context of a change in the entire international order. Therefore, the CDU had to abandon the last vestiges of its former attitude that a German settlement was the prerequisite to *détente*.

If the Federal Republic, it was then asked, should adopt a more active role in seeking a German solution, how would this affect other domestic policies, such as funding for scientific research and defence spending. (While the Federal Republic is an economic giant, she has limited authority in military and strategic matters and can expect to remain a junior partner in the Western alliance until she has a louder military voice.) This returned the issue to the externalization problem, i.e. to what level of activist foreign policy could appeal to both West Germans and their allies.

Conservative intellectuals pointed out that the historical constraints on Germany's foreign policy—the Scylla and Charybdis between seeking security or preserving the *status quo* —had not sufficiently diminished to warrant an ' open-arms ' policy in any direction and that an accelerated pace in contacts with the East risks the dangers of heightening these constraints. On the one hand, they acknowledged that an improvement in relations and relaxation in tensions required probing areas where contacts could be strengthened and where pressure could be supplied to demonstrate that more equitable arrangements in world order could be mutually advantageous. Only in this manner could Germany and Central Europe envisage genuine security. On the other hand, all Germany's neighbours held the aim of preserving and perfecting the existing order, which placed a high priority on maintaining the present *status quo*. Germany's friends showed in 1953, 1956, and 1968 that they placed such a high premium on the *status quo* that they were unwilling to jeopardize the gains of *détente* or risk a return to the cold war by supporting concretely the ' just ' aims of Eastern nations. Conversely, respect for the *status quo* has never been a Soviet virtue. Such asymmetrical respect for the *status quo* prohibits genuine security and prompts dissatisfied nations to upset the existing stability to gain satisfaction, leaving Germany with the unenviable prospects of alienating her friends and courting a perfidious adversary as she pursues her desires for security.

CDU supporters argued also that Bonn's position was further complicated by several uncertainties. The first uncertainty was the increasingly complex climate of opinion within West Germany itself. The election campaign was reawakening public interest in the government's German policy. As Karl Kaiser has observed, ' it is a characteristic feature of present-day Europe that accommodation to the *status quo* sets free forces that inherently challenge it '.[11] In no other country is this more apparent and potentially more dangerous than in West Germany. (The dimensions of the fear of extremism that dominates both public and Establishment thinking was demonstrated by university reforms introduced in the wake of recent, relatively minor, student protests. In the remarkably short period of three years, German university administrations were transformed from the most medieval to, in many respects, the most modern in Europe, clearly an unpredicted development.) Brandt himself has commented in this regard that in more than any other country, internal order in the Federal Republic is the preliminary condition for external security.[12] In the era of such changes, the stability of the *status quo* provided inner strength for the *bürgerlich und ordentlich*-minded Germans, but this stability was clearly no longer as durable as it was formerly.

A second uncertainty that troubled CDU policy planners more than the Social Democrats centred in the nature of Soviet leadership and the future transformations in Soviet society that could ultimately alter Soviet foreign-policy objectives. The continuance of the current Soviet collective leadership had not introduced an era of regularity, caution, and stability in Soviet policy, and the immediate future was unpredictable and could be dangerous. The conservatives concluded that Brezhnev was in a similar position to Khrushchev in 1964: embedded in the Chinese morass, tied down in Central Europe, confronted with schism in the world communist movement, and plagued by domestic difficulties. While the present leadership was still collective, its policies for these problems had often had a least-common-denominator appearance, leading frequently to unjustifiable conclusions of paralysis, or facile generalization about ' hawks ' verses ' doves '. Of course, internal strains were endemic to this form of leadership, but there was no evidence of a cataclysmic change in the near future. Yet there was also no basis for predicting the indefinite tenure of the present leadership or policies. This enigmatic element created uncertainty about the Kremlin's long-term

---

[11] *German Foreign Policy*, p. 50.
[12] DPA, 7 Jan. 1970.

goals. (The same uncertainties afflicted Bonn's estimates of the problems of East German leadership. Seventy-six-year-old Walter Ulbricht could not dominate GDR politics much longer, and although the struggle for succession might be relatively subdued, significant policy changes were possible.)

In the wake of the technological revolution it is even more difficult to forecast the future course of the Soviet social scene than it was under the former Stalinist rule. West Germany's leading Sovietologist, Richard Löwenthal, concluded: ' We are watching the outward expansion of an inwardly declining regime '.[13] Even Soviet intellectuals and academicians were condemning the regime's repressive measures and predicting domestic difficulties unless a drastic transformation could be made. Western analysts remained divided in their estimates, which ranged from the ' fumbling-crumbling ' course, leading to the collapse of committee leadership and the return of one-man rule, which would impose authoritarian, orthodox policies, to the evolution of democratic government espousing liberal society, or to the emergence of a technological élitist oligarchy, ruling a continuingly cloistered society. Clearly there were no agreed precedents that would indicate either the durability of the present regime and its social fabric or future alternatives.

A third uncertainty was closely related to these difficulties: the question of the continued application of the Soviet model for social development to Eastern Europe—an area of more immediate concern for CDU policy planners. If the Prague crisis demonstrated nothing else, it exposed the persisting ' mentality gap ' between Eastern Europe and ' oriental ' Russia. Polycentrism is a form of protest: manifest rejection of the Soviet formula for progress. As Joseph R. Starobin, a former party leader, has observed about the fragile adaptability of the Soviet models,

if there is any simple—or perhaps oversimplified—way in which Communism's crisis can be defined, I would stress first the enormous

---

[13] In *Adelphi Papers* (ISS), no. 66, Mar. 1970, p. 11. Walter Laqueur states that the Soviet Union was much stronger militarily during the last 20 years, politically it is far weaker than under Stalin (' Russia enters the Middle East ', *Foreign Affairs*, Jan. 1969, p. 306).

difficulty the Communist system experiences in making the transition from tasks of mobilizing underdeveloped societies to the more
complex and challenging problems of modern industrialization.
Wherever this stage has been reached, as in the Soviet Union itself,
or where it was the point of departure, as in Czechoslovakia, the
weapons of Communism have turned against the system . . . all the
techniques of dictatorship not only become outmoded but react
against the system and burst its integument.[14]

Such appraisals have led conservative analysts to question the
entire spectrum of future Soviet-East German relations and
their impact on proposed Federal policy.

Events in 1968–9, which indicated that the Soviet Union was
taking a more active interest in the German problem, raised the
question of whether this denoted a change in the Soviet attitude
towards East Germany. Moscow's stand on three basic
questions was cited as a significant indicator of policy changes.
First, was East Germany to continue deflecting and muting the
political influence of a revanchist Federal Republic by asserting
her own authority among fellow communist countries? In the
past, this approach had enhanced the GDR's stature at the
Kremlin's expense. Ulbricht's feud with Khrushchev during
the first attempted Soviet-West German rapprochement was a
contributing factor in the latter's dismissal. More recently, the
GDR's staunch hard line during the Czechoslovak crisis
actually led to competition with the Kremlin over the correct
definition of orthodoxy.

Secondly, was the GDR to continue posing as the economically sounder German state in comparison with capitalist West
Germany? The GDR had used this argument to demand
greater local autonomy and freedom for socialist innovation.
As a result, East Germany had established her position as the
world's most successful industrialized communist state. The
ascendancy of the East German model had in fact contributed
to the undermining of the formerly ubiquitous Soviet formula
for industrialization.

Thirdly, was East Germany to preserve her existing special
relationship with Bonn as an additional means of injecting
communist influence into the Federal Republic? From the

[14] In *Problems of Communism*, Jan.–Feb. 1970, p. 27.

Soviet viewpoint, this was potentially the gravest danger of all: both Germanies suffered the same handicaps in their relationship with their respective allies. Each had achieved the status of a major economic power, but was constrained in its political authority by the demands of the rival German state. Acknowledgement by both that their hard-line stances have been mutually detrimental could result in an understanding to minimize their antagonisms. Thus the GDR and the Federal Republic may not be able to reach a formal agreement on reunification or legal confederation, but they might gradually adopt a growing commonality of interests and views on selected foreign-policy issues. The emergence of a common European policy would allow both Germanies to exercise the authority of a third power in Continental matters. The negative tone of these appraisals led to searching questions of Soviet policy options. What new Soviet formula could Bonn expect? When the Federal Republic will soon represent Western Europe in the East, could the Soviet equation contain adequate restraints on the GDR's natural urges to extract maximum advantages as compensation for her exposed strategic posture and her potentially precarious political position *vis-à-vis* the West? Could Moscow devise a scheme for its relations with both Germanies that would provide sufficient elasticity to accommodate the natural interests of both states, but enough checks and balances to prevent the implosion of German nationalism across the present partition and alarm the allies of both states? Finally, if the changing nature of Moscow's relations with East Berlin were the most valid yardstick for measuring the dimensions of Bonn's *Ostpolitik*, what weight would Moscow be likely to place on West German demands in formulating its own option relating to East Germany?

Questions of this nature led sooner or later to the problem of East German viability. While the SPD tended to cite pragmatic economic and *de facto* administrative reasons to support its contention that the GDR was sufficiently viable to warrant an accommodation, the CDU argued in legal and political terms to justify its reservations. The CDU pointed out that no government of the Federal Republic could ignore its legal constitutional commitments to represent all the German people or abrogate the principles of *deutscher Rechtsanspruch und Recht auf Heimat*. These principles could not be compromised, and ultimately could not be avoided. Twenty-five years of abeyance had not weakened their legal and moral certitude. Any government that intentionally acted to contravene these obligations would be subject to strong censure. Within these legal restraints, there was only limited area for manoeuvre. Some CDU supporters, for example, argued that the Eastern territories should be regarded as a *quid pro quo* for reunification. Relinquishing territory under Soviet, Polish, and Czechoslovak administrations would be less onerous if it was a means of ensuring the reunification of all Germans. But the two principles could not morally be sacrificed simultaneously. The smaller, more immediate measures for relieving tensions should preferably be confined to issues alleviating the partition, i.e. to the humanitarian problems of the division. By relieving the emotions and tensions of the human aspects of the Wall, it was argued, normalization would follow naturally, leaving German claims in Eastern Europe unscathed and presentable for a final peace conference in an unmodified form.

But it was precisely on this argument that the CDU was least convincing. CDU supporters frequently cited the lack of intellectual and creative freedom in the GDR as evidence of the repressive practices of the regime and its artificial links with the society. In contrast to the scientific and technological intellectuals who had become incorporated into the Establishment as the new ' counter-élite ', practitioners of the creative arts had been subjected to rigid dogma and severe conditions. Accordingly, over the past twenty-five years they had contributed little to international art and thought that had been either distinctly East German or intellectually important. Especially since the Central Committee Plenum in February 1965, when the party reacted harshly to the resurrection of Franz Kafka in East German literary circles, increasingly strong and effective measures have been instituted to prohibit the infusion of liberal ideas from either Western or Eastern Europe. The GDR has become a bastion of orthodoxy through proscribing Western influences and banning the works of Karel Kosik, Ivan Svitak, Milan Prucha, and Ota Sik of Czechoslovakia,

Georg Lukacs of Hungary, Adam Schaff of Poland, and the *Praxis* school of Yugoslavia. These policies are regarded as the products of ideological brittleness that had relegated personal justice and civil rights to a subordinate priority in party objectives. To many West Germans, lack of intellectual freedom, therefore, was the most convincing proof that the SED control was patented only by Soviet tanks; they pointed re-assuringly to the Erfurt demonstrations during Brandt's visit as conclusive evidence.

But the insecurity of the Ulbricht regime no longer warranted a policy resembling that of ' maintained tensions ' as the preferred instrument for alleviating human conditions or inducing adjustment. It is on humanitarian questions, moreover, that the SPD has acted most decisively; it has reached a position where it can insist on its terms for reciprocity. The CDU's failure to produce a dynamic programme with which to confront the GDR either on humanitarian issues or substantive claims relating to sovereign interests was the main reason why it lost substantial ground to the SPD.

While the CDU maintained its plurality of 46·1 per cent of the total—a decline of 1·5 per cent over the 1965 election—the SPD increased its support by 3·4 to 42·7 per cent of the electorate. Ironically, the party that held the balance of power, as in the Erhard administration, lost the most parliamentary strength. Dropping from 9·5 per cent in 1965 to 5·8 per cent in 1969, the FDP lost 19 of 49 Bundestag seats. In the ensuing negotiations, the FDP agreed to join the SPD in the Federal Republic's first left-of-centre government.

The scope and intensity of the 1969 election campaign registered a new awareness among West Germans of the implications of alternative strategies in *Ostpolitik* and *Deutschlandpolitik*. A deeply aroused electorate had opted for the new SPD–FDP experiment (see poll cited on p. 94). With only a twelve-seat majority—subsequently cut to six by conservative FDP defections to the CDU—Brandt could neither ignore nor evade the pledges upon which his slim working margin was based. On the other hand, he was confronted with an opposition that was expected to learn quickly from its mistakes, to rejuvenate its party apparatus, and to exploit ruthlessly any errors he would make in dealings with the Pact countries. While the coalition won the election, its marginal political base unquestionably shaped the character of Brandt's *Ostpolitik*, yet it must be ranked as one of the most decisive political milestones in Central European affairs in the past quarter-century.

6

THE DIMENSIONS OF BRANDT'S
OSTPOLITIK

THE formation of the SPD–FDP coalition was viewed in both Eastern and Western Europe as an opportunity to intensify international consideration of the German problem. In one of the most graphic demonstrations to date of the externalization of domestic politics, the new government was given the strongest mandate yet by the West German electorate to seek an accommodation with Eastern Europe and the Soviet Union. The new charge was a firm refutation of the earlier policy of *détente* through reunification and a sanction to explore an accommodation through normalization. While the Grand Coalition had initiated this trend, the legacies of the former CDU position and the demands of its right wing had prevented it from probing in depth the East's terms for an adjustment. During the election campaign, the SPD and the FDP had promised to initiate an action programme to prosecute West German interests east of the Elbe energetically. The dimensions of this programme became apparent in the ensuing year of hard bargaining.

In general, the Warsaw Pact countries have historically made eight demands upon the Federal Republic as preconditions for normalizing relations: (1) legal recognition of East Germany; (2) abandonment of the Hallstein Doctrine and the concept of sole representation of Germany; (3) acceptance of the present Central European borders, especially the Oder–Neisse line; (4) abandonment of all claims to possession of nuclear weapons; (5) support of general disarmament proposals; (6) renunciation of the 1938 Munich Agreement as null and void *ab initio;* (7) recognition of the existence of West Berlin as an independent political entity; and (8) proscription of the ' neo-Nazi ' NDP. During the first weeks of the Brandt government new initiatives were launched to probe the realities of these demands and to determine if the Soviet Union and Eastern Europeans had altered their stand sufficiently to allow mutual adjustment.

The opening probes
In his initial speech before the Bundestag on 28 October

1969, Chancellor Brandt selected several of these issues to test the East's reaction. He offered to discuss outstanding differences on the basis of equality which could lead to contractually agreed accords with East Germany. While he acknowledged the existence of two German states, he insisted that his government could never accept another German state as a foreign nation. He advanced the thesis that two German states existed within the single German nation and that a special relationship should be formulated to accommodate these unusual circumstances. Brandt also offered to negotiate non-aggression pacts or renunciation-of-force treaties with East European states, including the GDR. These pacts, he stated, would ' acknowledge the territorial integrity of the respective partners '.[1]

The new government made other positive moves. Following the renewed communist call for a European security conference issued by the Warsaw Pact Foreign Ministers' meeting on 30–31 October, Bonn gave it the strongest endorsement of any Western capital, even when it was clear that the GDR would participate as a fully sovereign state. Yet Brandt qualified this endorsement in a statement on 7 December in which he observed that the convening of a European security conference would depend upon an improvement in relations between the two Germanies, thus emphasizing Ulbricht's reluctance to negotiate with Bonn. After all, he observed, if the two Germanies could not discuss their differences, there was little chance that the two halves of Europe would be more successful.[2]

In another major policy change, Brandt announced that the Federal Republic would no longer oppose recognition of the GDR by third states, provided East Berlin made some move towards inter-German co-operation. Yet, as an interim measure during the time when both Germanies were resolving their mutual interests, he stated that Bonn would regard ' premature action ' by third states as interference and act accordingly. (Bonn has, however, taken no action against the thirteen states that since then have opened diplomatic relations with East Germany.)

Thus by November Brandt had taken several significant steps

[1] *Bull.* & Suppl., 4 Nov. 1969 (*Survival*, Dec. 1969).
[2] Press interview, DPA, 7 Dec. 1969; see also *Bull.* 11 Nov. 1969.

to demonstrate the sincerity of his intent to seek accommodation and attempted to maintain the momentum of the opening with a speedy endorsement of the NPT—a major Soviet policy aim. The Federal Foreign Ministry formally asked Moscow about possible Soviet interference in West German domestic affairs under the pretext of nuclear inspections. The Soviet note of 9 November 1969 provided assurances of unhindered peaceful use of atomic energy. The Foreign Minister Walter Scheel stated before the Bundestag that this formal Soviet guarantee had been instrumental in Bonn's signing the treaty on 28 November.[3]

Scheel also implied that the West German signature had been the Soviet price for opening the joint renunciation-of-force negotiations. In the expectation of such negotiations, a West German note of 8 November accepted the proposed Soviet schedule for starting them. The first meeting on 7 December was heralded by the West German press as the first instance since Adenauer's visit to Moscow in 1955 in which German officials were negotiating in Moscow on key issues related to settling the twenty-five-year-old residual effects of World War II.

Both sides placed a high value on a favourable outcome of the Moscow meetings. From the German viewpoint, a Soviet accord would result in the forfeiture of her claim to intervene in West Germany under the ' enemy-state ' clause of the UN Charter. It would also represent a logical first step towards securing reduction of Soviet forces along West Germany's eastern frontier. From the Soviet position, West Germany's signature would strongly imply that the renunciation of force presupposed *de facto* acceptance of the existing territorial borders and the *status quo* in Europe. The conclusion of a renunciation-of-force or non-aggression pact with the most powerful European state would establish a precedent for Federal negotiation of similar accords with other Warsaw Pact members. Ultimately this could result in a network of non-aggression treaties between ' the main threat to peace ' (the Federal Republic) and Eastern Europe. Moreover, the conclusion of just one accord could represent an important

[3] *Bull.*, 18 Nov. & 2 Dec. 1969. See Ahlers's statement, DPA, 17 Nov., and Scheel's statement to the Bundestag, ibid., 8, 10, & 11 Nov. 1969.

step towards the convocation of a general European security conference.

This progression was viewed in the Pact countries as a process of confirming the *status quo*, while the NATO countries viewed it as a function of the normalization process. In other words, one side saw the negotiations as a form of consolidation, the other primarily as a means of relaxing tensions. The differences between non-aggression pacts and formal recognition of borders are small, if they are, indeed, logically discernible. The preference of one over the other is a tactical choice related to larger strategic issues. At that juncture, however, it was important that while both sides held opposing final goals they have agreed on an appropriate initial step—a non-aggression pact.

After the West German-Soviet negotiations were endorsed by both sides, Bonn responded to Gomulka's offer of 17 May for joint talks. In a note of 24 November Bonn invited Warsaw to negotiate on their differences. Poland accepted on 22 December, and a date in February 1970 was agreed upon for the first meeting.[4] In discussing the importance of the negotiations, Cyrankiewicz stated that Poland had made no preconditions (she dropped her insistence of recognition of the GDR), but placed priority on the Oder–Neisse issue as the most significant means of *opening* the normalization process.[5]

West German officials repeatedly expressed their sympathy for Poland's desire to gain maximum guarantees for her borders, and stressed the importance of providing tangible evidence of Bonn's respect for Poland's integrity. But they insisted that legal recognition would be more definitive and durable if it was the product of a multilateral accord or the long-awaited peace treaty. Further, the Potsdam Agreement imposed specific limits on the authority of the Federal Republic to conclude a border accord independently of a peace treaty. Accordingly, Bonn advanced the formula of a non-aggression pact, demonstrating the abandonment of its territorial claims

[4] The Polish response had been co-ordinated with the Soviet Union during a visit by Gomulka and Cyrankiewicz to Moscow on 1–2 October. One week later the Foreign Minister Jedryochowski announced that the Polish side was ready for talks with the Federal Republic.

[5] For the Polish argumentation see M. Naszkowski, in *Nowe drogi*, July & Aug. 1969; also M. F. Rakowski, in *Polityka*, 16 Aug. 1969.

to Prussia, Silesia, and Pomerania. Yet Conrad Ahlers asserted that the German side would not evade the border issue.[6]

As an inducement for progress on political issues, Bonn employed its powerful economic leverage. To meet her 1971–5 economic goals, Poland planned to purchase between $1,000 and 1,500 m. worth of producer goods in the West. This would require partial payment in scarce hard currencies or long-term credits. Trade negotiations between Poland and West Germany paralleled the political talks, and repeated press leaks indicated that Bonn was prepared to offer a $500 m. loan—the largest credit extension ever granted to a communist country. In response, the Polish Foreign Minister Jedryochowski, in an unprecedented West German television interview, expressed his confidence that the present trade negotiations would result in a substantial increase in total turnover above the DM 777 m. trade in 1969.[7]

As with the Soviet-West German negotiations, the serious, businesslike tone of the Polish side impressed the West Germans with the importance Warsaw attached to the proceedings. Its anxiety about a favourable outcome was estimated to be due to a genuine desire for an improvement in relations but also to concern about Poland's strategic interests as the *Ostpolitik* gathered momentum. For example, as the West German-Soviet dialogue broadened and intensified, Poland's anxieties increased over her geographic vulnerability and traditional isolation between the two dominant powers of Eastern Europe.

After three months in office, the acceleration of Brandt's *Ostpolitik* had lengthened the list of issues of mutual concern compiled over the preceding twelve months to a level unprecedented since the early 1950s. The length of the agenda and the importance of each topic represented a mutual desire to exploit the prevailing atmosphere to broaden contacts. Moreover, the breadth of the agenda permitted simultaneous negotiation of a variety of different issues and this, in itself, fostered a co-operative climate. This momentum created apprehension in several Eastern capitals, especially East Berlin, lest it allow

[6] See Brandt's interview with the Polish press, *Życie Warszawy*, 23 Nov. 1969, reported in *Bull.*, 25 Nov. 1969.
[7] *Handelsblatt*, 20 Oct. 1969.

Bonn to score points through inadequate co-ordination among communist negotiators.

After extensive bilateral and multilateral consultations, Moscow convened the summit conference of 3–4 December 1969 of Warsaw Pact leaders which had signalled a turning-point in the East's reaction to Bonn's diplomatic offensive. The participants attempted to establish a common policy by reflecting the individual national interests of each member, as well as their common concerns. All seven members, including Rumania, apparently concluded that their bargaining positions on broad European matters would be strengthened if they were anchored to a more unified, co-ordinated Pact position *vis-à-vis* Bonn. The Declaration was the strongest statement to date affirming that international security required all nations to recognize East Germany and the Oder–Neisse border on the basis of international law.[8] It also sanctioned bilateral negotiations with Bonn, but affirmed the members' desire to continue consulting with each other in carrying out concerted joint actions relating to European security. Soviet news media acclaimed the conference as convincing proof of the successful co-ordination of Pact foreign policy.[9] Since then it has become apparent that this co-ordinated effect established a division of labour along lines of national interest or comparative advantage, originally envisaged in the 1966 Bucharest Declaration. Polish sources commented that ' this division of labour reflected, not differences, but a well-understood, realistic, and correctly functioning unity, based on multilateral interests '.[10]

Upon their return from the Moscow conference, several Pact leaders made important policy statements which added evidence to the division-of-function thesis. In his most important foreign-policy pronouncement to date, the Czechoslovak party chief Dr Husak stated that the conference had established a co-ordinated platform and then expounded his delegation's position. He carefully sought to unfreeze West German-Czechoslovak relations, but stressed his country's demands that renunciation of the Munich Agreement was the price for

[8] See ch. 3, n. 16.
[9] *Pravda*, 6 Dec. & Radio Moscow, 7 Dec. 1969.
[10] *Życie Literackie* (Cracow), 11 Dec. 1969.

normalization. He referred to these demands in terms unknown since Novotny's reign, but concluded that he hoped for a favourable West German response.[11]

(Brandt responded two days later, stating in a press interview that he recognized the Munich Agreement as ' unjust and not legal '—a new formula—and that Bonn had formulated a plan for the settlement of the issue. He implied that this plan contemplated a formal renunciation of the Agreement and negotiations of the claims held by the Sudeten Germans. He said the plan had been shelved after the invasion of Czechoslovakia, but added that it would be reactivated at the appropriate time. Priority had clearly been given to dealings with the three other Pact members.)

In reporting to the SED Central Committee on the conference results, the East German Foreign Minister Otto Winzer stated that the Federal Republic would not be permitted to improve relations with other Pact members until she first accepted relations with the GDR on the basis of international law. ' We are acting in complete agreement with our brother states when we propose to the Bonn government completely equal ties on the basis of international law.' [12] Ulbricht later referred to this formula in his letter to President Heinemann as the product of ' concerted joint actions ' within the Pact.

Cyrankiewicz inferred in his acceptance of negotiations with Bonn on 22 December that Warsaw's slice of the concerted action contained the issues of recognizing territorial borders. It is now apparent that Hungary was responsible for conducting the Pact's campaign to convene a European security conference. On 14 December Ceausescu reasserted before the Rumanian party's Central Committee Plenum his traditional aims of fostering improved relations between East and West. He urged all Pact members to follow Rumania's lead in establishing diplomatic relations with Bonn and announced his intentions to expand commercial and technological contacts with the Federal Republic for the benefit of all East European peoples.[13]

[11] Interview with *Rude Pravo*, 10 Dec. 1969 (text *E-A*, 25th yr, 25 Apr. 1970 p. D184).
[12] *ND*, 17 Dec. 1969.
[13] Radio Bucharest, 14 Dec. 1969.

This apportionment of selected issues to individual members left the Soviet Union a freer hand in dealing with the more crucial matters affecting European security—strategic arms talks with the United States, and the test case for renunciation-of-force agreements with the Federal Republic. A Soviet Foreign Ministry statement of 13 January also clearly indicated that Moscow had divorced the status of West Berlin from the issue of GDR recognition and that it too would remain within the sole purview of the Soviet Union.

The degree of specialization within the Pact was more comprehensive than ever before and probably reflected both a sense of urgency to reach early border agreements and possibly also the desire of Moscow to reduce the restraints on its allies on issues within its purview. Accordingly, it was obliged to grant fuller jurisdiction to its partners over their respective national grievances, while improvising an improved form of consultation to accommodate the concerns of all interested parties.

Mounting East German intransigence was the most probable reason for the new attention Moscow paid to a more co-ordinated Pact policy. Even as late as the mid-1960s, East Germany merely sought *de facto* acceptance of her existence. But with increasing economic and political strength, she demanded greater guarantees of permanency. Ulbricht had maintained, for example, that the policies of the Kiesinger government were intended to ' isolate the GDR, then play off the socialist states against each other ', a view subsequently reiterated by Radio Moscow.[14] In his speech on 13 December 1969 before the Central Committee, Ulbricht rejected Brandt's two-states-in-one-nation thesis and reiterated East Berlin's demands for full recognition under international law as the precondition for conducting political exchanges. Such terms were obviously unacceptable to Bonn, yet East Berlin rapidly stepped up its demands. On 18 December Ulbricht trans-mitted to Heinemann a letter and a draft state treaty (see App. II, p. 220) to be considered the basis for Federal-GDR

---

[14] ADN, 15 Feb. 1967; Radio Moscow, 13 Apr. 1967. Ulbricht later charged that in the Prague crisis Bonn adopted a ' policy of encirclement to enable it to attack the GDR on its southern flank', *Der Spiegel*, 31 Aug., *Pravda*, 4 Sept. 1969.

talks—the form of a state treaty had been the point upon which joint talks had foundered in 1967. The GDR subsequently demanded that Bonn should renounce the 1954 Paris Agreements and its commitments to NATO. In early January 1970 she insisted that only the Potsdam Agreement governs relations between the two Germanies, and that Bonn must comply with its provisions requiring the abolition of monopolies and militarism before normalization could be expected. During a New Year reception Ulbricht called for the exchange of ambassadors and later for the abrogation of a long list of West German statutes regarded as ' imperialistic '. East Germany insisted that all technical accords between the two Germanies, e.g. those governing postal or communications matters, should be hereafter awarded the status of state treaties. Finally, she delivered two strongly worded warnings against holding Bundestag committee meetings in West Berlin.[15]

Thus roughly between mid-December and mid-January, East Germany insisted on the stiffest terms yet as the price for talks with Bonn. Apparently the intent behind this tactical manoeuvre was to force Bonn to respond to the new demands, which could give the impression that there was no ' new look ' in Bonn. On the other hand, Ulbricht told Western diplomats on 9 January 1970 that his minimum demand at present was recognition of the territorial *status quo* and existing borders.

The exaggerated distance between the GDR's maximum for *de jure* recognition and minimum acceptance of *de facto* approval was not merely the consequence of adroit bargaining techniques. It stemmed from her vital interest in securing sufficient international recognition from potential opponents of her autonomy and authority for her to exercise free control over her domestic policies and to guarantee indefinite East German national-communist rule. To East Germany, this means assurances against foreign subversion equated in the GDR with formal West German renunciation of the principle of self-determination, abrogation of all territorial claims through legally binding non-aggression treaties, and formal acceptance

[15] *ND*, 17 Dec. 1969, & 10 & 12 Jan. 1970. For Federal public responses see *FAZ* & *Die Welt*, 29 Dec. 1969.

of existing territorial boundaries. But additional measures are also necessary to ensure domestic tranquillity in a potentially restive society. These measures are largely undefined and have been identified in the past only as expediencies and coercive actions, but not as a comprehensive programme. The inability to prescribe a neat formula for domestic peace is a major source of insecurity for the GDR and of uncertainty for the Federal Republic. Bonn-sponsored measures that inadvertently complicate the GDR's dilemma or insecurity are likely to prove detrimental to the Federal Republic's long-term interests.

Bonn has shown a new understanding of the complexity of East Berlin's position and Brandt made notable gestures towards relieving Ulbricht's chief anxieties in his State of the Nation Report on 14 January 1970. Brandt called for talks between the two Germanies on the basis of complete equality and with an open agenda. For the first time, he stressed that the primary goals of these talks should be to ensure that both sides would undertake to provide assurances that neither would seek to alter the existing social structures of the other partner. This was a significant move, since the constitutional documents of both states uphold the legal responsibility of each government to reunite all Germany under the respective social system of each German entity.

Brandt reiterated known points regarding the two-state thesis and support for the four-power responsibility for the status of Berlin and Germany as a whole. The rights of self-determination, national unity within the framework of a European peace order, and ties with West Berlin were reiterated. But he put a new slant on earlier proposals by stating that relations between East and West Germany should be based on the generally recognized principles of international law and on the basis of equality and non-discrimination (abrogation of the Hallstein Doctrine), respect of territorial integrity, the obligation to settle all disputes peacefully, and respect of each other's borders.[16] Thus Brandt coupled a proposal for non-interference in each other's domestic affairs with suggestions embodying the mutual respect normally afforded friendly states. The GDR was offered at that time more generous

[16] *Bull.*, Suppl., 20 Jan. 1970. For a critique see *Die Welt*, 15 Jan. 1970.

terms than those contemplated for subsequent negotiations
with the Soviet Union and Poland. Further, Brandt gave a
strong warning against a GDR rejection of his offer when he
firmly linked West German participation in the European
security conference with ' some positive beginning in the inter-
German sphere '.

East Germany voiced obvious annoyance that Bonn had
circumvented her tactics by not responding specifically to her
increased demands.[17] (Brandt merely inferred that East
Germany's draft treaty was detrimental to the interest of both
states and refused to comment on the other proposals.) Moreover, Bonn had clearly retained the initiative by enriching its
inducements for talks while introducing a powerful coercive
factor in its threat to boycott the security conference. It was
subsequently announced that Ulbricht would conduct his first
press conference in nine years on 19 January.

Knowledgeable East European correspondents reported that
Ulbricht was under strong pressure from his allies to relax his
stand sufficiently to allow forward movement on the security
conference. While maintaining that the Federal Republic
must renounce her ties with the West as the price for normalization, he made several notable concessions at his press conference. He dropped both his traditional demand for legal
recognition and his demands for an exchange of ambassadors
as the preconditions for talks. He agreed that talks could begin
on an open agenda and set the tone for the East German
position. Full recognition was to become a final aim of the
discussions with Bonn, and, in the meanwhile, the conduct of
both states should be governed by international law: respect
for sovereign equality, non-interference in the internal affairs
of other states, and renunciation of the use of force.[18] This
position was closer to East Germany's minimum demands and
narrowed the gulf between them and the Federal proposals. It
also reduced the restraints on the GDR's allies of the Moscow
communiqué of 4 December 1969, which had stressed the

---

[17] *ND*, 15 Jan. 1970. Poland reacted positively (Radio Warsaw, 16 Jan. 1970).
[18] Within three hours Ahlers announced that Bonn would test East Berlin's
sincerity with a letter to Premier Stoph proposing a schedule for the talks. A
formal note was delivered three days later (see *ND*, 20 Jan. 1970).

common interest in ensuring East German recognition as the Pact's main priority.

Thus, in its first 100 days in office, the Brandt regime was credited with extending important concessions towards meeting the traditional Pact demands. (1) It had not legally recognized the GDR, but had officially accepted her *de facto* existence, and reunification—as it was understood in the 1950s—had been officially superseded by normalization. (2) It had tentatively abandoned the Hallstein Doctrine. (3) It had agreed to negotiate a formula providing for the sanctity of the Oder–Neisse border. (4) It had abandoned all claim to nuclear weapons through its signature of the NPT (ratification depended upon agreed verification procedures between Euratom and the IAEA). (5) Its most active support for general disarmament was its participation in negotiations for mutual reduction-of-force treaties. (6) It had devised a new formula for a solution of the issue relating to the Munich Agreement and was awaiting the favourable outcome of other diplomatic enterprises and a consolidation of the Husak regime before proposing talks with Prague. (7) It had reiterated its support for four-power responsibilities in Berlin, and had expressed reassurance about the Western allies' Berlin policy (a growing awareness of both Soviet sensitivity on the subject and Western determination to limit an excessive Western presence, while ensuring its continuing existence). (8) The September elections had reduced the NPD to an insignificant political group that could no longer be regarded as a threat to the East.

The Bundestag debate on the Chancellor's January Report was the liveliest in memory; an outbreak of slogans marked the opposition's difficulties in attacking the substance of his new concepts as well as in producing convincing alternatives. Charges of ' capitulation without cause ' and ' unilateral concessions ' were met with ' reunification may be dead, but long live the nation '.[19] None the less, Brandt's statement was at the time the most advanced formulation of a new *Ostpolitik*. And, as he unmistakably said, this represented his government's maximum bid. It emphasized, as did his policy statement of 28 October 1969, that the programme of action Bonn envisaged

[19] *Bull.*, 27 Jan. 1970.

was integrated into three interrelated component parts, dealing with Moscow, Eastern Europe, and East Germany. As Helmut Schmidt said,

our method is that of patient, persevering, matter-of-fact diplomatic dialogue, carried on in a spirit neither euphoric nor frustrated. That dialogue is being launched simultaneously with the Soviet Union, with Eastern Europe, and with East Germany. We see the situation realistically, as it is. Nothing important can be accomplished in Eastern Europe that Moscow does not agree to, it would be foolish to try to drive wedges between the members of the Warsaw Pact.[20]

But after Bonn had undertaken talks with the Soviet Union, agreed to discussions with the Poles and proposed top-level contacts with the East Germans, both the pace and the substance of subsequent deliberations were dependent upon the responses from the East.

The Federal–GDR dialogue

While initial advances in *Ostpolitik* were made with the Soviet Union and then with Poland, public and official attention was focused during the winter on relations with the GDR. Brandt decided to test the seeming loosening in the East German position, implied by Ulbricht's press conference, with a personal letter on 22 January 1970 to Stoph. Brandt proposed discussions between the two regimes at the ministerial level, the Federal Republic to be represented by Inner German Minister Egon Franke, and suggested that the agenda should cover three general topics: a contractual agreement between the two German states on mutual renunciation of force; an improvement in East–West German technical contacts; and an expansion of human contacts. Stoph responded on 13 February with a proposal that must have been a studied insult; he suggested that a meeting of the heads of government be held in East Berlin within a week or at the latest two weeks. At one stroke the GDR sought to embarrass the Federal Republic, enhance her *de facto* recognition, and gain acceptance of East Berlin as her capital. Bonn offered a qualified acceptance but its emissary, Ulrich Sahm, was outmanoeuvred on the protocol arrangements to the point of involving policy. The GDR insisted that the Chancellor could not stay in West Berlin in

[20] ' Germany in the era of negotiation ', *Foreign Affairs*, Oct. 1970, p. 47.

transit, a direct affront to a Chancellor, a citizen of the city, a former Mayor of West Berlin, and a member of the West Berlin Senate. The Federal Republic could not accept such a *diktat*. The ensuing month-long deadlock was broken when Bonn proposed alternative sites. The Chancellery representative was again outmanoeuvred, by agreeing to all the normal pomp and ceremony attributed to heads of foreign states, allowing Stoph in a subsequent letter to insist upon reciprocal protocol rights.

Herman Axen, a candidate member of the Politburo and SED Central Committee Secretary, explained the GDR's stand at the time. Recognition under international law by the Federal Republic was not a precondition for discussions but was a necessary prerequisite for a valid agreement on the renunciation of force.[21] (In contrast, Poland reversed the priorities in opening negotiations with the Federal Republic, i.e. an agreement first and then recognition.) During the interval of the stalemate, GDR diatribes against Brandt and West Germany reached new proportions, indicating possible anxieties about the unprecedented proposed contacts. On Bonn's side, Brandt replied that his government was working towards a *modus vivendi* that could prevent further alienation of Germany's two parts and keep the way open for a just approach to the problem of the divided nation in a future European peace arrangement.[22]

An important factor in breaking the deadlock was apparently the talks conducted simultaneously in Moscow between the State Secretary Egon Bahr and Gromyko (see p. 135). Brandt revealed on television during his visit to the United States in April that the talks had covered all points of mutual interest, not merely the proposed treaty. On 24 February Gromyko paid a quick visit to East Berlin, after which GDR polemics subsided and the alternative site for the conference was accepted, suggesting that Soviet influence may have been instrumental in promoting the subsequent meeting.

One of the most significant dates in modern German history is 19 March 1970, when the heads of the respective German

[21] *ND*, 7 Feb. 1970.
[22] *Bull.*, 17 Feb. 1970.

entities (Willy Brandt and Willi Stoph) met, for the first time since 1947 and for first time as heads of governments, in Erfurt. The public tone in West Germany was characterized by calculated optimism, protected against euphoria by a modest cynicism—the product of years of frustrated hopes. Yet it was the most important ' first ' registered by the *Ostpolitik* and warranted the closest attention.

Public reaction in Erfurt, however, was totally unexpected by both sides. With electrifying effect in West Germany, television cameras recorded uncontrollable popular enthusiasm for Brandt, who prudently refrained from encouragement or provocation. Upon his return to Bonn, Brandt told reporters: ' My short journey to Erfurt was certainly a powerful human experience. . . . It demonstrated that it was not a fiction but a reality when I spoke again yesterday about the continuing and living reality of one German nation.'[23] On the other hand, the demonstrations were also firm evidence for the CDU arguments about the artificiality of the SED regime that was difficult to ignore in policy matters. As the West German press repeatedly pointed out, relations between the two Germanies could never be the same after such spontaneous manifestations of the ' germanness ' of public sentiment in both states. The policies of both governments must now place a higher priority on the human element, a fact that inevitably complicated subsequent negotiations.

Stoph returned attention to the hard realities of power politics when he presented the Chancellor with a list of East German demands as the precondition for normalization. He suggested that they deliberate on the draft treaty which Ulbricht had submitted to Heinemann in December, including seven specific issues: full diplomatic recognition, renunciation of the Hallstein Doctrine, non-intervention in each other's internal affairs, renunciation of the use of force, acceptance of the principles of territorial integrity and the inviolability of existing borders, application for membership in international organizations, a 50 per cent reduction in arms expenditures, discussion of questions connected with burial of all vestiges of World War II, and the settlement of the debts and reparations

[23] Ibid., 24 Mar. 1970.

owed to the GDR, amounting to 100,000 m. marks. On the evidence of the prepared statements, Stoph added nothing new, but the presentation of all the former demands in a solid block did not augur well for the success of their private talks.

Brandt replied that his government could never consider the GDR a foreign country and proposed that they seek ways to collaborate in a ' neighbourly ' fashion. Measures towards peaceful coexistence could be regulated by agreements between the two regimes, and he offered several positive measures to facilitate this policy: Bonn would drop its claim to exclusive representation; both states should abandon discriminatory practices against the other, avow respect for existing borders and the peaceful settlement of disputes, and renounce attempts to change the social structure of the other entity; agreements should be negotiated on easing the human situation, and the responsibility of the four powers for Germany and Berlin must be reaffirmed. In a new offer he suggested that the two governments establish working-level secretariats in each other's capital to begin technical deliberations on their outstanding problems.

In reporting to the Bundestag, Brandt stated that the GDR had concentrated on the legal aspects of recognition, as she saw it, without recognizing the positive changes which it would mean in German coexistence and the co-operation of the two German states. The East Germans, he said, made a number of demands which could not be fulfilled because they had no legal or moral foundation.[24] The GDR responded by heightening the intensity of her polemical attacks against Bonn and Brandt personally. For example, *Neues Deutschland* maintained that Brandt had no higher standards than Stresemann, the Chancellor who had secured Germany's flanks with the Locarno and Berlin treaties (1925), a parallel the West Germans proudly accepted.[25]

The East German attacks were anomalies in the communist press at that time and probably reflected a bureaucratic reflex reaction against the public enthusiasm at Erfurt and the Federal Republic's propaganda victory, as well as growing nervousness about the strength of the GDR's bargaining position

[24] Ibid.
[25] *SZ*, 11 Apr. 1970.

at the forthcoming return encounter at Kassel in West Germany. But they also indicated to Germans in both states that insufficient grounds existed for a rapprochement. Indeed, in this atmosphere, it was openly asked whether Stoph would honour his commitment to a second summit meeting. But the tone of the attacks weakened, after Ulbricht made an unexpected trip to Moscow in mid-May, when the Soviet Union apparently pointed out that the onus for breaking off the dialogues would be intensified by contrast with the increasing contacts between Bonn and the Eastern Europeans.

Unlike the first meeting, the West German public attitude towards the second meeting (on 21 May) was marked, as Conrad Ahlers stated, by ' sound scepticism '. Whereas in mid-January 79 per cent of the West Germans polled supported the Brandt–Stoph meeting, only 67 per cent took a positive view of the second confrontation.[26] The pessimism pervading the Kassel meeting had been intensified by the Federal Republic's successful blocking of the GDR's application for membership in the UN Economic Commission for Europe and the World Health Organization. Bonn resurrected the Hallstein Doctrine and requested the three Western allies to lobby against the application on the grounds that the GDR was attempting to discriminate against the Federal Republic through exercising the Ulbricht Doctrine,[27] and that until formal relations between the two Germanies could be established Bonn remained the most representative German state. Brandt stated, in an address at Munich on 20 May, that this formulation was based on the desire for progress in the German dialogues through the elimination of mutual discrimination rather than on legal claims. East Berlin, however, viewed the move as a return to exclusive representation and a refutation of the measures of de facto recognition that Bonn had already extended to the GDR.

Apparently in response, in May the GDR increased the transit tax for goods transported between the Federal Republic and West Berlin by 30 per cent. This prompted a campaign

[26] Conducted by the Inst. for Applied Social Sciences (General-Anzeiger, 21 May 1970; also Kölner Stadt-Anzeiger, 10 Mar. 1970.)
[27] See above ch. 3, n. 9, p. 43.

in the West German news media to examine the details of interzonal and financial transactions between the two German states and their relationship to talks. During the 1950s interzonal trade represented about 11 per cent of the GDR's total trade, but the figure dropped by one-half during the early 1960s. After that it rose again, amounting to 8·6 per cent in 1969 or DM 3,600 m. (the same volume represented only 1.6 per cent of total Federal trade). Since the GDR is not considered a foreign country, she benefits from indirect participation in the Common Market. She pays neither foreign duty nor the value-added tax for goods purchased in the Federal Republic, which amounted to a profit of nearly DM 500 m. in 1969. This sum is inflated by an indirect profit provided by the permanent use of a ' swing ', whereby the GDR need not balance her trade on a yearly basis, in practice granting her an annual interest-free credit of about DM 380 m. Added to these net gains is a total of DM 270 m. for postal services above those already paid for the years 1967–73. The transit tax netted DM 40.5 m. in 1969 and was increased by DM 12 m. in 1970. Taxes on visas from January 1969 to June 1970 earned DM 92 m. and a special road tax for the same period netted DM 90 m. These direct and indirect financial contributions amounted to nearly DM 800 m. in 1969 and paid for a large portion of East German purchases in the Federal Republic. Because of the value of this preferential commercial treatment, it was widely held that the GDR could not afford genuine diplomatic recognition. Indeed, the East German draft treaty of 1969 provided that ' relations in special sectors will be regulated separately and contractually '.[28]

In contrast to the deterioration in relations between the two Germanies, Bonn's contacts with other socialist countries prior to the Kassel meeting had been readily growing. In the political field, the Soviet Union had accepted the Western Allies' proposal for talks on the status of Berlin; West German talks with Poland and the Soviet Union were progressing; the Hungarian Foreign Minister Janos Peter announced on 3 March in Brussels that his government had no preconditions for the complete normalization of relations with the Federal

[28] *Bull.*, 9 June 1970; & DPA, 1 Nov. 1969.

Republic, including diplomatic relations (but in Sofia he reiterated the usual Pact demands). The Soviet Union and the Federal Republic agreed on 22 March to establish Consulates-General at Hamburg and Leningrad, elevating West Germany to the diplomatic ranking of the United States; in consultation with Bonn, the three Western Allies agreed as a gesture of good-will after Erfurt to close the Allied Travel Board in West Berlin which formerly issued travel documents for NATO countries to East German citizens; and Poland opened a lavish campaign entertaining Federal politicians—the first two delegates, CDU Deputies Peter Petersen and Hans Dichgans, returned in May to present the Bundestag with a ten-point programme for normalizing relations with Poland.

In a related area, the Federal Federation of Trade Unions (DGB) launched its own *Ostpolitik* by sending its chairman to the Soviet Union, Poland, Bulgaria, Yugoslavia, and the GDR, and by accepting reciprocal visits. The purpose of these exchanges was to re-establish harmonious relations among trade unions (in the case of Bulgaria to open initial ties), and to cultivate a favourable political environment. In the words of the chairman H. O. Vetter, ' our constant task is an *Ostpolitik* marked by reason, patience, and strength of character '.[29]

Progress was equally impressive in the economic sphere. The Federal Republic signed the steel pipe–natural gas trans-action with the Soviet Union whereby she provided an un-precedented credit of DM 1,200 m., and opened negotiations for an even larger deal involving the construction of a heavy truck plant at Kama. Salzgitter AG was also contracting for construction of large steel mills in the Soviet Union. Progress was slow but noticeable on the Lufthansa–Aeroflot negotiation for a Moscow–Frankfürt air link. Joint Soviet-Federal scientific and technical talks had been opened, dealing with individual cases for the exchanges of technological expertise, licensing arrangements, and feasibility studies for joint-pro-duction chemes. A long-term, three-year trade agreement was signed with Rumania, but the proposed sizeable expansion was tied to the heavy Rumanian deficit (over DM 200 m. in 1969). The Hungarian Minister for Foreign Trade, Joszef

[29] *Welt der Arbeit*, 23 Jan. 1970.

Biro, arrived in Bonn in March to open negotiations for a long-term trade treaty, and the Federal Economics Minister Karl Schiller visited Yugoslavia for the same purpose a week earlier. Finally, trade negotiations on unprecedented terms were also being conducted with Poland and the Soviet Union.

The importance of many of these individual items was both their scope and their unique character. In most cases they represented new initiatives or significant breakthroughs from traditional positions. The cumulative effect was an acceleration in Bonn's diplomatic offensive in both Eastern Europe and the Soviet Union which emphasized the sterility of its contacts with the GDR.

The second inter-German summit meeting which opened in Kassel on 21 May was marred by several anti-East German incidents which Stoph immediately seized upon publicly to denounce the Bonn government's ability to maintain law and order; attacks which illustrated the hostility of the GDR towards the dialogue. Brandt went further than at Erfurt in meeting and satisfying East German demands. He presented 20 points (see App. III) which might serve as the basis for an accommodation between the two states. In summary these points offered: the renunciation of force, respect for borders, respect for each other's independence, the exchange of plenipotentiaries, and the settlement of membership in international organizations. Brandt even argued that if the GDR would grant concessions for the alleviation of human suffering, the desired East German goal of Federal recognition would be in sight.

Stoph remained even more adamant than at Erfurt. He summarily rejected all 20 points and demanded that legal recognition must be the precondition for the negotiation of other problems, even though the first three points provide for a full treaty that would meet all the constitutional requirements for a legal treaty. When a complete deadlock was obvious, both leaders agreed in a private conversation to salvage something from the meeting by suspending the dialogue so as to give a pause for reflection.[30]

The Brandt–Stoph talks produced no tangible results. The prospects for *rapport* were dimmer than ever and, as Brandt

[30] *Bull.*, 26 May 1970.

feared, the gulf between the two Germanies was widening. It is important, however, for the Germans to discover this for themselves without having to rely on the predictions of Moscow and Washington. The scope of the adjustments required for even a semblance of normality had become brutally apparent to the governments of both Germanies.

The SPD–FDP coalition had consistently inched their *Ostpolitik* and *Deutschlandpolitik* forward, but had developed no comprehensive plan when they sat down with their counter-parts. They expected that their generosity and magnanimity would induce 'reasonableness' and flexibility, but the Erfurt encounter demonstrated the weakness of not having a pro-gramme such as the East German draft treaty. The 20 points were drawn up to fill this gap, and to date remain the most detailed outline of Bonn's plans for coexistence.

While the 20 points marked a new level of West German understanding of the East German perspective, they also registered a nadir in relations between the two Germanies. This awareness produced a general depression in the Federal Foreign Ministry unknown since the cold war. It had been commonly believed that the 20 points had been the most generous, morally upright offer that could be extended, and their summary rejection prompted policy planners to focus greater attention on other proceedings that were already proving more promising.

The West German–Soviet Treaty

Since 1969 Bonn had placed its contact with the Soviet Union in the centre of its *Ostpolitik*. As has been seen, Egon Bahr was appointed to conduct initial talks with Gromyko. As Brandt had told an American television audience, these talks covered all aspects of East–West problems relevant to the interests of the two states, not merely the renunciation of force, as originally planned. The general West German objective in the talks, he explained, was to establish the same degree of contact with the East already enjoyed by other states. Indi-vidual issues could be successfully handled on a bilateral basis if the proper atmosphere existed. But larger questions of a regional character could be handled only on a multilateral plane. Therefore his government, to use Helmut Schmidt's phrase, was 'building agreement upon agreement', both for their intrinsic merits and their cumulative impact.

By the end of April Bahr had conferred ten times with his Soviet counterpart, and reports circulated in Bonn that five major obstacles had been identified in the Federal encounters with Moscow, Warsaw, and East Berlin that were being considered in these talks: (1) the inclusion of a clause into the planned German-Soviet agreement on mutual renunciation of force providing for revision of the agreement in the event of German reunification; (2) recognition of the Oder–Neisse line with reference to Article 7 of Schedule I to the Paris Agree-ments ('German Treaty') [31] of 23 October 1954, providing for the final settlement of Germany's borders by a peace treaty; (3) safeguards for the Berlin access routes by a four-power agreement and by complementary contractual agreements between the governments of Bonn and East Germany; (4) improvement of the situation in divided Germany before recognition of the GDR by Bonn; and (5) acceptance of Bonn's thesis that even in the event of recognition of the GDR by Bonn, the two German states should not consider each other as foreign countries and should make this perfectly clear by exchanging 'high commissioners' rather than ambassadors. [32]

Despite the obstacles, there was sufficient give for the Brandt government to decide on 7 June, after the Kassel encounter, to proceed with formal negotiations with the Soviet Union. Walter Scheel was appointed to conduct the negotiations, guided by the following principles:

1. German-Soviet relations should be based on the renun-ciation of force on the pattern of the Federal Republic's relations with the three Western powers.

2. The principles of refraining from using, or threatening the use of, force should apply also to differences of view that may continue to exist after the conclusion of a renunciation-of-force agreement with Moscow.

---

[31] The Paris Agreements of 23 Oct. 1954 (Cmd 9304), which terminated Germany's occupation status and admitted her to WEU and NATO, are referred to in Bonn as the 'German Treaty'.
[32] Die Welt, 1 Apr., Bull., 28 Apr. 1970.

3. The Bonn government assumes that the four-power talks on Berlin will secure West Berlin's close ties with the Federal Republic as well as unhampered access to Berlin.

4. The renunciation-of-force agreement must not affect the German people's right of self-determination.

5. The proposed agreements with the Soviet Union, Poland, the GDR, and possibly with other Warsaw Pact countries should contribute to *détente* and be considered as a package. The Preamble and contents of the West German Basic Law will not be affected by these agreements.[33]

Foreign Ministry officials privately stated that the meaning of point 3 was that none of the planned treaties with the East would be submitted for ratification without a satisfactory agreement on Berlin. This interpretation became the touchstone for Bonn's tactics in Moscow. Points 4 and 5 were intended to preserve both a ' national and a European option '. In other words, the agreement should not carry the connotation of a final peace treaty and should not preclude either peaceful efforts to restore German national unity or to establish a European federation.

On 18 June the CDU opposition attempted to challenge the government's decision with a vote of no-confidence. The attempt was unsuccessful because it could not obtain a majority or appoint an alternative Chancellor. Nevertheless, the government's bargaining position was soon altered. The scope of the treaty was expanded to include more than the renunciation of force. The Soviet Union argued that this would be useless unless it were accompanied by recognition of existing borders. On her side, the Federal Republic wanted a more precise definition of the Soviet-claimed right of intervention under the ' enemy state ' clause of the UN Charter. Bonn also sought some formula that would link settlement of Berlin with any agreement reached in Moscow.

Allied responsibility was increasingly used as the vehicle for surmounting the deadlock. Brandt placed growing weight on this aspect of the negotiations after January 1970. The applicability of the Potsdam Agreement and the Paris Agreements of 1954 was discussed at length during his visits to Britain in

[33] *Bull.*, 2 & 9 June, & 28 July 1970.

March, to the United States in April, and to France in May. These occasions were used in part to allay mounting anxiety in Western capitals about the substance and pace of Bonn's negotiations in Moscow. The French in particular voiced uneasiness, stating that the treaty must explicitly refer to the continued existence of four-power responsibility for Germany as a whole and that there must be a clarification about Berlin. William Rogers expressed American concern in a West German television interview when he asserted that the Allies had reservations under both the Potsdam Agreement and the Paris Agreements of 1954; ' so any final juridical decisions that are made would have to be made in the light of those reservations '.[34]

In a speech before the Bundestag on 17 June commemorating the East German uprising in 1953 Brandt reiterated the West German attitude towards four-power responsibilities for a German settlement. He said that these responsibilities had until then been unable to change political realities: ' The Federal Government still takes the fact of the existence of these legal obligations very seriously. . . . If we concluded non-aggression pacts, they will expressly include the statement that existing agreements and treaties of the pact partners will remain untouched. This includes the German Treaty [i.e. Paris Agreements] fully.'[35]

Brandt elaborated further in a French television interview: We cannot solve by ourselves the whole series of problems related to the subject of the present talks between the Soviet Union and Federal Republic. We are agreed with our allies that the responsibility for Germany as a whole and for Berlin continues to rest with the four victorious powers of the Second World War. The desire codified contractually by the Four Powers in 1945 to proceed from Germany as a whole and the necessity resulting from this type of a peace-treaty settlement for the whole of Germany form a decisive basis for our policy and that of our allies . . . Any initiative that we take with the objective of reconciliation with the peoples of Eastern Europe is closely coordinated with our Western partners.[36]

By citing the Paris Agreements, Bonn further emphasized the

co-ordination of policy. Brandt stated during his visit to Denmark in February that there could be no exclusive German *Ostpolitik*. He was referring to the provisions of the ' German Treaty ' whereby in Article 2 the three Allies reserved to themselves responsibilities for Germany and Berlin but in Article 7 pledged co-operation with the Federal Republic in seeking a final solution. Scheel observed on this ' that questions relating to Germany's Eastern boundaries can be dealt with by the Federal Republic only in conjunction with the Three Powers. The Federal Republic's freedom of action is thus restricted; but it is also subject to other limitations in so far as even an agreement with the Three Powers cannot stand in lieu of an overall peace arrangement.'[37] This did not preclude reaching agreements with other interested parties, but it required the consent of all four powers. Scheel concluded that it was up to the Federal Republic and the three Allies to decide what means would be the most appropriate for achieving the goals set forth in the Paris Agreements. (After Scheel visited Washington and London in July, it was agreed that Allied embassies in Moscow would be used as channels of co-ordination during the negotiations to ensure complete compatibility of interests in the final document. The three Allies also reportedly argued at that time that written guarantees in the German-Soviet treaty would not impair but would strengthen Western legal rights in Berlin and Germany by pointing to the relevance of the Potsdam accord and the ' German Treaty ' (Paris Agreements). This tactic would also demonstrate that the negotiations in Moscow were only for an interim measure and in no way foreclosed the option of a final peace treaty.

The relevance of these repeated references to Allied co-responsibility was not only to guarantee complete Western solidarity and present a united front in Moscow, but to illustrate the precise limits of Bonn's negotiating flexibility. Since the Federal Republic was not a completely sovereign state, she could not be expected to assume international legal obligations with the same degree of finality as the Soviet Union. Therefore she did not have the legal authority to recognize another German state or borders within the German nation. Likewise

[37] Ibid., June 1970; also *FAZ*, 13 & 16 July, *Die Welt*, 17 July 1970.

she did not have authority to recognize borders that came within the scope of the Potsdam Agreement, such as the Oder–Neisse line. If Moscow insisted on these provisions, she must refer the entire matter to the other signatories of the Potsdam Agreement. Moscow conceded on this crucial point, since it was less interested in the technical implications of international law than in securing a commitment to uphold existing political realities. Further, the Potsdam Agreement was the lynchpin of its position in Berlin.

On specific provisions, Bonn sought to uphold the terms of a reported understanding between Brandt and Nixon of April 1970 whereby none of its planned treaties would be advanced to a definitive stage until some progress was made on Berlin. Bonn tried to link these two considerations with the incorporation in the Moscow treaty of a Soviet commitment to seek an early agreement on Berlin. Moscow apparently refused, on the grounds that negotiations were already under way and would remain under four-power jurisdiction. Therefore, the issue was inappropriate for a bilateral accord. But for Bonn, Berlin was the cardinal issue for normalization with the East and, when Moscow refused to accept any mention of Berlin in a bilateral treaty, Brandt repeatedly stated in public before the final negotiations began that ratification depended upon progress in the Berlin talks. By this manoeuvre, Bonn unmistakably indicated that no accord could be made with Moscow that might in any way jeopardize its interests in West Berlin or those of the divided city.

From the West German viewpoint, the Soviet claim to the right of unilateral intervention in the Federal Republic under Articles 53 and 107 of the UN Charter had to be clarified in any provision for a mutual renunciation of force. In response to an opposition question on this issue, the government provided its formal interpretation of the proposed treaty provisions:

Mutual renunciation of force may not be qualified, let alone made valueless, by one side's reservation of force. In our judgment of the legal situation, the Soviet Union possesses no intervention rights vis-à-vis the Federal Republic of Germany. The Three Western Powers have expressed their joint agreement that none of the victorious powers has unilateral rights. . . . [This provision] is contained in the Final Act of the London Conference, in which the Three Powers . . . state that they ' will, in their relations to the Federal Republic, adhere to the principles contained in Article 2 of the United Nations Charter.' It was also stated that ' the Soviet Union has never expressly asserted that it possesses unilateral rights vis-à-vis the Federal Republic of Germany, even though it has expressly stated that [the two articles] are valid and applicable '.[38]

Since the Soviet Union had not formally registered these claims, she reportedly held that it would be inappropriate to include a legal provision in the draft treaty renouncing them. On the other hand, she pointed out that the mutual renunciation of force negated any individual reservations and tacitly placed the Soviet Union in alignment with the Western Allies' interpretation, i.e. that the draft treaty would be subordinate to Article 2 of the UN Charter, and that without a specific reservation she was not prepared to act alone.

Because of the one-sided strategic situation, however, where the Soviet Union could attack West Germany but the Federal Republic could not feasibly invade the Soviet Union, the issue of inviolability of borders was directly related to intervention rights. In exchange for the sanctification of its own frontiers, Bonn had to recognize the permanency and integrity of those borders between the Elbe and Bug rivers. In other words, without a contiguous boundary but with Soviet troops along the Federal Republic's eastern border, Moscow could demand Bonn's acceptance of the territorial *status quo* in Eastern Europe as the only plausible guarantee for its own western frontier. This line of argument returned the discussions to the Potsdam Agreement and the relationship of the proposed accord to the final peace treaty for which it provided. The West Germans tried to register the interim nature of the draft treaty and its subordination to the Potsdam and Paris Agreements by the proviso that the proposed accord would not negate provisions in the other documents.

On her side, the Soviet Union sought to maximize the importance of the draft treaty. She requested changing the title by dropping the renunciation-of-force clause so that the title would read simply ' Soviet-West German treaty ', introducing

[38] *Bull.*, 9 June 1970; also *SZ*, 6 June & 21 July 1970.

a much broader connotation. She could then insist upon the incorporation of the inviolability of existing borders, the renunciation of German territorial claims and abrogation of the Munich Agreement, the recognition of East Germany, as well as the renunciation of the use of force. These principles were to be the main factors in the ultimate peace treaty and clearly indicated that Moscow anticipated that the draft treaty would be far more durable than Bonn expected.

As late as the eve of his departure for negotiations in Moscow, Scheel amplified this point:

It is to be conceded that problems are neither eliminated nor anticipated in a treaty renouncing the use of force. Substantive solutions are not supplanted, nor are existing conditions made definitive. No claims are given up; all that is renounced is their forcible implementation. . . . Nonetheless, the renunciation of force is more than a gesture without material substance. It proceeds from the existing situation. It does not prescribe it but rather describes it, without attaching value judgments to it. It proceeds on the basis of the geographical status quo and offers a political modus vivendi within the bounds of this status quo. It respects and accepts the realities. It does not undertake to recognize them within the terms of international law and thus to legalize them.[39]

A clue to Soviet thinking on this matter was revealed during the four-power meeting on the Middle East on 24 June 1970. The Soviet Union proposed a new formula for the Arab-Israeli settlement. Rather than a final peace treaty, Moscow suggested that a cease-fire and renunciation of force should be extended to a 'formalized state of peace', similar to that existing between the Soviet Union and Japan. This condition was predicated upon a series of lesser agreements and under-standings that had fostered a normalization of relations, without the arduous task of negotiating a formal peace settle-ment or resurrecting all the residual problems unsettled by war. On the other hand, it assured a relatively durable relationship by increasing the penalties for breaches in normalized relations. The Soviet Union apparently sought to project a rationale into the draft treaty with Bonn whereby the explicit provisions

[39] *Bull.*, 21 July 1970.

would advance as far as possible a condition of 'formalized state of peace'.[40]

Two events had a direct bearing on the Soviet efforts to heighten the importance of the treaty. First the intentional leak to the press of the proposed draft treaty, known as the 'Bahr Paper' (see App. IV) at the end of June by Baron von Guttenberg, a right-wing member of the CSU. It was expected that the adverse public reaction against the 'capitulation' terms of the draft would embarrass the coalition government and either force it to abandon the more onerous provisions or demand more generous concessions. The least that the disclosure could do would be to complicate Scheel's bargaining position. Nevertheless, Brandt responded unruffled, and reiterated his government's pledge that whatever conditions were finally accepted, they would not be submitted for ratification until progress was made on the Berlin talks.

Brandt's estimation that he had successfully weathered the storm was indicated at the annual SPD Party Convention in July. Rather than hesitation, Brandt expressed confidence that the outcome of the negotiations with Moscow would prove to be the initial step in the establishment of a new European security system. The party had distributed on 1 June 2·5 m. questionnaires asking whether the *Ostpolitik* should be continued as outlined. At the time of the Convention 79 per cent of the West Germans polled supported the government's position, despite the revelations of the Bahr Paper.[41] The Convention voted near-unanimous endorsement for the party leadership and its policies in the East, putting Brandt in the favourable position of enjoying firm partisan support as well as a determined parliamentary opposition, that could serve as an important trump. From this posture, Brandt could attempt to focus the negotiations on the Federal Republic's priority interests: the Berlin question, the German right to reunification and Europe's right to unite, and the reaffirmation of Allied responsibilities.

[40] *International Herald Tribune*, 24 & 25 June 1970, also *FAZ*, 19 June 1970.

[41] After the treaty was initialled, 81 per cent supported it according to the Federal Press and Information Office (*Handelsblatt*, 14 Aug. 1970), but the Deutsche Fernsehen Erste Program conducted an independent poll on 28 Sept., indicating that only 70 per cent of the interviewees favoured the treaty, 13 per cent opposed it, and 17 per cent were undecided.

Moscow apparently told the Ambassador Allardt, however, that it was prepared to consider only verbal changes, a Preamble, and the supplementary declarations, and not modifications of the principles involved. To emphasize this point, after Scheel held a press conference before his departure to stress Bonn's shift in emphasis, Tass announced that the West German delegation would be in Moscow only three days, when no deadline had actually been fixed. After twelve days of hard bargaining and thirty-eight hours of face-to-face negotiation, Gromyko and Scheel initialled on 7 August the Soviet-West German treaty (see App. V), which was signed on the 12th.

The Chancellor subsequently admitted that the Bahr Paper had constituted an authentic draft of each article, minus the Preamble. The first four draft articles were incorporated into the treaty with only minor verbal changes, e.g. Article 1 of the treaty omits the words ' on this basis ', in Article 2 the term ' bilateral relations ' was replaced by ' mutual relations ', and in Article 4 the term ' agreements ' was replaced by ' arrangements '. In a concession to Bonn, the phrase ' in accordance with the foregoing purposes and principles ' was inserted in Article 3, linking it to Article 2 and strengthening the presumption that the renunciation of force did not obviate the prospects of peaceful border revisions.

More important, the Germans were able to refer to the vehement CDU opposition and reported strong Allied reservations as the reason for dropping Articles 5–10 of the Bahr Paper, which were converted into supplementary declarations by each party. While the provision for expanded economic and technical co-operation was transferred to the Preamble, the deleted articles had provided that the treaty to be signed, and corresponding agreements between the Federal Republic and other socialist countries, in particular the agreements with the GDR, Poland, and Czechoslovakia, would form a single whole; that the Federal Republic was pledged to conclude a normalization treaty with the GDR as binding as other treaties concluded by *both West and East Germany* and establishing the full independence of both states; that both the Federal Republic and the Soviet Union were to take action to promote East

German membership in international organizations; that the Federal Republic would undertake to settle problems resulting from the invalidity of the Munich Agreement; and that both states welcomed the plan for convening a conference on European security problems.

The omission of these major provisions was a significant curtailment in Moscow's design to secure a ' formalized state of peace '. The Western Allies reportedly argued that the conclusion of such a sweeping document on a bilateral basis would negate the grounds for a multilateral solution as envisaged in the Potsdam Agreement. Indeed, the 1945 documentation would be so weakened by such a definitive stand on all major issues that the entire basis of Allied responsibility for Germany and Berlin would be undermined, forcing the four powers to seek a completely new foundation for *modus vivendi* in West Berlin. This rationale was apparently persuasive and only general references were made in the final treaty of West Germany's problems with other socialist countries—the specific provisions were confined primarily to German-Soviet affairs. However, a tacit understanding may have been reached whereby the Allies would not object to Bonn's dealing with other regional problems on a bilateral level.

The main points of the treaty were that the Preamble accepted the precedence of the 1955 formula for preserving the right of German self-determination, supported by a similar letter from Scheel to Gromyko re-establishing this principle (App. V, p. 227). Article 1 provided that the parties would proceed from the ' actual situation existing in this region ' as the basis of normalizing relations with all European states. Article 2 provided for the renunciation of force and the peaceful settlement of disputes under Article 2 of the UN Charter. Article 3 obliged the two parties to ' respect unreservedly the territorial integrity of all states in Europe in their present frontiers '. They renounced all territorial claims ' against anyone ' now and in the future and promised to respect the inviolability of existing borders, including the Oder–Neisse line and the frontier between the GDR and the Federal Republic. (This formula fell legally short of unqualified border recognition, as the Poles subsequently pointed out.) A joint accord that the provisions within the treaty would not affect bilateral and multilateral treaties previously concluded by either party was contained in Article 4.

At the Western Allies' request, a formal note was issued in conjunction with the treaty by the Federal Foreign Minister in which he elaborated on the unimpaired four-power responsibilities for Germany and Berlin. The continued Allied rights had not been a subject of the present negotiations and he stated that ' the Soviet Foreign Minister had made a similar declaration '. (In an apparent concession to upgrade the ceremonial importance of the truncated Soviet-designed ' formalized state of peace ', it was agreed that the treaty would be signed by the heads of government, rather than by Foreign Ministers as is customary in the West, e.g. the NATO treaty. While in Moscow Brandt called for a summit conference with the Western Allies as a demonstration of Bonn's solidarity with the West, and to offset the historical significance or successful conclusion of one portion of Brandt's *Ostpolitik*, but the offer was quietly rejected as unwarranted.)

The fundamentally differing viewpoints on the treaty and its implications were illustrated in the news media. Whereas the West German press called the occasion of the signing ceremonies ' a step towards *détente* ', ' an opening of the door to the East ', and said that ' the Russian bear has given the paw ', the Soviet press soberly remarked that the importance of the historic milestone was Bonn's acceptance of commitments that bind it to the *status quo* in Europe on terms that amount to a permanent basis.[42]

Scheel amplified these differences when he returned from Moscow:

I return today with results that safeguard the preservation of national interests of the German peoples; help to anchor the peace in Europe; place the future relations of the Federal Republic with the Soviet Union on a new foundation; [and] bring our people more security . . . Sheltered under the protection of the Alliance and in our friendship with the West, we have now opened a door toward the East and, through the reciprocal renunciation of the application of force, have arrived at a modus vivendi that leaves our right to

[42] Tass, 12 Aug. 1970.

self-determination untouched. We have not left the Soviet Union in obscurity regarding our views on the necessity of satisfactorily settling the Berlin question. We have formally declared that the treaty will not be put into effect as long as such a satisfactory solution for Berlin has not been reached by the four powers.

Both ' the right to self-determination and our national goal of German unity' and European integration, he concluded, remained beyond doubt. [43]

In his address to the German nation from Moscow, Brandt stressed the dual themes of Western integration and Eastern *détente*. He called the treaty a success of German postwar policy. ' Nothing is lost with this treaty that was not gambled away long ago.' He concluded that a new chapter had been opened in the realization of German objectives, based upon integration in the West and reconciliation with the East. [44] (The Mayor of West Berlin, Klaus Schütz, added a shrewd comment on the occasion. The *Ostpolitik* was not a matter of making policy *with* Moscow. There were too many differences of principle. But if relations become normal interstate ones, tensions in Europe would be reduced.)

From the West German perspective, there were both gains and losses embodied in the treaty. On the positive side: (1) the renunciation of force was mutual, meaning that no unilateral reservations of rights of intervention could be maintained outside the treaty. (2) The basis for the Soviet commitment was its acceptance of the respectability of the Federal government as a responsible administration and the implied abrogation of its former charges that Bonn's policies were the main source of European tensions. (3) The reduction of the German threat would facilitate the process of normalization with Eastern Europe. (4) The four-power rights remained intact, providing a plausible basis for a Berlin settlement and the general framework for an accommodation with East Germany. (5) Moscow was now committed to a solution to the Berlin question, if it expected to see the fruition of the treaty provisions. And by complying with the Soviet demands for accepting the ' existing realities ' in Eastern Europe, Bonn had advanced a powerful

[43] *Bull.*, 13 Aug. 1970.
[44] Ibid., 18 Aug. 1970.

quid pro quo for demanding Soviet acceptance of the *status quo* in Berlin. (6) The economic and cultural union between West Berlin and West Germany had not been challenged, implying Soviet acceptance of some form of association short of legal, sovereign ties. (7) In the supplementary documentation, Bonn had secured Moscow's concurrence in the continuation of Allied responsibilities in Germany and the validity of a multi-lateral peace treaty as the ultimate source of normalization in East–West European relations. (8) Bonn had accepted a European security conference, however, for its own intrinsic merits and not as a substitute for peace settlement. (9) The dilution of the legal terminology on border recognition did not inject qualifications about German territorial claims in the East, but ensured that they could be settled through mutual negotia-tion, e.g. the sizeable deviation from the Oder river west of Szczecin. (10) both the German and the European options had been preserved as future policy options. (11) The Soviet Union had not pressed any reparation claims for herself or on behalf of any other East European state. (12) While the door to the East had been opened, Soviet access to Western Europe was now more secure, which raised the possibility of a gradual europeani-zation of the Soviet Union. (13) This mutual opening would offer important economic possibilities, both for investment and markets. (14) The omission of the commitments specified in the Bahr Paper relieved Bonn of any time limit for an adjustment with the GDR. More important, the deletion of the latter provisions of the Bahr Paper left Bonn freedom of movement in formulating its tactics within the conditions it had already im-posed upon itself for negotiating with the GDR. In other words except for guaranteeing respect for East European borders, Moscow had substantively distanced itself from inter-German negotiations. (15) The parliamentary opposition agreed that the treaty should be regarded as constitutional and did not alter the state's legal responsibilities towards the East. There-fore, it did not require a two-thirds majority in the Bundestag for ratification.

Opponents of the treaty, however, charged: (1) that it un-questionably confirmed the *status quo* in Central Europe, a region of traditional German manoeuvre. (2) It compromised, without reference to those whose interests were involved, the right to return to their homeland or to claim realistic personal reparations. (3) For all practical purposes the solution to the Berlin question now depended upon the Soviet Union; the initiative had passed in this vital issue to the East. (4) There was insufficient distinction between the terms 'inviolability' and 'recognition' for diplomatic manoeuvrability, and Bonn had lost its leverage against the East to induce border revisions. (5) Acceptance of the existing borders also implied acquiescence in the existing power relationships in Eastern Europe and the tacit endorsement of the Brezhnev Doctrine of 'limited socialist sovereignty' or hegemony over one-half of Europe. While this was today a political reality that cannot be denied, it was historically unnatural and incompatible with contemporary public sentiment in the East. (6) West German complacency had denied the East Europeans important leverage in increasing their options against Soviet centralism. (7) The timing was inappropriate: the Soviet consolidation programme in East Europe was at a crucial point and Bonn's relaxation of pressure increased Moscow's flexibility in other regions of important interests to the Federal Republic, e.g. in contrast to 1967, the East Europeans had not objected to the Soviet Union's unprecedented venture of actively participating in the defence of Egypt. (8) Rather than enhancing the stature of West Germany in the West, the treaty was more apt to engender reservations among Bonn's principal allies, ultimately increasing its estrangement from the West, without strengthening its option in the East. The danger of such a development was that Bonn would inevitably be forced to adopt a see-saw policy, playing the East off against the West and compromising its credibility in both quarters. (9) The pace of Western integration will almost certainly be affected, either through Bonn's preoccupation or growing rivalry with its partners for Eastern markets and resources. And (10), there is no sign of the Soviet Union agreeing to a military *détente* or disengagement; tanks and barbed wire remain more convincing indications of Soviet intentions than their diplomatic overtures.[45]

It is less clear how the Soviet Union interpreted the impact

[45] For excerpts from the Bundestag debate see ibid., 22 Sept. 1970.

of the treaty. She had not achieved her maximum aims of a conclusive 'formalized state of peace', but had gained a treaty sufficiently definitive indefinitely to delay a final peace accord. In other words, a final multilateral settlement would more than ever be a product of Soviet discretion. By reducing for the time being the chief threat to Central Europe, Moscow had potentially diminished the freedom of manoeuvre for its allies but yet had preserved the importance of its strategic position in this region. On the other hand, through the treaty the Soviet Union was able to guarantee the security the Central European countries required by border recognition and thereby introduced a new element of regional stability essential for her own strategic needs. Thus the treaty represented an important gain for Soviet requirements of both security and stability and cost little in terms of the sacrifice of any important Soviet national interest.

The main loser was East Germany. The Soviet Union violated the key axiom of East German policy that had apparently been reiterated at the Pact PCC meeting on 3 December 1969: that no move towards normalization of relations with the Federal Republic would be made without reciprocal concessions by Bonn towards recognition of East Berlin. Moscow had attempted to maintain this line during the initial Bahr–Gromyko talks. But when faced with strong CDU and Allied opposition, it agreed to minimize the demands of East Germany, while upholding the interests of Eastern Europeans as a whole. In the light of this setback for East German policy and in conformity with the provisions of the 3 December 1969 communiqué, the Soviet Union convened a Pact summit meeting on 20 August to explain its interpretation of the treaty (the East Germans were the only delegation to send all Central Committee Secretaries, indicating the seriousness they attached to the new developments).

On balance, both the Federal Republic and the Soviet Union made important gains for their immediate respective national objectives; the long-term advantages are more difficult to assess, but the Soviet Union potentially stands to lose less than the West Germans. It is too early to predict whether the pace and direction of European security arrangements have

been directly affected by the treaty, or whether Soviet hegemony in Eastern Europe will be gradually relaxed. The most
visible impact of the treaty had been on Bonn's relations with
East Berlin and Warsaw: the GDR recognized that the support
of her allies for her maximum demands had been substantially
weakened, raising the need for a revised position that could
receive broader endorsement, and Poland interpreted the
treaty as a manifestation of Bonn's increasing willingness to
reach an accommodation with Eastern Europe, stiffening her
bargaining position in the negotiations over the Oder–Neisse
border.

The West German-Polish Treaty

In many respects the West German-Polish discussions over
mutual differences were the most simple yet the most difficult
of Bonn's dealings with the Pact. Brandt reiterated in his
address to the nation on 14 January that ' the Federal government has the intention shortly to start an exchange of views
with Poland '. During the ensuing parliamentary debate,
Scheel stated that both parties had agreed to discuss all outstanding questions, including the Oder–Neisse line. He pointed
out that twenty years ago the GDR had already recognized the
Polish western frontier in the name of all Germans, but the
Polish government had not accepted this interpretation. The
parliamentary State Secretary, Ralf Dahrendorf, stated in a
public interview that the permanent recognition of this border
remained outside the jurisdiction of the Federal government.[46]
The vehicle for an adjustment of views was to be an agreement
on the renunciation of force, similar to the accord under
negotiation in Moscow. It was envisaged that the agreement
with Poland would provide for the sanctity of the boundary
through pledges of ' respect ' and non-use of force against
Polish territory. Thus renunciation of force was regarded by
Bonn as the main agenda item.

Poland, on the other hand, held the opposite viewpoint.
The then Deputy Foreign Minister Adam Willman stated that
recognition of the Oder–Neisse frontier was, for the Poles, the
starting point for the process of normalization of relations

[46] *Hannoversche Allgemeine Zeitung*, 21 Jan. 1970; see also *SZ*, 28 Jan. 1970.

between the two countries.[47] The Poles viewed Bonn's repeated arguments about a final treaty as ' a used-up commonplace' sentiment. Two days before the first session Ryszard Wojna, a semi-official spokesman of the government, argued that the frontier should be recognized within the lifetime of the generation which knows both its price and what this frontier stands for if its durability is to be ensured. He concluded that the present talks ' may end either in recognition of the Oder–Neisse frontier by the Federal Republic or the continuation of the present situation '.[48]

On 5 February 1970 the State Secretary of the West German Foreign Office, Georg Ferdinand Duckwitz, met the Polish Deputy Foreign Minister, Josef Winiewicz. The first round of talks concluded with both sides convinced of the other's sincerity and the difficulty of the task ahead. The second session opened on 8 March with both sides presenting proposed draft treaties for the solution of their problems. It was at this point that the distance between the two positions became clear.

Unlike the Soviet negotiations, where there had been substantial give and take on an expanding agenda, the Polish position steadily hardened and concentrated on a single issue. The Polish press was an accurate barometer of the government's toughening line. Radio Warsaw claimed on 8 February that the Polish stand was consistent: ' The recognition of the frontier of the Oder–Neisse as final is a basis for the process of normalization of relations between Poland and the Federal Republic.' Again on 2 March it asserted that the only basis for the talks was Gomulka's offer of 17 May to conclude a treaty on the final and permanent character of the present border. Ryszard Wojna insisted that the only possible outcome of the talks could be the final West German recognition of Poland's Western boundary.[49]

Duckwitz publicly acknowledged after the second round that

---

[47] *Trybuna Ludu*, 15, 22 & 23 Jan. 1970; also *Życie Warszawy*, 22 Jan., *Żolnierz Wolnosci*, 23 Jan., & Radio Warsaw, 16 Jan. 1970. See *Polityka*, 25 Jan. 1970, for a wide-ranging public-opinion poll, in which 80 per cent of the interviewees regarded West German recognition of the Oder–Neisse line as an essential condition for establishing diplomatic relations with the Federal Republic.

[48] *Życie Warszawy*, 3 Feb. 1970 (quoted by SWB, pt. 2, 3 Mar. 1970).

[49] *Życie Warszawy*, 1 Mar., & *Trybuna Ludu*, 3 Mar. 1970.

it was clear that Bonn had made false assumptions about the prospects for an agreement with the Poles. The Federal Republic was not prepared for the fact that the Poles would view ' the unconditional and final recognition of their western frontier as a precondition necessary for fruitful talks '.[50] The Federal formula of relating respect for frontiers with renunciation of force was regarded as irrelevant to the higher priority of securing unquestioned guarantees of the border's permanency. Gomulka restated his tough line on 19 March: the Bonn government ' can either recognise this frontier as final in accordance with the principles of international law, thus expressing its peaceful intentions, or it can stick to its old revisionist positions, thus actually continuing, in these or other forms, the policy of its predecessors '. The then Secretary of the Central Committee and leader of the ultra-nationalistic faction, known as ' Partisans ', Mieczyslaw Moczar, amplified this. Gomulka's position was the only acceptable platform, he stated. Renunciation of force was of little importance, since the borders ' are absolutely sufficiently safeguarded . . . by the policy of our party, through the Warsaw Pact, the treaty of friendship with the Soviet Union and the bilateral treaties with the other socialist countries '.[51] The anxiety of the Poles was about future governments and generations who could not remember the price of aggression but who could recall the 700 years' occupation of Polish lands. In the twentieth century alone, Poland had experienced thirty-nine border changes; this had bequeathed an acute sensitivity with regard to the perfidiousness of political proclamations. Moczar concluded that the formation of an SPD regime in Bonn was the most propitious indication to date that a satisfactory settlement could be reached.

On 22 April Brandt attempted to move the third session out of stalemate by presenting a new formula in a personal letter to Gomulka. The new proposal was reported to be very close to final recognition—probably similar to the wording in the Soviet-German Treaty, i.e. ' unreserved respect ', but was short of unqualified recognition. The press on both sides was

---

[50] Interview with *Der Stern*, 22 Mar. 1970.
[51] *Zolnierz Wolnosci*, 25–26 Apr. 1970; also ibid., 19 Mar. 1970.

pessimistic about success and increasingly bitter about the frustration. (It was believed that Brandt was seeking traditional German goals through new means—economic enticements; and ' it is one thing to know that the German eastern territories are lost, and quite another to confirm that loss in writing '.)[52]

The impasse in the talks was compounded by Brandt's commitment in April to President Nixon that Bonn's negotiations would in no way impair the Allies' rights to Germany and Berlin. Acceptance of the Polish terms would clearly contravene the Potsdam Agreement and the Paris Agreements. Yet Polish fears were intensified as the debate within the Federal Republic gathered momentum and the opposition increased its demands that the ' Polish option ' must be kept open. Moreover both West Germany and Poland had heavily invested national prestige in the talks. From Bonn's viewpoint, some progress was important to prevent the deadlock from having a weakening effect on the other negotiations. Accordingly, Bonn reopened the suspended bilateral economic talks, reportedly with an offer of even more favourable terms, and attempted to explore in greater depth the Polish attitude on side issues at the political talks, such as establishing consular rights, diplomatic recognition, and the European security conference. Finally, a concerted effort was made to examine possible ways of strengthening rather than weakening Allied rights while meeting Poland's terms.

Bonn's task was complicated by a 90-minute speech by Gomulka in Breslau on 9 May dealing broadly with German relations and announcing the most intractable demands to date. Poland would not accept any attempts to settle her problems with the Federal Republic in some form of a temporary agreement. The basis for normalization of relations was unequivocal recognition by Bonn of the existing Polish border as final and unchangeable. ' We also demand that this recognition be regarded as binding for all agreements concerning peace and security in Europe ', i.e. for the Potsdam Agreement and the ' German Treaties ' [53] Gomulka's statement was a clear

[52] M. F. Rakowski, *Polityka*, 25 May 1970; also *Die Welt* & *General-Anzeiger*, 21 Apr., *Frankfurter Rundschau*, *Trybuna Ludu*, & *Życie Warszawy*, 15 Apr. 1970.
[53] *E-A*, 25th yr, 25 July 1970, pp. D329–32.

indication that Warsaw viewed any border agreement with the Federal Republic as a substitute peace treaty and that it had no interest in perpetuating the commitments of the Potsdam Agreement. Such an unambivalent stand threatened the interests of the four powers and was regarded with alarm in Bonn. The fourth round of talks was delayed until 8 June. The West German delegation was reported to have presented several new proposals at the June session: it was prepared to accept the ' Zgorzelec ' formula in the GDR–Polish treaty of 6 June 1950 which omits the term ' recognition ' and refers only to the ' established and existing ' frontier; [54] it sought an understanding on the ethnic Germans living in Poland who might desire to emigrate to the Federal Republic; and it placed a high priority on establishing diplomatic relations between the two countries.[55] Poland refused to accept a compromise formula on the border or to consider alternative issues until a satisfactory agreement had been reached on the boundary question.

Bonn had apparently exhausted its alternatives, and Scheel went to London and Washington before the next session to test the strength of the Allied reservations in face of Polish intransigence. When the fifth round opened in Warsaw on 23 July, Duckwitz was visibly optimistic, replying to questions by reporters that it was possible for an agreement to be reached during that session. The Allies had firmly rejected Gomulka's demands for a negation of the Potsdam Agreement and had devised an equation whereby Allied responsibility would be preserved which was to be applied in negotiations with both the Poles and the Russians, i.e. the written acceptance by all parties concerned that the provisions of the proposed treaty would not abrogate earlier commitments, in exchange for stronger wording on recognition.

The Federal Republic presented this revised Allied position as the last stand and then concentrated on a modified position on her own interests that could improve prospects for ratification. Accordingly, she shifted the emphasis from renunciation

[54] Zgorzelec (Görlitz) was the town bisected by the Oder–Neisse line where the treaty was signed (*Survey of International Affairs 1950*, p. 194).

[55] *Le Monde*, 7–8 June; and DPA, 11 June 1970.

of force to the ethnic Germans. Bonn expected reciprocal concessions, but Warsaw rejected the revised Potsdam formula —accepted several days later by the Soviet Union—and insisted that there was no German minority problem in Poland. With apparent pique, the West Germans asked that the talks be recessed until September and focused attention on a successful conclusion of the Soviet treaty.[56]

Despite the immediate departure after the session of Adam Willman for extensive briefings in Moscow, Poland was apparently surprised and embarrassed by the rapid conclusion of the West German-Soviet treaty. The Polish press promptly assumed a more conciliatory tone towards the sixth round of Polish-West German talks, scheduled to begin on 10 September. In a traditional harvest speech on 6 September Gomulka omitted further allegations about equality between a border treaty and the Potsdam Agreement, and the press called on both parties to adopt ' concepts of good faith which, as we know, is the foundation of any treaty '.[57] But Bonn proposed postponement of the September date and took the opportunity to authorize a visit to Poland by the West German Red Cross to ascertain more precisely the number of outstanding emigrant applications and the personal reparation claims by private Polish citizens (750 claims had already been settled and a reported 6,000 remained unredeemed).

Progress was implied in a press conference by Winiewicz before his departure for New York on 20 September for a scheduled exchange with Scheel. He referred to Gomulka's proposal of May 1969, which acknowledged the existence of the Zgorzelec formula between the GDR and Poland as the proper guidance in talks with Bonn. This led to Bonn's confirmation of the opening of the decisive sixth round on 5 October. The Federal Republic insisted upon provisions for the repatriation of ethnic Germans, but Poland declined on the ground that this was a domestic issue and an inappropriate subject for an international treaty. Proposals for an alternative agreement were taken under advice by both sides. They also

[56] Radio Warsaw, 23 July, *Trybuna Ludu*, 25 July & DPA, 26 July, 1970.
[57] Polish Press Service, 6 Sept., Radio Warsaw, 7 Sept., *Slowo Powszechne*, 26 Aug. & *Zycie Warszawy*, 27 Aug. 1970.

agreed to transform the former Polish demand for a unilateral German confession of war guilt into a statement referring to the sufferings of both nations. Reflecting a possible adjustment in the West German position on the border issue, Scheel reported to the Bundestag:

There exists a close interrelation between the responsibility of the Big Four and the peace treaty [referring to the legal restrictions of Potsdam]. The Federal Republic has no common frontier with Poland and, although the Federal Republic is ready to recognize the right of the Poles to live within stable frontiers, nevertheless a confirmation of this by a peace treaty is necessary.[58]

The Bundestag opposition maintained that this view equated with the Polish value attached to the proposed treaty and adopted a resolution which virtually condemned the negotiations: ' Peace treaty settlement must not be anticipated, either intrinsically or formally; the whole German people must be able to act in free self-determination.'

In an equally important development, after nearly one year of intermittent negotiations Poland and West Germany signed on 15 October a five-year trade agreement on the most beneficial terms yet extended to a communist country. The German representative stated on the occasion: ' We hope this treaty will be a sort of inspiration '. Poland was granted most-favoured-nation privileges and an annual credit of DM 500 m. for five years. Federal trade restrictions were fully removed from 80 per cent of Polish imports (1,200 items) and relaxed on 4,000 additional items. Plans for industrial co-operation and correlated production were envisaged. While only a modest growth in trade was expected because of Poland's economic and financial difficulties, the long-term treaty was regarded by both sides as a major step towards normalizing relations between the two countries.[59]

In the light of these advances, it was agreed at the sixth session of the talks to convene formal negotiations in Warsaw on 3 November. While this denoted real progress, there was no fundamental agreement on the central issues. The Polish

---

[58] *Münchner Merkur*, 10 Oct., Radio Warsaw, 9 Oct. 1970; and *Życie Warszawy*, 14 Oct. 1970.
[59] *Bull.*, 21 & 30 June 1970.

press reflected the anticipated travail. The determination of the CDU opposition and Scheel's continued reference to 'legalistic argumentation ... must flabbergast the Polish public'.[60] The negotiations over the Oder–Neisse were clearly going to be the toughest to date in the entire *Ostpolitik*.

The talks opened against a background of steadily improving relations between West Germany and Eastern Europe which must have influenced negotiations on both sides. For example, on 22 June the Rumanian Premier Ion Gheorghe Maurer paid his first visit to the Federal Republic and Conrad Ahlers accepted an invitation to visit Bucharest after the signing of the Soviet-West Germany treaty; he is reported to have briefed the Rumanians on Bonn's interpretation of its provisions and to have reaffirmed the two countries' preferential relations. On 25 May Egon Emmel, who negotiated the successful West German-Polish trade treaty, had arrived in Prague to open talks that led to the initialling of a new five-year accord on 12 June. Federal-Czechoslovak trade had increased by 50 per cent between 1968 and 1969 and was expected to make similar gains in 1970. Growth under the new agreement will probably not be so spectacular, although substantial increases in West German import quotas were approved. This accord was followed by an announcement that Prague was ready to open political talks with Bonn on their outstanding differences. On 21 June the Pact PCC met in Budapest and agreed to inject new impetus in the European security conference scheme by advancing the most detailed proposal to date for an East–West gathering. Poland and West Germany opened talks on 7 July for upgrading their respective trade missions to consular status, and Poland initialled a treaty with Austria on 11 July settling 1,100 claims. Finally, on 27 October the Economics Minister Schiller visited Budapest to initial the Federal Republic's first long-term trade agreement with Hungary. The Federal Republic is Hungary's first Western trading partner, total trade amounting to DM 1,000 m. in 1970, a 40 per cent increase over 1969. Moreover, Hungary is the only East European country that has achieved a favourable trade balance with West Germany. On these grounds, Schiller predicted significant

---

[60] *Slowo Powezechne*, 13 Oct. 1970.

increases over the next five years and stated that the Federal Republic was prepared to make major financial investments in Hungary. (In this treaty, as in all other trade accords signed in 1970, the clause including West Berlin within the Federal Republic for trade purposes was incorporated.)

During the final West German-Polish negotiations which began on 3 November in Warsaw, the Polish side persisted in its demands for final and unequivocal recognition of the border, while agreeing to the Soviet formula for reaffirming Allied rights. The West German side replied that even its own proposed draft treaty was likely to be ratified by only a one or two-vote margin, and that under West German constitutional law the Polish demands would require a two-thirds majority for ratification. (Article 79 of the Basic Law provides for parliamentary approval by a two-thirds majority of international agreements on a peace settlement. Further, since the Basic Law presumes jurisdiction over the Eastern territories, the Polish demands could require an amendment of the constitution and the endowing Allied documents, an unlikely prospect.) The Poles were asked what would be the use of accepting a document that meant the downfall of the Brandt government and the treaty's non-ratification.

When Scheel returned to Bonn on 9 November, the diplomatic moves had been exhausted and top-level political decisions were required by both parties. Both sides had invested too much national prestige not to reach a successful agreement. The Poles were apparently impressed with the senselessness of signing a non-ratifiable document, and the Deputy Bundestag Speaker Carlo Schmid, the SPD 'high priest', met the Chancellor and stressed the need for attaching prime importance to the moral considerations of the treaty. Accordingly, both sides met the next day and agreed to assure a saleable package by augmenting the treaty with supplementary documents and declaratory statements.

With this enhanced flexibility, after an all-night session on 12 November accord was finally reached on one of the most historic documents since World War II. (See App. VI.) On the key issues, the Poles accepted the Zgorzelec formula (see above, p. 155) on border agreement. In Article 1 the two parties ' state in mutual agreement that the existing boundary line, the course of which is laid down in Chapter IX of the Decisions of the Potsdam Conference . . . shall constitute the western State frontier of the People's Republic of Poland '. In Art. 1 the states also reaffirm the ' inviolability of their existing frontiers now and in the future ' and declare that they ' have no territorial claims whatsoever against each other and that they will not assert such claims in the future '. In Article 2 the two states pledge their adherence to the principles of Article 2 of the UN Charter, i.e. the peaceful settlement of disputes, and undertake to ' refrain from any threat or the use of force '. In Article 3 they express their mutual intention to normalize relations and to enlarge economic, cultural, and other links of common interest. Article 4 contains the important provision that the treaty ' shall not affect any bilateral or multilateral international agreements previously concluded by either Contracting Party or concerning them '.

The Moscow formula was adopted formally to reassure four-power rights under the Potsdam and Paris Agreements; consequently a note from the West German Foreign Minister was delivered to the Western Allies on 19 November reaffirming the fact that the negotiations had not dealt with Allied rights and that the treaty in no way diminished these prerogatives. The three powers noted the proceedings and the documentation with approval.

On the humanitarian aspects of the package, the Federal Republic agreed that the question of the ethnic Germans remained within the purview of Polish domestic policy and Poland undertook to furnish official information about the disposition and desires of this group and to facilitate repatriation and reparation claims of other Polish citizens through national Red Cross organizations. According to the official Polish statement, about a quarter of a million ethnic Germans left Poland between 1955 and 1959 under the auspices of the Red Cross, and in the subsequent ten years another 150,000 emigrated under routine procedures. There remained an unidentified number of persons with unmistakable German nationality and partners of mixed marriages. These persons could emigrate in compliance with existing Polish regulations. Scores of thousands of persons may be entitled under the family-reunion criteria to emigrate, and the Polish government pledged to facilitate such transfers through the Red Cross. Finally, after the treaty became effective, Poland agreed to apply the same regulations to Germans wishing to visit relatives as exist for other Western countries. (In private and in the press, however, Polish authorities made a clear distinction between Germans meeting the above criteria and those who sought emigration ' merely for economic gains '. The latter would not be granted permission, leaving open a point of potential friction.) On the reparations issue, the Polish Red Cross appealed on 18 September to the Bonn government for a lump-sum settlement of DM 120 m., claiming that the original offer of DM 56 m. was inadequate. Thus humanitarian issues were excluded from the treaty, but both sides had made qualified moves to demonstrate the genuineness of their willingness to meet each other's wishes before the document was initialled. (Poland honoured her pledge. Within a month after signing the treaty Warsaw repatriated the first ethnic Germans. Over 51,000 immigrants were processed by Federal authorities during the spring of 1971.)

At the signing ceremonies, Brandt expanded his government's position in a declaratory statement. The treaty was, as its title implied, the basis for normalizing their mutual relations, and was not a substitute for a formal peace treaty. The treaty did not mean that ' we recognize injustice or have legitimatized expulsion '. A clear consciousness of history did not ' tolerate unrealizable claims '; nor did it tolerate ' secret reservations '. ' To subscribe to the treaty, to reconciliation, and to peace, is to accept German history in its entirety.' He also revealed a major Polish concession, undisclosed by his hosts: ' I would confirm with a sense of satisfaction our agreement to take up full diplomatic relations immediately after the treaty . . . comes into force.'[61] Finally, he reaffirmed that the efforts to normalize relations with Poland and Eastern Europe would be incomplete unless agreement is reached on improving the situation in and around Berlin.

Brandt also pointed out that the utility of a normalization

[61] *Bull.*, 8 & 15 Dec. 1970.

treaty depended upon the extent and manner of its implementation. Public reaction to the treaty is an indication at least of
its short-term impact on the policies of both states. West
German public reaction was predictably cataclysmic. ' In the
thousand years of Polish history, no Polish prince or head of
state achieved what Gomulka has achieved towards the
German state.' The ' contractual surrender ' of 40,000 square
miles, one-quarter of Germany, that had been German for 700
years, will divide the Federal Republic; mistrust will mount;
disagreement will degenerate into enmity, the Springer firm
alleged. ' From enemy to partner in seven short lessons, à la
Scheel.'

A centre-right paper pointed out that it would be counterproductive to try and pacify the refugee groups by explaining
that the treaty did not ' recognize ' the border, but merely
described it. The Poles had made their interpretation perfectly
clear, and introducing a conflicting viewpoint would only prevent accommodation and complicate achieving the goals
envisaged by the treaty. The treaty had precipitated ' heart-
rending inner conflicts in most Germans ' of the magnitude of
the national decision over establishing a separate state and
accepting rearmament, but, as in the past, siding with reality
did not fracture the society—the government should be com-
mended for its courage to make such a decision. ' That he knelt
down on Polish soil honours Brandt, the man [he knelt before
the memorial in the former Jewish ghetto of Warsaw]. But this
gesture also symbolized the fact that the treaty is not based on
reciprocity . . . it represents recognition of the Oder–Neisse
border.'

Implementation will require clear respect for the integration
of Poland and the Federal Republic firmly into opposing social
systems; the challenge will be to establish a tolerable and
tolerant relationship. While an unprecedented constitutional
question exists, the government has outmanoeuvred the opposition: to vote against the ratification would be considered, both
at home and abroad, as a refusal to accept the consequences of
the war, and would have an admittedly disastrous impact on
West Germany's image abroad and ' fan real domestic tensions '
—the end-result might be an accelerated move towards

neutralization, a modest resurgence of the NDP and other extremist parties, and the further alienation of youth.[62]

Polish sentiment was most graphically expressed during the signing ceremonies. Chancellor Brandt was greeted by the public throughout his visit with respectful silence. The recognition of the Oder–Neisse line had been the single most unifying factor in modern Polish society and the presence of the West German Chancellor symbolized the victory Poland had achieved through patience and perseverance. It was a solemn occasion when thoughts of previous sacrifices were foremost. The public was too overwhelmed with the magnitude of the moment to visualize its long-term implications clearly.[63]

The broad ramifications were indeed difficult to perceive in an atmosphere of traditional animosity balanced by only a distant vision of *détente*. The Bonn government had only extended *de facto* rather than *de jure* recognition of the Polish frontier and had not ceded to the Polish government its legal claims to the Eastern territories, though it renounced the desire for their restitution. The normalization treaty was subordinated to the Potsdam and Paris Agreements, thereby upholding the Allies' reservations about the final disposition of the respective territorial claims. Further, no action had been taken to abrogate the legal jurisdiction of the Basic Law over the Eastern territories. Until the endowing Allied authorization was changed or the goals of the Basic Law are achieved (reunification), it is questionable whether the Federal Republic has the legal sovereignty to initiate action to curtail this jurisdiction, even through amending the Basic Law. These were the grounds for the Federal qualifications during the negotiations: that it could speak only on its own behalf, not for a reunified Germany, the Allies, or an integrated Europe.

Poland countered on equally sound juridical grounds that the provisions of the treaty were binding on all possible legal successors of the Bonn government. Her declaratory statements clearly registered the finality Warsaw attached to solution of the border issue. The underlying reason for her entering the

---

[62] *Die Welt*, 4 & 12 Dec., *FAZ*, 23 Nov. & 8 Dec., *SZ*, 9 Dec., *Rheinische Post*, 8 Dec. 1970.
[63] Polish Press Service, 7 & 8 Dec. 1970.

negotiations had been specifically to preclude loose interpretations. [64] (East Germany had recognized the Oder–Neisse line in 1950 for *all* Germans, but this had not alleviated Polish fears.)

While Poland had not achieved final recognition of her border, she had secured as definitive phraseology as possible. The border formula in the normalization treaty is substantially stronger than in the Soviet treaty. The distance between this formula and ' final ' recognition is theoretically unbridgeable without the consent of all the Allies, but the gap has been narrowed legally to the extent that it could largely be closed through conscientious implementation of the treaty's other provisions. But herein lay uncertainties for both sides. When could Poland safely open her borders to unrestricted tourist travel and the dissemination of literature and culture ? When could West Germany encourage the periodic return of the expellees without stimulating dangerous irredentist sentiments ?

While the compromise accepted by both sides—*de facto* recognition of the border—imparts an inestimable potential for future Central European affairs, some guidance may be found in the possible explanations for Poland's acceptance of terms less than her maximal demands. Several grounds seem plausible.

1. Soviet interests in Berlin are firmly anchored to the Potsdam Agreement, and any theoretical diminution in credibility of one portion of the document would weaken the authority of the other sections. Moscow probably placed strict upper limits on Poland's expectations.

2. The Poles may have seen the normalization treaty as the best possible agreement and have hoped, with the cumulative effects of other East–West accords, to be able to continue to advance their own interpretation, independent of the specific treaty provisions.

3. Once committed, she could neither accept defeat, protracted haggling, or a weakening of the Brandt government; each option would have been detrimental to Polish interests. Thus she had little choice but to press for an early settlement within these conditions.

4. As the speed of both bilateral and multinational negotiations between the Pact nations and the Federal Republic

[64] Ryszard Wojna, *Życie Warszawy*, 19 Nov. 1970.

increased, Poland was compelled to maintain an active interest in a broader settlement, lest agreements in other areas—such as a European security conference—might either diminish its relevance or influence an unsatisfactory solution.

5. As the German threat receded in Pact councils, especially after the March 1969 Budapest meeting of Foreign Ministers, Poland could advance her national aims under the mantle of socialist-endorsed programmes. Moreover, the trend towards West German respectability provided growing confidence that Poland could accept the risks associated with a less than absolute guarantee.

6. When they foresaw the possibility of having to compromise, the Poles graciously accepted generous economic compensation. Though there are limits to trade with the Federal Republic the trade treaty will be an important contribution to the Polish economy, especially in view of the food riots two weeks after the normalization treaty was signed.

7. The position of the GDR may have been a consideration. Gomulka was the only Polish official to call for the recognition of the GDR when referring to the border question. Omissions by the other authorities, and comments that German reconciliation should be achieved based on ' internal laws ', suggest that this repeated citation was a personal conviction rather than a national policy. None the less, Poland's negotiations with the Federal Republic indirectly strengthened the GDR's claims for equal status for both Germanies. But the equalization process would be imbalanced if it appeared that Bonn had exclusive and absolute authority over the disposition of the eastern territories and, accordingly, the relaxation of tensions. A less-than-final solution that was not linked to reunification would be in East Germany's interests.

8. The degree of consultation and co-ordination between Polish, East German, and Soviet negotiators was unprecedented in Pact history. Either before or immediately after each important session, leading officials would confer directly with their counterparts, particularly Soviet representatives. As the Polish delegates acknowledged, this procedure was in accordance with the resolutions of the Warsaw Pact Moscow conference of 3 December 1969. But the frequency of the Soviet

consultations was particularly noticeable, and this may have been viewed as a sign of a new Soviet respect for the interests of her allies which might augur well for the adoption of more genuine coalition politics within the Pact. It may also have been regarded as an indication of growing Soviet anxiety about the pace of events in Eastern Europe. At any rate, the new camaraderie could be quickly stifled if Warsaw exploited the latitude granted by Moscow and the other allies.

9.   During the summer months, a number of Polish intellectuals participated in a press discussion of ' New Polish Concerns '. The thrust of a series of fourteen articles in leading journals was that as *détente* leads to a shift in forces within the blocs, Poland should examine changing attitudes towards the communist system, European integration, political organization and leadership, and new social needs.[65] These penetrating articles were not reminiscent of those of the Czechoslovak writers in 1967–8, but they imparted an air of uncertainty which culminated four months later in the sweeping changes in the leadership. This new trend in public sentiment may have influenced the negotiators to accept a quick compromise rather than hold out for maximal demands and accept the risks of public disenchantment.

These conjectures do not diminish one central fact: the compromise represents a very significant milestone in both Polish and German history. Its precise dimensions are currently unpredictable and will remain heavily dependent upon progress on other interrelated international problems. The policies of both states remain ultimately subordinate to those of their respective protectors, whose interests in turn converge on broader vistas than the Oder–Neisse line. But even in Central Europe, the externalization of domestic sentiments projects an interdependency of national interests that serves both as a regulator and an accelerator of regional accommodation: an adjustment between any two rivals cannot be fully implemented without achieving a high degree of *rapport* with the others.

---

[65] The series appeared primarily in *Zycie Warszawy* from 4 June to 27 Aug. 1970.

Czechoslovak-West German Relations

Before the treaty with Poland was initialled, Bonn had opened official contacts with Prague, as the next facet in the normalization process in Central Europe. This modest opening was the culmination of sporadic efforts at reconciliation most seriously made by the Kiesinger government. In January 1967 a West German delegation was sent to Prague, authorized to discuss all outstanding issues between the two countries, to offer negotiations on a renunciation-of-force accord, and to determine the feasibility of establishing diplomatic relations. ' Other meetings followed this first discussion, but suddenly the atmosphere changed again. After the agreement between Rumania and the Federal Republic was signed a sharp polemic erupted in the pages of *Neues Deutschland* and *Scinteia*.'[66] Further formal contacts on major political issues were suspended.

However, on 3 August 1967, a three-year trade agreement was signed, including provisions for exchanging trade missions. Czechoslovakia was the last of the Pact countries to establish a permanent trade mission with the Federal Republic and maintained an unusually tough stand during the negotiations: she refused to accept the clause recognizing West Berlin as economically integrated in the Federal Republic, imposed stern restrictions on the functions and activities of resident West German representatives, and even refused to adopt the official title of the Federal Republic in formal documents. The Dubcek regime guardedly expressed its willingness to improve relations in the April 1968 party Plenum and unofficially expressed its interest in a major hard-currency loan. But both sides realized the dangers of immediately resuming the 1967 dialogue, and no measures towards normalization were initiated under the Action Programme.

The Husak regime has been consistently ambiguous on the subject of normalizing relations with the Federal Republic. On the one hand it has repeatedly stated its desire to open talks with Bonn with a view towards solving their differences. On the other hand it has maintained a steady polemical campaign

[66] Jan Riecan, *Vyber* (Bratislava) 29 Sept. 1969.

against the 'revanchist and imperialistic policies' of the Federal Republic with an intensity surpassed only by East Germany. In contrast in 1969 the other socialist countries shifted the focus of their propaganda attacks from the policies of Bonn to 'certain revisionist and reactionary circles and influences', indicating a desire to deal with the government but a continuing apprehension about conservative tendencies within West Germany. Further, until mid-1970, Prague remained the most ardent supporter in the socialist camp of the recognition of the GDR.

The conclusion of the Soviet-West German treaty on nationalistic lines and progress on the Polish treaty on the same principles was the turning-point in Prague's propaganda policies. Orthodox attacks were suspended and occasional comments about normalizing relations were now accompanied by only periodic calls for East German recognition. Prague began stressing that its terms for improved relations with Bonn were exclusively Czechoslovak grievances about the consequences of the war.[67]

The chief obstacles to normalization from both the Czechoslovak and West German viewpoints are the legal and political legacies of the 1938 Munich Agreement. In his initial speech to the Bundestag on 13 December 1966, Kiesinger had repudiated the agreement as no longer valid on four grounds: (1) it was concluded under duress; (2) it was never constitutionally ratified by the competent Czechoslovak political organs; (3) it was in violation of existing treaties; and (4) it was voided by the German occupation of March 1939. James H. Wolfe has conclusively argued that none of these points is legally sound and that the agreement constituted a valid and legal international document that cannot be declared invalid *ab initio*, as the Czechoslovaks have consistently demanded.[68] Kiesinger's argument was an attempt at political appeasement, as is demonstrated in a further passage in the same speech: 'problems still exist which must be settled, for instance the problem

[67] For indications of this changing emphasis see *Rude Pravo*, 10 Dec. 1969, & 27 June, 27 July, 12, 13, 14, & 19 Aug., 10, 19, & 21 Oct., *Ceteka News Service*, 14 July & 12, 14 Aug., *Mlada Fronta*, 29 July & 13 Aug. 1970.

[68] 'West Germany and Czechoslovakia: the Struggle for Reconciliation', *Orbis*, Spring 1970, pp. 154–79.

of the right of citizenship '. Jan Riecan, a prominent Slovak intellectual, points out that this is the core of the entire Munich dispute and cannot be as facilely dismissed as the Chancellor hoped.

As Robert Dean pointed out, the question to be resolved is the legal relationship of the Sudeten Germans to the Czechoslovak state, specifically between 1938 and 1945. The minimum goal of the Sudetendeutsche is to prevent a settlement between West Germany and Czechoslovakia which would preclude the possibility of their being recompensed for lost property and damages suffered because of their expulsion, and which could expose them, as former Czechoslovak citizens, to legal proceedings by the Prague regime. Both Prague and Bonn are caught in a legal imbroglio as they attempt to rectify claims of over 3·25 m. expellees, totalling nearly DM 65,000 m. Both Prague and the expellees maintain that the expulsion and the confiscation of property was a legal government action and the basis of the claims for compensation. The question remains which government is legally accountable for these claims.

If one proceeds from the premise that the Munich Agreement is invalid *ab initio*, then the Sudeten Germans could hardly be regarded as having been German citizens. The naturalization acts of the Hitler government, according to which the Sudeten Germans became German citizens (10 October 1938 and 16 March 1939)—and which are recognized by the West German government under the federal law of 22 February 1955—would also have to be considered invalid . . . a Czechoslovak decree (no. 33/1945) stipulated that the Sudeten Germans had lost their Czechoslovak citizenship when they acquired German citizenship as the result of the occupation regulations. Only the Czechoslovak government's recognition of adherence to the Munich Agreement could have provided the basis for this (judgment).

The dilemma may be summed up as follows: If the Munich Agreement was in fact valid, the occupation statutes had a binding effect and the Sudeten Germans were indeed German citizens. This is an interpretation which would appear to be not wholly unacceptable to the Czechoslovak leadership, because it would tend to legalize the expulsion and its effects, if not to mitigate the responsibility which would hypothetically accrue to the Czechoslovak government from the claims of former Czechoslovak citizens. If it was never valid (the present position of the Prague government)

then the Sudeten Germans remained Czechoslovak citizens who . . .
were unjustly expelled by their government and who are entitled to
compensation for property lost and damages suffered (by the
Czechoslovak government).[69]

In a related issue, Czechoslovakia maintains sizeable personal
and property claims against the Federal Republic for war
damages and individual suffering. In 1945 Prague advanced
claims of $11,500 m. and received $15 m. from the Allied
Reparation Agency. Since the Federal Republic insists that
she is the sole and rightful heir of the Reich, Prague maintains
that she must assume responsibility for the balance of the
claims.

The legal complexities of these claims and counter-claims
have frustrated and delayed a satisfactory solution. Movement
towards normalization is now a function of political attitudes
rather than jurisprudence. Provided that there is a continuation of the atmosphere that was observed during the visit of
Jürgen von Alten from the West German Foreign Ministry to
Prague on 13 October 1970 to re-establish the 1967 dialogue,
several formulas for normalization are plausible. Both sides may
be encouraged to put legal questions aside or to accept *pro forma*
statements if a satisfactory political equation can be substituted.
In May 1969 Brandt had announced the most likely West
German offer. He stressed the moral aspects when he asserted
that the Munich Agreement was an immoral and therefore
illegal document, avoiding the question of validity or application. Riecan has suggested that both sides should be allowed
to retain their respective interpretations of the causes and
implications of the Munich Agreement, but that they should
seek a political solution of its legacy without invoking its legal
injunction. Both sides might then pursue the precedent of the
Rapallo treaty, whereby their respective counter-claims would
be declared mutually compensatory, with each government
assuming responsibility for the claims of their respective citizens.
Or a variation on the scheme adopted in the recent Polish
negotiations might be applied, namely that only personal
claims of those victims of Nazi surgical experimentation would

[69] ' West German-Czechoslovak Relations: Problems and Prospects ' RFE
Research Memo, 9 Oct. 1970, pp. 24–5.

be honoured and the Federal Republic would provide massive long-term financial credits or investments at low-interest rates on the grounds that the entire contemporary society would benefit from past tragedies. Again, following the Polish precedent, when an agreement on normalization has been concluded, diplomatic relations might be established.

The negotiations are likely to be as difficult and protracted as those with Poland. This will depend largely on the stability of the Husak regime. As Brandt stated earlier, ' Czechoslovakia still has certain problems, and it might be wise for us not to give the impression that we were adding to her difficulties '.[70] Yet he also publicly stated in the wake of the normalization treaty that he expected an agreement with Prague within a year.

In view of the accelerated trend towards the pursuit of national interests among East European countries, the Czechoslovak government concluded that to open negotiations on a settlement of the Munich Agreement might constitute an important distraction of public sentiment, still distraught in the aftermath of the Prague Spring. And for the Husak government to open negotiations might be viewed abroad as a positive sign of the regime's confidence and determination to concentrate on its most pressing foreign-policy problem instead of on its former obsession with internal ills. Thus the mere agreement to talk is likely to have symbolic importance for both governments: for Czechoslovakia a demonstration of legitimacy of her rule, and for West Germany evidence that she is prepared to cope with probably the most intractable legacy of World War II.

[70] Radio Prague, 4 Mar. 1970.

7

THE CONSEQUENCES OF ADJUSTMENT
AND OF INTRANSIGENCE

IN just over one year of office, the Brandt government scored
two major diplomatic triumphs in the Soviet-West German
treaty and the Polish normalization treaty, reopened a dialogue
with Czechoslovakia, and substantially increased commercial
activities by signing liberalized five-year trade agreements with
all East European countries except Bulgaria. These and related
developments gave a greater potential impetus to improving
relations with the Warsaw Pact countries than had the cumulative efforts of the Western Allies over the previous quarter-
century. The impressive successes of the *Ostpolitik*, however,
have been compromised by the failure to establish *rapport* with
East Germany or to achieve a viable solution for divided
Berlin. Thus the chief source of European tension—the
'German problem'—remains largely unaltered, and the
reconciliation established between the Federal Republic and
Eastern Europe has so far been denied its full fruition.

Nevertheless, sufficient accommodation has been registered,
to make it impossible for political relations in Central Europe,
even between the two Germanies, to return to the level of
distance and distrust witnessed even as late as 1968, let alone
the cataclysmic upheavals and tensions of the 1950s. While it
seems safe to speculate that recent events have probably pre-
cluded a direct reversion to the Stalinist era, when threats and
reprisals virtually froze diplomatic activity, it is less possible to
indicate the most likely course of future relations. This is a
period of change on a scale unknown since before World War
II; there are no reliable precedents in the memories of contemporary statesmen and diplomats, and the available evidence
upon which to base even tentative answers to questions that
have plagued analysts for years, and to new ones that have
arisen very recently, is scant. For example, is the Warsaw Pact
now a more or less reliable political instrument than it was
following the Czechoslovak invasion? Now that Bonn's
policies no longer constitute the 'main threat' to East European security, and West Germany is considered politically
respectable, what new cohesive doctrine can be supplied to

ensure Soviet discipline in Eastern Europe? Has a greater degree of coalition politics, à la Rumania, been accepted by the Kremlin, and how should this be measured? The Eastern Europeans now enjoy greater mental security than at any time in the past thirty-five years, through the reduction of ' the German menace ' and Bonn's renunciation of territorial claims and recognition of existing borders, but does this inject more or less latitude into the formation of national policies? As her measure of security increases, will the Soviet Union's top priority aim of stability be proportionally enhanced? Are there natural levels, much beyond the present level, to the extent of West German influence acceptable in the East? With Germany's traditional avenues for influence partially curtailed, what can be drawn upon to fulfil Bonn's desire for political stature? Since Western integration has not achieved German reunification, and if Bonn cannot use its *Ostpolitik* to achieve this aim, what options are open? Since in the past the German problem and divided Berlin have had the effect of increasing international tensions, whereas the initial success of the *Ostpolitik* has had that of reducing them, how can the mechanism of thrust in ' the German problem ' be controlled? What are the limits of German reconciliation acceptable to Bonn, East Germany, Moscow, and the Allies? Has the relevance of Allied authority and influence been weakened or strengthened by the *Ostpolitik*? Have signs of US withdrawal from Europe contributed to or impeded a solution of the German problem? Now that military expenditure is being scaled down, what new NATO strategy and aims could best demonstrate the Allies' support for Bonn's goals? In the light of the success of its *Ostpolitik*, are Bonn's Western partners likely to reappraise their attitudes towards inter-German reconciliation? What is the effect of strategic nuclear parity on intra-European and great-power relations, and has Moscow's enhanced global stature induced a more lenient German policy? Or can Moscow be expected to employ its new power to cultivate a deferential West German attitude towards Soviet interests? Finally, can German nationalist sentiment endure the losses inflicted by the *Ostpolitik* and the continued frustrations in the *Deutschlandpolitik* for much longer without demanding such drastic action as a more aggressive policy towards the GDR, a more Gaullist line towards the West and a neutralist stand towards the East, and firmer demands for greater political power in European councils, or conversely a gradual detachment and indifference about the interests of Bonn's allies?

Such questions must be answered in the 1970s if Western policy is to exert reasonable control over the historical Russian-German love-hate relationship. A survey of the implications of both the *Ostpolitik* and *Deutschlandpolitik* may not provide appropriate solutions, but it might afford guidelines for further research and additional queries.

A leading figure among German expellees, Johann Baptist Gradl, stated in 1964 that the Germans could not overcome the division of Germany by recognizing it. Remarks in this vein were typical for the time, but in the light of recent developments they appear to have been short-sighted. Indeed, only through recognizing the partition and accepting the existence of two Germanies has sufficient progress been made in improving relations with the East to produce the present stilted dialogue across the Elbe.

For many years the West European leaders formed their Eastern policy in terms of promises and visions, but without a concrete programme for achieving these aims. After 1956, however, it was frequently argued that the most durable solution to the German problem would be within the context of a new European order. The immobility of policy in both East and West stemmed from the inability to devise workable models for the new order. When individual East European states attempted in 1956 and 1968 to formulate their own programmes, the Western nations demonstrated such circumspection that they implied acceptance of the Soviet understanding of spheres of influence. On the other hand, the Soviet Union was unable to implement her plan for a new Europe beyond stabilizing her own security system in Eastern Europe; her programme did not elicit wide support among the NATO countries, where the lack of immediate tangible results fostered passivity and public apathy, whereas in Eastern Europe the public remained more aware of the legacies of war.

In general, Western hopes for a new order were based on

achieving a German peace treaty to resolve the residual post-war problems, and correspondingly to reduce the sources of European tensions. General disarmament and later arms-control schemes were seen as measures to remedy the potential imperfections of these solutions. The unfortunate legacy of ' package deals ' persisted longer in the NATO countries than in those of the Warsaw Pact. (For example, in 1963 Khruschev proposed a non-aggression pact similar to the recently concluded treaty, but it was rejected by both the CDU and the SPD as superfluous and dangerous—without solutions to the political problems, military *détente* would reduce most important leverage that could be exerted by NATO.) Only gradually was it perceived that a policy of confidence-building measures by small steps could advance ultimate aims.

A number of influences generated the new awareness and the shift in orientation. The domestic pressures that had made the Grand Coalition and the SPD/FDP victory imperative, i.e. the combination of hopes and frustrations and the now-or-never atmosphere, released new demands for an activist platform. (It is noteworthy that the SPD rank and file became more assertive than the national committee in seeking an opening to the East.) The changing nature of the policies of Bonn's allies also had a crucial bearing: de Gaulle's flanking movement to the East, Kennedy's search for alternatives to confrontation, Johnson's obsession with the Far East, the run-down in Western integration, and NATO's acceptance of Soviet strategic equality and the ending of asymmetrical deterrence. On the other side, signs of polycentrism in the Pact countries gave rise to speculation that policies directed towards the individual East European countries could foster the growth of nationalistic aims, allowing greater latitude for a policy of small steps. Rumania's independent policy had been instructive. For a year and a half after establishing diplomatic relations with each other, both Bucharest and Bonn had been subjected to concerted polemical attacks and discriminatory policies. But after the Prague crisis, it became apparent to many East European leaders that it was in fact necessary and desirable to deal directly with the West Germans in further stabilizing developments in Central Europe.

In Brandt's view, there were four main reasons for the change in Moscow's German policy. First, its growing concern with the Chinese threat. Secondly, the desire for broadening economic and technological contacts with the more advanced Western industrial countries. Thirdly, the necessity to reach a *modus vivendi* with the United States. And finally, the realization after the Prague crisis of the need to participate in the *détente* to the same extent as its allies. ' What makes the present process of *détente* so important is the fact that it is going on with the Soviet Union and not against it.'[1]

While it is difficult to identify the relations between cause and effect witnessed in the policy changes of both the Federal Republic and the socialist countries, one decision was cardinal in the transformation of policy in Eastern Europe. Bonn's gradual acceptance of the *status quo* and abandonment of its policy of strength generated forces in the Pact countries which inevitably challenged the traditional stand. In turn, these forces fostered responses which allowed the Federal Republic to reduce still more her own terms for accommodation. (In contradistinction to this cyclical motion of adjustment, the East Germans increased their terms in rough proportion to the diminution of those of their allies.) More than any other single issue, the loosening in the Federal position, especially since 1969, seems to have been the prime catalyst.

This new awareness became most evident among the SPD, yet the party had no Grand Design. Even after taking office, Brandt expressed ideas and aims but had no comprehensive programme of action. The lack of a plan was most evident in the inter-German talks, where the distance between the two parties could not be bridged even on single issues. The willingness of the other socialist states to explore an agreement on limited topics minimized the need for a broad perspective. The claim of being guided by realities and the need for more intermediary steps [2] were no substitutes for a general strategy the public could grasp. A more elaborate formulation could have

---

[1] Interview in *L'Express (Bull.*, 15 Dec. 1970).

[2] Katharina Focke, ' New Ways to Cope with Old Problems of Divided Germany ', ibid., 16 June 1970.

minimized the popular shock over the results of the three-pronged West German offensive. What have the West Germans actually gained from the first year and a half of Brandt's *Ostpolitik*? Were the Soviet and Polish treaties successes or sacrifices?

From the NATO standpoint the long-range impact of the treaties appears in early 1971 to be mainly beneficial:

1. By placing ratification within the context of a favourable Berlin solution, the entire normalization process has been refined to a single frame of reference. The Federal Republic has accepted the existing realities in the Pact countries, and now requires them to follow suit in Berlin. This should significantly strengthen the Allies' bargaining position in the Berlin talks. Both sides must now both extend and accept concessions largely within the context of the German-Soviet treaty.

2. Federal aims of national self-determination coupled with non-intervention in domestic affairs, and the refusal to recognize the GDR, have been upheld. No important issue or principle was traded or weakened, except the commitment to an international peace treaty. While Bonn initially argued that the German-Soviet treaty would neither prejudice nor anticipate a final settlement, the acceptance of the Soviet and Polish demands has conveyed a *de facto* peace arrangement.[3] But if these and subsequent accords are firmly linked to a solution of the Berlin question, the necessity for a final peace conference will have been substantially reduced.

3. The Soviet Union has now accepted the respectability of the Federal Republic. Bonn's political aspirations in both the East and West can no longer be construed by the socialist countries as a potential disturbance of the peace. This is the most significant contribution to date towards intra-European co-operation.

4. Bonn learned from its attempts in 1967-8 to make gains in Eastern Europe at Moscow's expense. In 1969 it started at the top and made an adjustment with Moscow its leading priority. This new configuration was more acceptable to Moscow, and as Bonn gradually expanded the scope of mutual co-operation with Eastern Europe, its stature in both East and

[3] See Scheel's extensive argumentation, *FAZ*, 15 July 1970.

West substantially increased. After integration in the West, the opening to the East was the second step towards establishing a political authority commensurate to the Federal Republic's economic status as the world's third industrial power. These co-ordinated steps allowed Bonn for the first time to extend its policy aims beyond those of the Weimar Republic, through offering political integration in the West, and security and settlement in the East rather than manipulation and expansion. It is too early to predict the durability of the new normalization policy, but as it is now exercised, it represents one of the most important changes in Germany's traditional Eastern policy in this century.

5. The strategy of small steps and the piecemeal approach to stability and security have proved more successful than the former comprehensive peace plans. The *Ostpolitik* has been the best example in the history of East–West relations of the merits of confidence-building through micro-diplomacy. It is likely to influence the strategy of other West European countries and NATO as they seek a military disengagement and political *détente*.

6. In the wake of the Soviet and Polish treaties, there is a growing feeling among West German analysts that Moscow is attempting to return its European policy to the context of the nineteenth-century Concert of Europe. It has recognized that the Federal Republic is the chief source of European stability and instability and has elected to replace a policy of ostracism by one of mutual co-operation. While the distance between co-operation and condominium of the 1939 variety remains wide, it is essential that the Federal Republic, as the second European power, should act positively to establish and preserve leverage against the Soviet Union. The German-Soviet treaty marked Bonn's first substantial initiative, which can be expanded and secured as the West's main prerogative in a future Concert of Europe.

7. The sacrifices embodied in the Soviet and Polish treaties are more than symbolic gestures (welcomed by friends and foes alike) that the Germans have at last accepted the consequences of their aggression. They are an essential step towards rectifying the war guilt and political paranoia that have afflicted so many

Germans and their foreign policy. These treaties afford a real measure of international rehabilitation and restoration of self-respect that are indispensable for a durable solution to the German problem.

8. Critics have stated that the treaties also represents a moral step backwards: the acceptance of injustice and a new climate of cynical relativity of values in which the communist system is regarded only as different from, but as good as, a free society. But the futility of the twenty-year-long anti-communist campaign warrants a new approach. Its barrenness was not due to lack of humanity or moral virtues, but to the misuse of anti-communist arguments, stemming largely from confusion between national communism and Soviet expansionism. The available evidence indicates that peaceful competition between the two political and economic systems can reasonably be expected to lead to a better perspective for human rights than in the era of anti-communism and international tensions.

9. The *Ostpolitik* has undoubtedly opened up new economic opportunities. Otto Wolff von Amerongen, President of the German Chambers of Commerce and Industry, has predicted that the percentage of Eastern trade in total West German foreign trade may increase from a present 4·2 per cent to 8 or 9 per cent. But he has also warned against immediate optimism, because of the natural restraints experienced by the socialist countries, namely the lack of convertible currencies and strict bilateralism, poor-quality industrial goods, and inadequate marketing techniques to stand up to competition in the West. He pointed out, however, that there are several largely unexplored additional areas of co-operation, such as buying and selling licences and technological know-how, marketing East European products by Western firms within Eastern Europe itself and in third countries, and financing correlated production in the socialist countries.[4] If such activities prove profitable traditional restraints may gradually be neutralized and West Germany might become the dominant technological power in Eastern Europe.

10. The responses of Bonn's allies to the *Ostpolitik* are critical for its success. Fears have been expressed that either

[4] *Die Welt*, 12 Aug. & *Bull.*, 4 Aug. 1970.

Moscow would not appreciate Brandt's delicate domestic balance and therefore would not endorse his claims to preserve the *status quo* in Berlin, or, conversely, would tempt him to make excessive concessions in a desperate effort to succeed both at home and abroad. An analysis by Acheson, Clay, McCloy, and Dewey presented to Nixon asserting that Bonn's centre of gravity was being shifted to the East by Brandt's ' mad race to Moscow ' was viewed with alarm in the Federal Republic. (Fearing that Acheson was saying what the White House could not, in December Brandt sent his personal envoy, Horst Ehmke, on a ' blitz ' visit to Washington.)

American concern was partly due to the decline of Western countervailing forces, e.g. the eclipse of French authority and the still uncertain utility of the British-West German rapprochement. Thus the *Ostpolitik* has made important gains but has also aggravated many traditional apprehensions.

Adalbert Weinstein has sympathized with these fears.

The *Ostpolitik* is made by us instead of by the Americans. When confronted with possible consequences beyond its control, a world power cannot but worry. . . . In our situation one cannot seek a fair opening towards the East and pursue classic Western policy without creating suspicion. . . . Hence the American decision to maintain the US troop presence in Europe can also be interpreted as a precautionary move not only towards the Soviet Union.[5]

Other West German analysts were less sensitive to Western concerns and cited a long history of Federal grievances against her Allies' indifference towards her important and vital interests.

The Western position in Germany first cracked when the Kennedy government gave preference to its relationship with the Soviet Union over its policy of alliance . . . When Washington abandoned the project of a joint NATO nuclear force; when McNamara started looking for new pseudo-rational concepts for the defence of Europe, the idea of equal protection for all NATO members waned and the Federal Republic's faith in NATO received a shock from which it has never fully recovered. . . . [This was amplified by] the Allied passivity at the erection of the Berlin Wall; the American campaign against the formation of German-French bloc; the French campaign

[5] *FAZ*, 23 Dec., *Die Welt*, 12 & 14 Dec., *Rheinische Post*, 15 Dec. 1970.

against an intimate German-American relationship . . . Gaullist resistance against West European integration; and British opposition to the WEU. . . . Even before it had digested the reorientation of de Gaulle's European policy toward Moscow, the Federal Republic was confronted with Washington's and London's signing of the NPT, even though they knew that the Soviet Union interpreted it as an anti-German pact. Today Senatorial pressure for troop withdrawals spreads doubt about the alliance to the most remote German village. It is surprising that despite so many blows the Germans have remained reliable partners. . . . [But] unless the West, particularly the US, is prepared to lose the struggle over the Federal Republic, it must correct past errors. . . .[6]

Such complaints by a right-of-centre analyst, Dieter Cycon, make the pledges of solidarity by Federal leaders inadequate for men like Acheson. Brandt has affirmed many times that the opening to the East is important but not vital to West Germany; though West European integration is a vital interest. For example, Brandt termed the EEC Hague summit meeting of 1–2 December 1969 ' the most important event in foreign affairs since I have come to office '.[7] And Helmut Schmidt has remarked, ' without a firm foundation in NATO there can be no sensible policy of *détente* in Europe. It would be sheer folly if one attempted to conduct one's policy in the East from any other basis than that of firm Western solidarity.[8]

The differences between the three positions—apprehension, grievances, and allegiance—should not impugn the sincerity of each conviction. Closure of the gap will depend increasingly upon the prevailing Western, especially the American, attitude towards the Federal Republic. The United States must adjust her thinking and accept the realities of Europe in the 1970s. The Federal Republic is the dominant military and economic Continental power. Her stunted political stature in part stems from the preservation of artificial Allied restraints through fears of latent German nationalism and Soviet expansionism. But each year, West Germany becomes less a Western dependency, over which certain sovereign rights must be retained.

---

[6] *Die Welt*, 28 Sept. 1970.
[7] *Bull.*, 10 Mar. 1970.
[8] ' Perspectives of the Alliance ', speech at the WEU Assembly, *Survival*, Feb. 1970, p. 43.

Since the peace treaty provisions in the Postdam Agreement have been diluted for all intents and purposes by
the bilateral treaties with the socialist states, the Allies' legal
prerogatives will remain technically binding but increasingly
less applicable. The demands of the 1970s are that the Western
Allies should parallel Soviet realism and accept the Federal
Republic as a fully sovereign partner, and proceed to establish
a more genuine relationship, based on equality and independent national interests. Unfortunately, the key to implementing
greater equality and responsibility lies in the outcome of the
Berlin negotiations.

The final argument over the merits of the *Ostpolitik* from the
Western viewpoint is the impact it has had on the citizens of
West Germany. Before the signing of the Soviet treaty, the
semi-official Institute for Applied Social Sciences revealed that
79 per cent of those interviewed in a recent poll favoured the
government's conduct of the *Ostpolitik* and only 8 per cent
dissented. But more revealing of public sentiment and the
durability of the government's policies were the results of six
provincial elections held in 1970.[9]

Party Gains and Losses in the Federal Länder Elections in 1970
Compared with the results of the 1969 General Elections
(per cent)

Land	CDU(CSU)	SPD	FDP	Electorate
Hamburg	−1·2	+0·7	+0·8	1,381,000
North Rhine–Westphalia	+2·7	−0·7	+0·1	11,875,000
Lower Saxony	+0·5	+2·4	−1·2	5,085,000
Saar	+1·8	+0·9	−2·3	783,000
Hesse	+1·3	−2·3	+3·4	3,835,000
Bavaria	+2·0	−1·3	+1·4	7,265,000

Source: German Tribune 10 Dec. 1970.

[9] *German Tribune*, 10 Dec. 1970. Many analysts compared the results with those
of 1966, but this is highly inaccurate because of major changes in the issues confronting the electorate. For Polish reactions and correlation with negotiations in
Warsaw see *Kurier Polski* & Radio Warsaw, 15 June, and *Trybuna Ludu, Zycie
Warszawy*, 16 June 1970.

In the 1969 general elections the CDU/CSU received 46·1 per cent, the SPD 42·7 per cent, and FDP 5·8 per cent of the votes. Since the SPD/FDP coalition only had a 2·4 per cent majority, the CDU claimed that the coalition did not reflect the public will. Its platform during the six *Länder* campaigns was based on proposals to rectify this 'trick' and to curb excessive inflation. The SPD/FDP campaigned primarily on the progress of the *Ostpolitik* and economic reforms. The first test in Hamburg in March was a major disappointment for the CDU. Rather than a groundswell against the government, both coalition parties received gains. In the next three elections in June, 'the little general election', the results were inconclusive; losses were traded for gains by the two larger parties. Only the FDP sustained heavy damage, but the CDU had to shift to the opposition in Hanover. The November elections in Hesse and Bavaria were more crucial. The SPD lost significantly in Hesse, its traditional stronghold, but the FDP made impressive gains in both contests.

The details of the Hesse campaign are the most revealing since it was the weather vane for the collapse of the 1966 coalition. The SPD lost 8–9 per cent in the industrial precincts of southern Hesse, but only 0·5 in the more rural north. The reason for these sharp drops was worker dissatisfaction with price instability (a traumatic issue in Germany), the usual by-election woes of the ruling party and the loss of youth to the CDU, but not foreign-policy matters. Herbert Wehner acknowledged after the defeat that, for the first time in recent history, the SPD could no longer call itself the 'young' party. The CDU had successfully remodelled its image and attraction and fought a vigorous campaign with young, energetic local candidates.

Several conclusions can be drawn from these elections that will affect the conduct of West German foreign policy. First, the CDU does not have the electoral strength to overthrow the present government before the 1973 general elections (though defections from the FDP deputies could reduce the coalition majority). Likewise the SPD is not strong enough to call a general election before 1973 to increase its working majority. Yet the new strength of the FDP has injected greater reliability into the coalition itself. The SPD is likely to give increasing priority to price stabilization at the expense of other issues (the inflation rate had been cut from over 5 to 3·9 per cent by the end of 1970), but will interpret its generally strong showing against the CDU as a mandate to continue the pace of the *Ostpolitik*.

Equally important, the revitalization of the CDU led to some significant local victories. Yet the national leadership remained seriously disabled through the rivalries of established personalities. (The inability of the existing leadership to agree upon an alternative Chancellor after one and a half years in opposition and their bungling of the affair of the Bahr Paper, where they presented government with the opportunity to harden its demands in Moscow and at the same time undermine the CDU's opposition to the treaty, were widely regarded as marks of immobilism and indecision.) This paralysis at the top has encouraged the rise of more youthful leaders, like Dr Helmut Kohl, Mayor of Mainz. A younger group of Bundestag deputies will be less susceptible to traditional conservative arguments regarding the *Ostpolitik*. Indeed, it may be concluded from the 1970 *Länder* elections that should the CDU win in 1973, it will not be interested in or able to reverse the gains which have accrued from the SPD's offensive in the East. The most feasible CDU alternative will be to control and pace the extent of the rapprochement.

It is more difficult to plot the long-range profits and losses for the Soviet Union and Poland in their new relationships with the Federal Republic. Traditionally, Moscow's aims in Eastern Europe have been to consolidate and legitimize its rule. An important instrument for this purpose was the strongly negative cohesive factor of the spectre of West German imperialism which was raised to doctrinal proportions and became the primary *raison d'être* for Pact solidarity.[10]

These tactics were so successful that after the construction of the Wall, Moscow was able to change its German policy and to offer to open a dialogue with Bonn in 1964. Prague, Warsaw, and especially East Berlin reacted so sharply, however, that

[10] Fritz Ermath, *Internationalism, security and legitimacy: The challenge to Soviet interests in East Europe 1964*, RAND Corp., RM-5909-PR, Mar. 1969.

Moscow accepted their argument that the Pact could only deal with the Federal Republic from a position of strength, or unequivocal solidarity. West German diplomacy in Eastern Europe up to that point had had the effect of aligning the northern-tier countries—those who feared Bonn's territorial claims—directly behind East Germany's growing assertiveness in challenging both Bonn and Moscow. Rumania viewed this collusion among the northern-tier countries as a dangerous step towards greater Soviet hegemony and a sound reason for formulating a two-Germanies policy, a precedent subsequently adopted by other East European countries.

This success for Bonn was jeopardized by rising uncertainties in Czechoslovakia and the determination of its own conservative political factions. But the Prague crisis forced a growing appreciation in Bonn that its policy of strength had proved unsuccessful and that Moscow's consolidation programme was so complete that it could not be reversed, thereby denying Bonn expected leverage against the GDR. The Federal Republic gradually accepted the fact that the realization of her principal national aim, a reconciliation with the other German entity, could be made only on Moscow's terms, namely the endorsement of the *status quo* in Eastern Europe as the core of the Soviet Union's stabilization programme. (However, grasping the dimensions of this fact was a slow process, as late as his address of 14 January 1970, Brandt stressed the opportunities for political gains afforded by the disarray in Eastern Europe.)[11]

At the same time Moscow was becoming increasingly aware that it could not complete its consolidation in Eastern Europe without dealing with the West Germans, who would not agree to a multilateral approach because this would imply full recognition of the GDR. The courtship of de Gaulle had demonstrated the futility of trying to bypass Bonn in settling Central European problems. West Germany's central position in European affairs, her prodigious technological capabilities, and her position along Moscow's strategic security frontier made direct contact with her unavoidable. But the Soviet Union could not invite the Federal Republic to participate as

[11] *Bull.*, Suppl. 20 Jan. 1970. For a rebuttal on this point see *Frankfurter Neue Presse*, 15 Jan. 1970.

a peace partner in Central Europe—the long-standing Gaullist desire—without making important concessions to West German interests. The initial concessions, and probably the most durable ones were the removal of any ' West German threat ' and the Pact's formal commitment to West German respectability. While the East European people will continue to fear and hate Germans for many years, this commitment has introduced such a fundamental change in East–West relations that diplomacy in Central Europe will probably never be the same again. It is important to note that these changes in Soviet policy were made without West Germany either manufacturing her own nuclear weapons, as did France, or receiving substantially greater support through NATO's nuclear posture (with the exception of the Lance missile, no major improvements in the Organization's tactical nuclear capabilities have been made since about 1965, and participation in the Nuclear Planning Group had not increased Bonn's access to nuclear weapons).

Changes in traditional Pact aims and methods of policy formation were fraught with uncertainties about the entire fabric of solidarity and raised questions about appropriate conditions for autonomy, policy co-ordination, and security. Could the Pact's decision-making apparatus be decentralized along the lines of Rumania's demands for genuine coalition politics without impairing Moscow's interest in preserving regional stability? Did Moscow's gradual deference towards the national interests of its allies represent a trend or merely a momentary expediency? What were the dangers of establishing such precedents and how would they affect new power relationships within the Pact?

The use of force against Czechoslovakia and its threatened employment against Rumania established the upper levels of tolerance for East European manoeuvrability. The Brezhnev Doctrine of limited socialist sovereignty has been denounced by ruling and non-ruling Communist Parties alike, but its implications have been clearly understood and accepted by countries like Rumania. Bucharest's return to Pact councils and deliberations was a sign that it acquiesced, however reluctantly, in the priority Moscow attached to socialist discipline on issues of vital interest to the Kremlin. Rumanian diplomacy since Prague has been designed to establish new areas of manoeuvre and wider freedom of action within the Soviet level of tolerance. A *modus vivendi* was worked out in the bilateral defence accord of July 1970, which confirmed the interests of the respective allies and met important demands of both sides. While Rumania accepted the importance of conformity and discipline on selected issues, and Moscow could proclaim that the Brezhnev Doctrine was successful, the Soviet Union recognized Bucharest's special status within the Pact and its right to establish national priorities within the general framework of socialist policy.

With Rumanian conformity, Soviet policy in the Pact became more clear. Its chief demand was apparently that its allies remain 'little Europeans' and refrain from undue objections to Moscow's great-power policies. As a result, all the Pact members, minus the GDR, accepted legal commitments to aid the Soviet Union in the event of Chinese aggression and have assiduously refrained from contesting Moscow's unprecedented Middle East venture in actively participating in the defence of Egypt. (In contrast, it should be noted that the protest at the Czechoslovak Writers' Congress in July 1967 against Moscow's Middle East policy was a crucial reagent in the movement to oust Novotny that began three months later. The anti-Semitism which swept Poland in 1967 and 1968, stemming from the Middle East war, was a contributing factor in the country's mounting economic stagnation. Finally Rumania seized on the Middle East crisis as a major point of challenge to the Soviet leadership.)

In response, the Soviet Union agreed to greater co-ordination of regional policies and to introduce new impetus into its allies' hopes for a European security conference, as seen in the Pact meetings from March 1969 to July 1970. The failure of the NATO countries to accept the Pact's terms for an all-European gathering and the growing indications of a moderation in Bonn's *Ostpolitik* prompted a change in priorities in December 1969, agreeable to all except the GDR. The Pact decided to place a greater emphasis on bilateral solutions to national problems while holding the multilateral approach in reserve;

to be used as a means of exerting pressure on the West, but to be employed mainly as the vehicle for maximizing the gains made in the bilateral agreements. The preference for the bilateral approach, however, opened the way for a broader application of the normal processes of diplomacy and the adjustment and compromise required for its effective application. It also required new methods and instruments for the co-ordination of policy. To date, this has been most noticeable in the accelerated pace of individual contacts among leading national figures; no institutional modifications have yet come to light.

But the immediate implications of the nationalist approach to foreign policy readily became apparent. In the first of the new treaties, Moscow virtually abandoned the policy aims of its allies. No mention was made of the Munich Agreement, recognition of the GDR, or of the sanctity of borders in terms acceptable to its partners. This was a betrayal of the Pact's aggregate demands for *détente*, regularly reiterated since the 1966 Bucharest Declaration. In establishing such a powerful precedent for separatist national contacts with the chief European ' antagonist ', Moscow was forced to grant similar prerogatives to the East Europeans. Further, by accepting something less than what the Czechoslovaks, Poles, and East Germans regarded as non-negotiable terms, the Soviet Union will no longer be able to pose as the absolute guarantor of East European interests, as she did before August 1970. While the physical security of the three allies was not immediately endangered, their negotiating position on one of the most important national commitments since the war was seriously undermined. The East Europeans could only conclude that they had been left to their own resources; an important beginning had been made in transforming the processes of conflict resolution and political *détente* from international to national preferences.

It is not strange, therefore, that each of the principal negotiations conducted during 1970 gradually assumed individual characteristics. The case of Poland was instructive. From 1956 to 1958, Poland proffered almost unconditional terms for establishing normal relations with the Federal Republic, and shifted the emphasis to military disengagement in the various

Rapacki plans of 1958, 1960, and 1962 and the Gomulka plan of 1964. After that date, however, Warsaw became virtually harnessed in tandem with the GDR on all aspects of the Pact's German policy. When Bonn's policy began to loosen in the mid-1960s, Polish policy aims had become firmly subordinated to those of the GDR, whose main objective was to ensure Pact solidarity for the legitimization of the SED's rule. Poland was thus unable to assert an independent initiative.

Gomulka's speech of 17 May 1969 reflected a willingness to sacrifice this link with the GDR in return for firm guarantees of West German recognition of Poland's security interests through the renunciation of all claims to Germany's former eastern territories. But once the talks were firmly under way, Poland's national prestige became so heavily committed to a successful outcome that she had no choice but to continue negotiating for the best possible terms. She could not afford to overlook such an important opportunity to advance her traditional aims, and therefore could not return to her former preference for securing East German goals. Poland rejected the Moscow formula of West German ' unreserved respect ' for her present borders and continued to hold out for ' final, unequivocal recognition '. The compromise wording was substantially stronger than the Soviet position, indicating the different values both allies placed on the same issue. Poland in addition not only dropped her former demands for West German recognition of the GDR but reversed former policy by agreeing to establish full diplomatic ties with Bonn in return for a ratified treaty.

The shifting position of Poland does not as yet indicate a desire for autonomy on the scale asserted by Rumania, but it suggests a growing reluctance to pursue the demands of others at her own expense. Coupled with the consequences of the December 1970 food riots, Warsaw can be expected to adopt a more assertive policy in both political and economic areas which may assist Czechoslovakia to formulate a more nationalistic policy and induce East Germany to modify her intransigent aims.

Thus those forces of rapprochement in Eastern Europe that have sought solutions to national grievances have gained an ascendancy over those demanding solidarity of purpose. Moreover, by accepting the commitment to long-term *détente* Moscow has opened Eastern Europe to penetration by West German influence, and to an infusion of new standards and criteria for proper socialist behaviour and appropriate relationships between great and small powers. Indeed, West German influence may become an important factor in shaping these modalities in intra-Pact relations. Yet it would be unwise to imply that the Soviet Union will remain insensitive to these new, potentially dangerous, forces in her vital sphere of influence. She can be expected to improvise new checks and balances to supplement those of the Brezhnev Doctrine and bilateral defence treaties; and Soviet armour will remain the basic guarantor of East European respect for Soviet vital interests. Nevertheless, in the next decade, Moscow will have to assess and accept to a greater degree than before the individual interests and demands of its allies. Consensus will now have to be negotiated rather than imposed. It remains to be seen whether this process will strengthen or weaken the military potential of the Warsaw Pact.

The chief obstacle to the further improvement of West German-Pact relations has become not the fundamental policies of either antagonists, but those of East Germany. By the early spring of 1971, East Germany had successfully blocked ratification of the treaties Bonn had concluded and thereby prevented the fruition of the *Ostpolitik*. She had also become the principal opponent of the Soviet Union within Pact councils. She had amplified her former role as the monitor of Pact policy and relations with West Germany, and had assumed the role formerly largely played by Rumania, of the focal point of dissent. East Germany can be expected to play an even more adroit and determined game than Rumania, for the stakes are higher; she is threatened with isolation by her allies' indifference, subversion by West German liberalism, and the dissent of a potentially restive populace. Thus the pace of accommodation in East European affairs has become increasingly dependent on East German foreign policy.

During 1969 and 1970 the GDR pursued an assertive foreign policy unprecedented in her short history. It was directed against both the Federal Republic and her allies and was an inevitable by-product of the new challenges from both quarters. As the threat from the West diminished, the GDR's strategic leverage against the Pact was proportionally reduced; she could no longer demand the unequivocal support of her allies for her interests in compensation for her exposed position. (In October 1970 the Pact conducted its largest peacetime military manoeuvres in history, involving 100,000 men from all seven member nations. Holding this exercise for the first time in the GDR was regarded as a gesture of support for East Berlin. However, it remained only a gesture, unrelated to important political priorities, and is likely to be the last of its kind, both in location and scale.)

A more important gauge of the changing nature of the GDR's relations with her principal partners were the treaty provisions they recently negotiated. East Germany's allies decided to compromise with the Federal Republic on issues of vital importance to the GDR rather than make sacrifices on matters each regarded as important to her own national interests. The new trend was confirmed at the Pact summit conference of 2 December 1970 called to ' ratify ' the Polish and Soviet treaties and to consider the latest Western bid for *détente*. The conference did not adopt the customary vindictive declaration against West German militarism; it advocated pursuit of *détente* rather than confrontation; it paid tribute to the Soviet and Polish treaties; it called for *de jure* recognition of the GDR, but not as a precondition for any additional moves towards *détente*, such as a European security conference; and for the first time it did not oppose Bonn's formula for relations between the two German states. This latest Pact position indicated that Ulbricht had lost substantial influence, especially since the fall of Gomulka, the next most senior Pact party leader—and that his allies would continue to place national interests above East German objectives, even after gaining major successes with the Federal Republic.

Ulbricht has been sensitive to this new environment. Speeches delivered since August have been noteworthy for their omission of many maximalist demands and lack of recrimination for his partners' perfidy. When the Soviet Union agreed to drop the last five points in the Bahr Paper, East German policy had to be substantially recast so as to place greater emphasis on unilateral initatives and national resources. The new tone became apparent at the SED 13th Central Committee Plenum in June, when Ulbricht adopted a remarkably con- ciliatory tone and admitted that the West German government might be subject to serious pressure through the opposition to the Bahr Paper.[12] In conformity with practices already adopted by other Pact members, East Germany's vitriolic denunciations were shifted from Bonn's policies to the oppo- sition's intentions and the subversive designs of the imperialist class. Further hints were offered at the Rostock festival a month later, when both Ulbricht and the Foreign Minister Otto Winzer stressed the adoption of peaceful coexistence as the basis for improving relations with Bonn.[13] The efforts of other socialist countries were termed important contributions to coexistence and normalization of relations with the Federal Republic. Such conciliatory remarks were in sharp contrast with those associated with the earlier German summit meetings and were generally regarded as an attempt to alert the party cadre of impending changes. Indeed, the East German Cabinet officially stated that ' normalization of the relations between the GDR and the Federal Republic, on the basis of equality, has become a realistically soluble task ' because of the Soviet treaty. The statement erroneously said that ' the obligations entered upon by the Soviet Union and the Federal Republic in the treaty consequently require that normal diplomatic relations between the GDR and the Federal Republic be established henceforth ', but it implied that interim solutions were now feasible.[14]

Ulbricht followed the Pact summit meeting of 2 December with a speech to the 14th party Plenum. Reflecting the altered stand taken by his allies, he omitted any reference to West Berlin as an independent entity and called only for a lowering of the Federal Republic's profile in the city. The main thrust of the speech was a plea for negotiations on ' mutual transit

[12] *ND*, 16 June 1970.
[13] Ibid., 14 & 17 July 1970.
[14] Ibid., 15 Aug. 1970.

traffic' between the German states as equals. His conditions, however, were that Bonn must suspend all 'illegal state interference in West Berlin'. While these terms were unacceptable to Bonn, they represented a substantial shift in East Germany's position. Finally, he expressed 'agreement' with the Polish reversal of policy in establishing diplomatic relations with the Federal Republic, clearly contravening the former 'Ulbricht Doctrine' which proscribed recognition by Pact nations until the Federal Republic established relations with the GDR.[15]

The revision in East German policy since the Kassel encounter in May suggests that a reassessment had been made along several lines. The lack of recrimination against her allies may have stemmed from the conclusion that the trend was both irreversible and could win important gains. The breach in the common front made by her allies' insistence on a higher priority for national interests than international commitments would allow East Germany to demand the same prerogatives. Indeed, greater emphasis upon the individualist approach might strengthen the GDR's bargaining position against both East and West; she had unique leverage in Berlin, and after her partners had resolved their own national grievances against Bonn, she would have a freer hand in balancing the Soviet Union against West Germany. (This widening freedom of action was enhanced by the timely arrival of a potentially powerful ally, the reappointed Chinese envoy who may aid Ulbricht's orthodoxy and manoeuvres against Moscow.)[16] This new pressure can be used most effectively, however, if the GDR modifies the intransigent stand she took at Kassel. Accordingly, during the summer of 1970, she set the stage for a more flexible policy towards Bonn and the basis for her own *Westpolitik*.

After Gromyko visited both the Federal Republic and the GDR in October, it was announced that the dialogues between the two German states would be reopened. Bonn refused to reopen the talks at the summit level, as East Germany suggested, and Egon Bahr was designated its representative for the exchanges conducted in East Berlin on 27 November and

---

[15] Ibid., 10–14 Dec. 1970; see above, p. 43.
[16] V. Kostov, in *Otechestven Front* (Sofia), 17 Nov. 1970; see also above, p. 62.

23 December. It was agreed that only practical problems should be discussed at that level. East Germany sought to discuss acceptance of the status of West Berlin and access rights, but Bonn refused on the grounds that these items remained under the purview of the Allies, and preferred to discuss improvement in matters such as communications. Little was achieved and the talks were temporarily suspended.

The talks in East Berlin between Bahr and Michael Kohl, a senior official in the GDR Council of Ministers, suggested that the GDR had made important tactical changes which might improve the prospects for a long-range adjustment, primarily on the issues of recognition and West Berlin. In October Stoph firmly rejected Brandt's thesis of 'unity of the nation' and denied that there could ever be anything like inter-German relations.[17] And the 14th party Plenum reaffirmed the unique aspects of East Germany's national character as the grounds for international recognition. This reiteration indicated that there had been no erosion in the ultimate value the SED placed on these issues, but the party realized that they can no longer be placed in the forefront of its *Westpolitik*. This awareness was due to the pace of its allies' adjustment, as well as the unofficial raising of Bonn's terms for recognition.

As early as January 1970 the SPD's deputy leader and its most flexible spokesman, Herbert Wehner, predicted that a situation will arise in which people will no longer argue about the recognition or non-recognition of the GDR but will ask whether contractual agreements between East and West Germany can be concluded. Opponents maintained that Wehner had accepted recognition in principle but supporters developed his argument. Recognition alone has several drawbacks: (1) Bonn could not make a case for recognizing the GDR under German public law rather than international law; (2) recognition under international law connotes that both countries consider each other as foreign states; (3) refusal by one country to recognize another is not identical with considering the other non-existent; (4) full recognition of the GDR would entitle East Berlin to consider all refugees living in the Federal Republic as citizens of the GDR and subject to her

[17] *ND*, 7 Oct. 1970.

public and criminal laws; (5) recognition of the GDR would virtually negate four-power responsibility for all Germany and would undermine West Berlin's legal basis and security; (6) after obtaining diplomatic recognition, the GDR could cut all remaining links between the two parts of Germany and thereby reinforce the partition rather than perforate it; (7) partition is a political, not a constitutional, matter and recognition of the GDR as a fully sovereign state would reduce Bonn's opportunities to mitigate the division; and (8) there is no evidence that Moscow will accept full independence until legal guarantees assuring its political influence in German matters can be provided by both German states.

The importance of such exchanges was the gradual public acceptance that, in Wehner's words, ' recognition of the GDR would be too little ', or that the formulas of the legal accords were less important than the political content behind them. West German recognition would have to be dependent upon the GDR's acceptance of important additional political conditions for mutual accommodation. Coexistence is not enough, a degree of inter-German settlement is required. While a peace treaty seems no longer probable, the German people must seek an adjustment that relieves their grievances but does not obviate their claims to a more durable settlement.[18]

Thus while the GDR was hardening her position on recognition during the period of the German summit talks, the West German public was becoming increasingly aware that recognition was not the main issue involved in a mutual accommodation, as East Germany claimed. Accordingly, the Federal political parties were able to close ranks and deny the GDR any tactical leverage on this issue. In view of this united West German stand, the GDR was forced to put a lower priority to recognition and either to elevate the importance of practical questions or side with her allies on the crucial place of Berlin in the whole German problem and European *détente*.

Berlin's role in East-West détente
Brandt firmly linked the fruition of his *Ostpolitik* with a

[18] *Die Welt*, 28 Jan. & 18 Feb., *Telegraf*, 8 Mar., *FAZ*, 16 May, *Die Zeit*, 29 May 1970.

solution of the Berlin question as the key to a durable, long-term improvement in Soviet-German relations. When President Nixon visited West Berlin in February 1969 he proposed a fresh attempt to resolve the city's long-standing problems. In July sufficient progress had been made in Soviet-West German bilateral talks for Gromyko to suggest that Moscow was interested in limited talks on Berlin. The Western Allies probed these intentions in August in formal notes to the Soviet Union. When the Soviet Union concurred, protracted discussions ensued over various protocol matters and the substantive aspects of the agenda. The West finally agreed to accept the ambassador to the GDR, rather than the ambassador to the Federal Republic, as the Soviet representative and to conduct the sessions in the former Allied Control Commission building on the Potsdamer Platz as a symbol of continuing four-power responsibility for Greater Berlin.

The Soviet Union insisted on confining the discussions to four-power responsibility for West Berlin, arguing that East Berlin had been legally incorporated into the GDR by the 1964 Soviet friendship treaty, and that Allied authority should be used to curtail Bonn's continuing illegal activities in West Berlin, i.e. the suspension of national political activities. This view was supported by the rationale that West Berlin was an autonomous political unit within the GDR's sovereign territory.

The Western allies rejected this proposal, insisting that they retained ultimate authority over the Western sectors, which had been legally, politically, and economically integrated into the Federal Republic as an interim measure, pending a final settlement. The three Allies were prepared only to negotiate a legally binding agreement governing the access routes between the Federal Republic and West Berlin, i.e. three air corridors, three railway lines, four highways, and two canals. For her part, the GDR had argued since 1964 that West Berlin was an independent political entity on her sovereign territory and that she exercised administrative authority over the access routes as a function of her sovereign rights. She had legally incorporated the Soviet sector into the GDR, designated it the state's national capital, and in March 1969 had integrated its political representatives into the national Volkskammer in violation of Allied directives. But in the light of the repeated references to the sanctity of the responsibilities enshrined in the Potsdam Agreement, the GDR was obliged to allow the Soviet Union to defend her interests in any discussions over Berlin.

The West German position was that the Basic Law and the enabling Allied documents prescribed West Berlin's legal status and connection with the Federal Republic. These documents and the constitution of the *Land* of Berlin define West Berlin's special status. Berlin cannot be governed by Bonn, and does not possess the characteristics of a normal *Land*. The laws of the Federal Republic are not applicable to West Berlin until the city parliament has adopted them as local statutes. West Berlin does not participate in Federal elections and sends delegates to the Bundestag as observers only; it is exempt from conscription for the *Bundeswehr* and some other provisions of the Federal constitution. Thus the Allies and the West Germans have created West Berlin as a semi-autonomous political entity.

During the recent negotiations in Warsaw and Moscow, Bonn attempted to avoid the legal tangles and clearly stated that its acceptance of the *status quo* in Eastern Europe, as defined in the treaties, was contingent upon Soviet and East German concurrence in the existing realities in West Berlin. Soviet compliance was to be in the form of a legally binding document, prohibiting interference with the access routes, and guaranteeing the viability of the city and the transit of its inhabitants between the East and West sectors.

On 10 February 1970 the Soviet Union finally agreed and the four-power talks opened on 26 March. This was the first time since 1959 that the four powers had come together to discuss Berlin, and the first occasion that such talks were not the result of Soviet threats and pressures. In the fifteen sessions conducted over the ensuing year, however, some progress was noted in the differing interpretations of authority, status, and rights.

The key to the dispute is the relevance of the Potsdam Agreement to existing realities and the importance each party attaches to legal as opposed to pragmatic considerations. The Soviet Union and Poland stressed acceptance of the *status quo* in negotiations with Bonn, but agreed not completely to abrogate the provisions of the Potsdam accord pertaining to the eastern territories. On the other hand, the Soviet Union cited the Potsdam Agreement as justification for her claims to equal status in the Western sectors of Berlin, and the three Allies referred to the same document as grounds for their rights in East Berlin. Yet both Germanies placed a higher priority on Allied acceptance of the existing circumstances, though neither was completely satisfied with the provisions for her allotted share of the divided city. Thus the emphasis on the *status quo* in the Polish and Soviet treaties, reinforced by that of both Germanies on existing realities, undermines the moral authority and political relevance to an eventual settlement of the Allied documentation. Progress towards a durable settlement of the Berlin problem cannot be made until all six parties agree on new terms of reference, based on a mutually acceptable formula combining elements both of the *status quo* and of Allied responsibility. This new formula must include guarantees for continued Soviet influence in Berlin, for the viability of the Western sectors, for the rights of its citizens to determine their political destiny, as well as for the national interests of both the East and West Germans.

In a public interview Wehner referred to the forthcoming Berlin talks as being ' the most difficult and probably the most important ones '. He predicted that they would soon arrive at a point where, as happened in 1959, the question of what should be permitted in West Berlin would be crucial. The Soviet Union would presumably insist that this question could be decided only by the four powers, including herself. Wehner also expected that attempts would be made to ignore ' East Berlin's incorporation into the GDR '. The Western powers permitted that incorporation, but they ' cannot digest it ' without abandoning their position.[19] Wehner's sagacity soon became apparent.

The Western negotiating position was explained in detail by Klaus Schütz. The West hoped that the talks would provide: (1) an end to East German interference with traffic between West Berlin and West Germany; (2) formalities at crossing-points into East Germany that accorded with international custom; (3) agreement

[19] *Die Welt*, 2 Mar. 1970.

to allow West Berliners to go to East Berlin and East Germany; (4) acceptance of the city's status as it has developed up to now, West Berlin being part of, although not belonging to, the Federal Republic's legal, financial, and economic system.

Schütz expected that ' Soviet acceptance of West Berlin's attachment to West Germany would be the toughest problem on which to reach agreement'.[20] Chancellor Brandt amplified this point.

The security of this city and its access routes is a three-power responsibility. We bear a high degree of responsibility for the viability of the city. We are not considering giving any of this up. We are determined to convince our Eastern partners too that the ties as they have grown between West Berlin and the Federal Republic are part of the realities from which one must proceed.[21]

Finally, the Allies insisted that their presence and authority in all Berlin was a fundamental right which could not unilaterally be abrogated or impaired by any interested party. The Allies intentionally had sought to preserve the legal and moral context of Berlin's special status, while the Soviet Union had delegated her authority over East Berlin to the GDR. This action was rejected by the Allies as illegal. They also claimed that the agreements of 1945 and 1949 were the source of their responsibility for the access routes to Berlin from West Germany and that the Soviet Union's delegation of her authority to the GDR in 1964 was illegal. Such decisions could only be made in conjunction with the other three partners.

For her part, the Soviet Union insisted that four-power authority was confined to West Berlin and did not pertain to East Berlin. This argument was based on legal premises and the *de facto* effectiveness of the transfer: the Allies no longer exercised any administrative control over the eastern half, and West Germany had extended *de facto* acceptance of East Berlin as the GDR's capital. Further, as early as 1955 the Soviet Union had argued that the transit of goods and persons was a matter for inter-German negotiations: she maintained the same position in 1970.

The Soviet stand began to harden as early as the second

[20] *Bull.*, 5 May 1970.
[21] Ibid., 23 June 1970.

session of the talks in April. The Soviet Union maintained that she could not interfere in the matters of a sovereign state (the GDR) and could not recommend the restoration of the customary transit regulations until the GDR's desire for full international recognition had been met. (The GDR underlined the importance of this argument on the opening day of the second session by increasing the toll rates for goods crossing her territory by 30 per cent, or DM 12 m. per annum.)

The fourth, fifth, and sixth sessions in June and July focused on the Soviet viewpoint of the status of West Berlin. The Soviet ambassador Abrasimov was reported to have stated that the Allied presence in West Berlin could no longer be justified on the grounds of military victory, but only at the sufferance of the Soviet Union. And he presented a long list of ' illegal ' West German political activities in Berlin which must be suspended. The Soviet Union would accept the economic and cultural ties between West Berlin and the Federal Republic but not the legal and political relations hitherto maintained.[22]

The Allies responded that they were prepared to make far-reaching concessions in exchange for reciprocity. In agreement with Bonn, they offered to reduce the demonstrative Federal presence and constitutional transactions in West Berlin by restraining the Federal President from conducting official actions and the Bundestag from holding sessions in the city. In return, the Allies expected concessions on normalization of the access routes.[23] (President Heinemann has intentionally observed this practice, and the Bundestag no longer holds sessions outside Bonn. Moreover, the Allied offer would not have impaired the current practice whereby the Chancellor, ministers, and parliamentary working groups travel to West Berlin to debate and conduct routine business. The Allies were apparently not prepared to accept the Soviet demand that the Berlin-located Federal agencies be dismantled and their 23,000 employees discharged.) The Soviet Union apparently did not respond; and there was thus an impasse.

[22] West German spokesman denied numerous other accounts of the confidential proceeding, but refused to comment on this one (*Christ und Welt*, 3 July 1970).

[23] In an address in Berlin on 1 July, Ambassador Rush omitted any reference to legal and political ties, while stressing economic integration as the basis for continuing stability, an omission that was noted by many West German papers.

At the seventh session in September the Allies tabled a
'working concept' pertaining to their priority issue, Berlin
access routes. It was designed mainly to reduce untimely
delays and unwarranted interference, yet still to provide the
East Germans with adequate assurances against the smuggling
of refugees by sealing all goods containers crossing East German
territory. Autobahn visas and taxes would be paid in a lump
sum by the Federal Republic rather than individually. An
international authority, including both East German and Soviet
members, would be created to mediate grievances and complaints. And the 'Berlin clause', incorporating West Berlin
into the Federal Republic for commercial reasons, would
automatically be accepted by all socialist states in transactions
with Bonn.[24] Thus in the first six months both sides had stated
their broad positions and presented their initial proposals for
meeting their respective demands.

During this period several peculiarities emerged in the
negotiations. As it became apparent that not even a margin
of agreement existed between the four powers on the larger
issues of rights and status, the Allies sought to divert the focus
of the talks to smaller pragmatic problems that could substantially be resolved at the working level. The Soviet Union
refused to do this, insisting on continuing top-level meetings
dealing with fundamental issues. She is reported even to have
introduced various proposals that would tend to 'institutionalize' the talks. The Allies employed the device of presenting
working papers on specific matters, but the Soviet responses
tended to avoid details and commitments on specific items.
(The first working-level session was authorized only in December, and throughout the first year of the talks the Soviet Union
apparently did not table a single itemized reply to Western
proposals.)

A second feature was the increasingly tough stand the Soviet
Union took on fundamental issues in Berlin at a time when
obvious progress was being made in the bilateral negotiations
between the East European countries and the Federal Republic.
Moscow attempted to erode the linkage Bonn had established
between ratification of the Soviet treaty and a solution in

[24] *The Times*, 2 Sept. 1970.

Berlin, when Supreme Soviet member Zhukov said in a German TV statement that the Berlin problem could be solved only after ratification. And Tsarapkin told the CDU delegate Philipp von Bismarck that ' you must ratify the treaty because we have the power '. The Soviet Embassy Secretary Popov, in an address at Eichholz near Bonn, stated that Moscow categorically rejected any West German political claims to West Berlin and would not accept West Berlin's representation by the Federal Republic in foreign policy. A settlement of the access problems was possible, he said, but the normalization of relations with the GDR was a prerequisite. Finally, Abrasimov asserted in a discussion with Schütz that the Soviet Union indeed had greater authority in Berlin than the Allies because she had conquered the city single-handed at heavy cost.[25] These scattered reports were viewed as an unexpected hardening in Moscow's stand and were supported by analyses of Soviet and East European news media, which indicated that since mid-September an increasingly antagonistic tone against Western and especially American policy was being adopted in broadcasts and news items.[26]

This sharp deterioration in the Soviet attitude on Berlin was accompanied by a resumption of harassment of Western traffic during military field manoeuvres, by Soviet cease-fire violations along the Suez Canal, and by the establishment of a submarine shore-supply point at Cienfuegos in Cuba. The cumulative impact of these seeming breaches of good faith prompted President Nixon to request a State Department review of Soviet intentions and to conduct prolonged discussions with Gromyko during his visit to the United Nations in October.

The Nixon–Gromyko talks apparently convinced the Soviet Union of the firmness of the American stand and the necessity of seeking alternative approaches to achieve her goals in Berlin. This was manifested in the lack of progress made in the next four sessions of the Berlin talks. Secretary Rogers told his NATO colleagues that in view of this immobility, the four Western partners had ' agreed that there is no need to acceler-

---

[25] Die Welt, 29 Sept., General-Anzeiger, 28 Sept., & Christ und Welt, 15 Oct. 1970.
[26] RFE, Research Memo, 9 Nov. 1970.

ate the pace of the Berlin discussion because there is no pressure on the Allied side to compromise '.[27]

The Soviet Union apparently adopted another approach, namely the decision on 28 October to reopen the inter-German dialogue and the introduction of direct East German claims into the Berlin dispute. Following the ninth session of the four-power talks, *Neues Deutschland* carried an article suggesting that the ' transportation of West Berlin's persons and goods . . . can only be regulated between the GDR and the Senate of West Berlin '.[28] This was followed by a similar comment the next day and driven home by Ulbricht himself when he said:

The government of the GDR has stated its readiness to start negotiations with the Federal government on questions of reciprocal transit of people and goods on the condition that any activities of other states in West Berlin which contradict the international status of this city and which violate the interests of the GDR and of other Socialist states be discontinued. Every word in my formulations, incidentally, is significant.[29]

Ulbricht elaborated at length on this theme at the 14th party Plenum in December, using the term ' mutual transit traffic '.

The East German formula raised several new questions by proposing to deal with West Berlin for traffic on the access routes and with the Federal Republic for mutual transit traffic (goods between the two countries and beyond to third states). In this manner, East Germany could contribute to a *de facto* acceptance of its three-Germanies thesis. Further, by establishing as a precondition the termination of ' any activities of other states ', which could only be the Allied powers, the GDR introduced a direct challenge to Allied responsibility for West Berlin and to the Potsdam Agreement. This is a logical consequence of the three-Germanies thesis, but it is the first time such a direct assault has been made on a document used ambiguously but so far not disregarded by the Soviet Union.

The Soviet reaction was difficult to analyse. At Erivan, in November, Brezhnev made his first public reference to West

[27] USIA *Bull.*, Bonn, no. 233, 4 Dec. 1970.
[28] *ND*, 5 Nov. 1970.
[29] Ibid., 9 Nov. 1970. This thesis was referred to again on 9, 20, & 28 Nov. & 10 Dec. 1970.

Berlin since the four-power talks began, which was later in-cluded in the communiqué of the Pact summit meeting of 2 December. The hope was expressed ' that the current negotia-tions on West Berlin are concluded with a mutually acceptable agreement serving the interests of *détente* in Central Europe as well as the needs of the population of West Berlin and the legiti-mate interests and sovereign rights of the GDR '.[30] Was this a sign of disarray or co-ordination? Referring to the December 1969 Pact decision to improve policy co-ordination, Brezhnev stated at the Hungarian Party Congress in November 1970, ' We have now developed the sound practice of consultation on current affairs '. But Ulbricht had complained of inadequate consultations.[31]

Brandt, on the other hand, quickly took up Ulbricht's offer. Recognizing the GDR's willingness to discuss transit problems, he stated: ' We could discuss a good number of such questions, including those concerning traffic through the two states to third states . . .'. Transportation problems were being dis-cussed in principle by the four powers. Only when agreement was reached among them could the Federal Republic open dis-cussions on a supplementary accord with the GDR.

Thus we differentiate between general traffic questions between the two states, which can be discussed soon, and questions relating to Berlin traffic, on which the Four Powers must reach a settlement of basic principles, which then can be supplemented by a German agreement on details.[32]

As the government spokesman von Wechmar stated in response to Ulbricht's proposal, agreement between the incom-patible views of Bonn and East Berlin could not be found over-night. Yet inter-German discussion of transit problems might be an important first move in the Berlin entanglement, which has been characterized to date by the difficulty in distinguishing between purely administrative matters and issues that could impinge upon national prerogatives and the interests of any of the six parties concerned.

Several proposed solutions for the status of Berlin have been

[30] Tass, 2 Dec. 1970.
[31] *German Tribune*, 24 Dec. 1970.
[32] *Bull.*, 8 Dec. 1970.

made officially and unofficially by both sides. These are: (1) The Liechtenstein model, whereby West Berlin would maintain economic, legal, and financial ties with the Federal Republic, and Bonn would represent West Berlin in foreign affairs. (2) The Luxembourg model, whereby the same ties would exist except in foreign affairs. (3) A six-party agreement guaranteeing the *Freie Stadt* status of all Berlin, with joint supervision by East and West Germany of common facilities and access routes. (4) *Freie Stadt* status for West Berlin with access routes and facilities either guaranteed by the great powers, constructed extra-territorially, or placed under international supervision. (5) A ' minimum settlement ' providing for *de jure* recognition of the *status quo*, or the ' maximum settlement ' providing for West Berlin's full integration into the Federal Republic. (6) The ' *status quo* plus ', whereby access routes would be internationalized in return for a ' higher degree of conditional recognition ' of the GDR. (7) *Freie Stadt* status under Allied sovereignty, with freedom to establish economic and financial relations with either German state, but with foreign policy conducted by the Allies. (8) The designation of West Berlin as a UN Trusteeship, with status and access routes guaranteed by the UN Trusteeship Council in which both East and West Germany would be represented.

In evaluating the feasibility of each model, several factors must be weighed. (1) The most crucial consideration is the continued viability and right of self-determination for West Berlin. (2) Continued survival depends ultimately on an American physical presence and military deterrence. (3) A degree of permanent Soviet influence in West Berlin will be the price for a lasting settlement; the model should both permit and contain Soviet authority. (4) In no other aspect of Soviet-German relations is the adage ' recognition of the GDR is too little ' as applicable as in Berlin. While the two Germanies adhere to such divergent political ideologies, the GDR will be able to harass West Berlin unless adequate political constraints are incorporated into the model. (5) No other problem in Soviet-German relations is as interrelated with other international issues as is the Berlin question. The West intentionally preserves Berlin's special status as a means of bringing the

Soviet Union to account on a variety of complaints. This has not always been successful and is likely to become less so as the East European national interests gradually increase. (6) The Allies have been relatively constant in their stand on Berlin and are likely to remain so. As strategic parity between the Soviet Union and the United States has increased, France has gradually closed ranks with the West, denying Moscow the tactical advantages it formerly enjoyed. (7) The Soviet Union regarded the city as a source of political influence, but the access routes as a source of instability. She has repeatedly stated that she will not accept another Danzig corridor between the Federal Republic and Berlin. Thus a settlement may depend upon distinguishing between the two problems and on how the four powers finally agree to delegate authority for supervising the access routes. (9) The chief reason for East Germany's obsession about eliminating Bonn's political presence in West Berlin is the Federal Republic's continuing insistence that this serves the former capital's all-German function. The incorporation of East Berlin into the GDR has firmly denied the city this role; Bonn's continued pretences are only a source of tensions and should be relinquished. (10) West Berlin's present function as an outpost could be converted to a bridge without any infringement of Western interests. Indeed, it could substantially improve the viability of the city and enhance Bonn's international political stature by diminishing a major restraint on its options.

The most feasible of these possible models currently appears to be a combination of several options negotiated in several stages—a variation of the ' agents ' thesis in which the four powers delegate specific responsibilities. In the first phase, the four powers would establish in a written agreement the general outline of a final settlement. This would provide that West Berlin would be linked with the Federal Republic economically, culturally, and juridically: but the demonstrative political Federal presence would be substantially reduced. Both parts of Berlin would remain under four-power authority, but the Soviet Union would state in a separate note that she regarded East Berlin as the capital of the GDR, and the Allies would issue individual notes affirming their jurisdiction over East Berlin and acknowledging their shared responsibility with the

Soviet Union for West Berlin. (This device would be the key to both assuring and containing Soviet influence in West Berlin. The Allies could retaliate against Soviet obstructive policies either by asserting their claims in East Berlin or restricting Soviet functions in the western half.) Internationally accepted customs regulations and transit fees would be guaranteed for all access routes. Western traffic through the Wall would be the subject only to normal rules of border crossings. West Berlin would be represented abroad by the Federal Republic but a Berlin representative would be attached to Bonn missions in socialist countries.

In the second phase of a Berlin settlement, the East and West Germans would be authorized by the four powers to discuss technical details; Bonn and East Berlin dealing primarily with transit-traffic problems and West Berlin and East Berlin concerned with inter-city facilities. To prevent protracted wrangling, the four powers' concepts would be precisely outlined and a rigid timetable provided for the conclusion of technical negotiations. In a third phase, the technical agreements reached between the two Germanies and West and East Berlin would be consolidated into a final enabling treaty signed by the four powers.

Such a formula would allow both the great powers and the two Germanies to retain their respective claims in Berlin, while ensuring a high degree of security and stability for West Berlin. The four powers would preserve their occupation authority, and in the event of violation or non-compliance with the enabling act by either German party they could theoretically mediate or impose a settlement on the Germans. The above formula meets more of the parties' interests, and closes more loopholes, than other proposals. As in other treaties embodying divergent viewpoints, the most difficult task is not the negotiation but the implementation of the agreement. More than any other settlement since the war, an adjustment in Berlin will depend on the extent of the goodwill of all six parties.

8

CONCLUSIONS

POLITICAL developments in Central Europe from 1968 to 1971
allowed both West Germany and the Soviet Union to advance
their historic national aims. Both powers were able to proceed
on parallel paths, rather than at each other's expense as was
attempted during the previous quarter century. For nearly
twenty-five years after her defeat, West Germany pursued the
policy aims of gaining integration and respectability in the
West while preserving her options in the East. Her international stature was considered a product of the two factors.
But the political standing of each Germany was reduced by
the challenge from the rival German state. When Bonn in
1969 opened an era of reconciliation with Eastern Europe, it
was able to mitigate the debilitating consequence of demanding
an international solution to the German problem on its own
terms, and to exceed the aspirations of the Weimar Republic
by promoting stability and security in the East. More than any
other European development since the end of World War II,
for example the collapse of the British Empire or the fall of de
Gaulle, the reconciliation between Eastern Europe and Bonn
has contributed to West Germany's stature as the leading
European power, second to the Soviet Union, in the 1970s.

Bonn's diplomacy has been skilful. After making concessions
unthinkable merely a year before, it firmly linked implementation of negotiated agreements to counter-concessions which
directly affected the growing *détente*, such as Berlin, and a
mutual reduction of armed forces. These tactics tended to
promote the *détente* and to force upon the opponent the onus
for delays and raising tension. After successfully negotiating
treaties normalizing relations with the Soviet Union and Poland
and opening a dialogue with Czechoslovakia, Bonn agreed to
reopen direct contacts with the GDR. The initial confrontations at Erfurt and Kassel had proved abortive because of East
German insistence upon full diplomatic recognition, a concession West Germany could not extend for emotional, moral, and
legal reasons. Bonn fell back on a hard line, pointing to its
opposition to recognition by third countries and East German

entry into international organizations as a demonstration of firmness on the issue. The result of the confrontation over recognition in the Federal Republic was to bring the main political parties into a virtually bipartisan position towards the Pact countries and to end the prospect of parliamentary in-fighting which both Poland and the Soviet Union hoped to be able to exploit. The effect in East Germany, on the other hand, was to encourage the SED to consolidate its rule and establish a more dynamic foreign policy to assert its own interests and consolidate its national identity.

Each German rival sought initially to constrain the other's influence and assert its own, but by different means. The GDR viewed recognition through participation in multilateral East–West conferences as the most acceptable way of gaining equal status with the Federal Republic in the West. On the other hand Bonn sought to isolate East Berlin through opening bilateral contacts with its allies. Rumania proved a valuable collaborator, and the GDR's priority aim of gaining recognition by creating an anti-West German front was irretrievably lost. Bucharest's two-Germanies policy was subsequently endorsed by its allies but not until, after the Czechoslovak crisis, Bonn modified its intentions of making gains at Moscow's expense. When Moscow acknowledged the sincerity of this new orien-tation, Poland was able to break out of her long-held tandem position, supporting East Germany. During the late 1950s and early 1960s she envisaged her security as a function of Soviet protection against ' the German menace ', but her diplomatic manoeuvrability as a result of the various regional arms-limitation schemes she sponsored. With the failure of these proposals and the growing military power of NATO, she viewed her defence against West German territorial claims in terms of unquestioned Pact solidarity. Accordingly, she sacri-ficed her former desire for manoeuvrability between the Soviet Union and the Germans.

The treaty Poland subsequently signed with Bonn, more than the German-Soviet treaty, thrust the Berlin question into the foreground. The three Allies retained their rights under the Potsdam Agreement, but in the light of West Germany's renunciation of territorial claims against Poland without the prescribed peace settlement, the utility of all the postwar documentation based on this accord became highly questionable. Further, the practices and behaviour of both Germanies, stressing acceptance of existing realities, also jeopardized the applicability of the Allied writ. Consequently, if the Allies wished to retain their status and influence in Berlin and to a lesser extent over ' all Germany ', they had to revise their legal terms of reference.

On the Soviet side, the long-term objective of extending Moscow's influence in German affairs was achieved through several major policy changes. After the Czechoslovak crisis, Moscow was able to shift priorities from its demands for regional stability to its allies' requirements of security through reconciliation. This shift was due in large part to Rumania's rejection of the common Pact claim that West Germany was ' the main threat ' to European peace. Denied a consensus, the other partners were inclined to view security in terms of settling national grievances. Moscow eventually endorsed the bilateral approach for the resolution of national problems and opened the door to West German penetration of Eastern Europe; but was itself thereby enabled to use the same aperture to enter the West. It is not possible to predict whether the elimination of the West German threat and the confirmation of Bonn's respectability will strengthen Moscow's position in Eastern Europe. The Polish food riots in December 1970 indicate that, after twenty-five years of socialist rule, domestic issues are still more gripping than those of foreign policy. This suggests that the obsolescence of the Soviet model for socialism in Eastern Europe is the chief challenge to Soviet authority. In this light, will West German economic penetration, however limited, be a dependable trade-off for the still unpredictable degree of influence Moscow can expect in trans-Elbian affairs? While the value and risks of this exchange are still largely indeterminable, Moscow has probably concluded that it has enhanced its global flexibility by reducing a source of continuous challenge and potential instability through its adjustment with Bonn.

In the 1970s the German problem is likely to become largely an inter-German dispute, with tensions between the two states remaining relatively high. The GDR cannot humanize the partition until she liberalizes her rule and bridges the economic gap—processes that are unlikely to be completed in this decade. Thus the chief sources of tension are likely to persist, albeit at a more subdued level than in the 1950s and 1960s, and the inability to humanize the division and deprive the Wall of its emotional impact will continue to be the grounds for acute frustration in West Germany, especially after witnessing the enormous concessions Bonn granted the East. What price can the Federal Republic be expected to demand if the frustrations become unacceptable—a variation of a Rapacki Plan, neutrality *à la* Sweden, or the return of a national conservative government?

The Soviet Union viewed the German-Soviet treaty as a means of stabilizing Eastern Europe, but its implementation could be used as an instrument for advancing her ultimate aim, loosening Bonn's ties with the NATO countries. If Moscow can raise the price for Berlin settlement, either by exorbitant demands or by protracted bargaining, the Brandt government may feel compelled, if it is to survive, to raise counter-claims with its allies, namely that greater emphasis be placed on accepting the existing realities at the expense of the diluted postwar Allied responsibilities. Without the conclusion of a new contractual accord governing Berlin and the limits of all parties' interests and obligations, Moscow could continue to exercise the vestiges of its postwar authority in the divided city as a negative influence over Federal policy in West Berlin. A contest of this scale suggests that the SPD's vision of a new order in Central Europe is more complicated than confidence building through negotiating a series of legal treaties and outlining a framework for the demonstration of goodwill; it must be based solidly on power politics, a game the Soviet Union has mastered. The recent adjustment in Soviet and West German policies has moved relations between the two past the most important milestone since Germany's defeat. But in the continuing rivalry, search for security, and influence in European affairs, these relations will remain transitional, with new dimensions added to the judgements and policies of both sides, projecting new uncertainties into the calculus of European *détente*.

Long-term implications

Legal and constitutional arrangements are clearly not sufficient to ensure a durable settlement for so contentious a problem. The solution must incorporate those provisions which will make it in the interest of all parties, especially East Germany, to promote its implementation. Identification of these provisions will require insight into the broad future developments likely to affect the six states' interests in Berlin. In the mid-1970s the potential political role of the Federal Republic and her security requirements are both likely to be the most dynamic and controversial changes facing the other five parties. This generalization is based on the assumption that her economic and political growth potential is greater than that of any one of the five. Broadening economic integration in Western Europe and the recent expansion of her commercial activities in Eastern Europe are likely to enhance her stature as the leading European industrial state. Further, her recent negotiation of the main East European grievances and the expected gradual amelioration of her differences with East Germany will remove these former obsessions and constraints on her political options. As the leading spokesman for Western Europe, with growing latitude in Germany's traditional area of manoeuvre, Eastern Europe, the Federal Republic may enjoy greater freedom of political action by 1975 than has been enjoyed by her or by any other European state, except the Soviet Union, in the past thirty-five years.

The durability of any negotiated settlement, therefore, will depend on future developments in two broad areas. First, will the Pact countries see in the emergence of the Federal Republic as the leading European industrial and political power an inevitable threat to their national interests: a resurgence of German dynamism and a harbinger of potential German domination? Are they likely to conclude that the expected steady expansion of her influence will move her back into Germany's traditional position between Eastern and Western Europe without solving the classical German problem; to secure the optimal frontiers and social order for the Germans which are also acceptable to all their neighbours? In other words, should not the Federal Republic begin now to think as much about how to diminish her neighbours' anxieties as about how to employ her new international authority?

The second consideration is the degree of security Western Europe can expect over the next five years. Over the past two decades, the communist threat has provided the cohesive reagent for Western security arrangements. But the nature of the East–West military balance in the 1970s, characterized by great-power parity, has fundamentally altered the nature of the threat to the West and the Federal Republic's role in collective defence. Bonn's future military posture appears to be the most acceptable instrument for ensuring favourable conditions in two areas of potential instability: the apprehensions of Germany's neighbours and Western security interests.

As the Federal Republic becomes the focal point of non-Soviet Europe, she will still not be the military equal of the Soviet Union, even though she may exercise unprecedented power. The challenge facing her during the early 1970s will probably still continue to be how to accommodate the East and at the same time reassure the West. But thereafter she may again chafe under the continuing domination and shadow of a power whose values she does not respect. Priorities may again be reversed, in favour of a more overt challenge to Eastern influence and ideals. A continuing grievance that may prompt this change will be the persisting, though somewhat mitigated, division of Germany. In pursuing such a more assertive foreign policy, the Federal Republic must be guided by the lessons of the Prague crisis: that there will be no basic changes in Eastern Europe until there are changes in Moscow, and that the extension of influence into this region must start at the top, not the bottom. Accordingly, Bonn will probably be forced to view its national salvation increasingly through a Soviet perspective. Herein lies the root of the continuing German-Soviet confrontation.

Naturally this challenge to Federal interests will not take an aggressive turn, even if the frustration reaches unprecedented heights. More likely, other goals may be changed, i.e. the present dependence on US strategic deterrence. The conversion of European NATO's forces to a highly effective defensive force equipped with usable tactical nuclear weapons would be an important first step in restoring the alliance to its original purpose, if the United States were to allocate only sufficient resources to support European provisions for self-defence. Such modernization of forces and doctrinal change would increase security and introduce sizeable economies. Existing forces could be reduced by one-third if the availability of tactical nuclear firepower were proportionately increased. By the mid-1970s a European Nuclear Force could become operational if planning were started at once. A regional nuclear force, based on French and British physical assets and West German financial resources, could permit a posture of armed neutrality resembling that of Sweden. While the Atlantic Alliance would remain intact, the formation of an integrated European nuclear deterrent would eliminate the hostage value of US troops in Europe without impairing regional security or weakening the credibility of US commitments.

American interest in preserving European independence will remain constant, with or without troops on the Continent. British interest in the Low Countries was maintained for several centuries without a military presence. To pursue the analogy of Swedish neutrality, the United States has made it clear that she regards Swedish independence as an important American interest. In recent cases when a US President has considered that his country would have to go to war sooner or later, he has in fact decided in favour of prompt action. Moreover, if one accepts the premise that the most likely great-power contests in the age of parity will be the deployment of nuclear submarines, then the United States will have to be prepared to pay an extremely high price to prevent Soviet access to the Atlantic. Finally, with the creation of an integrated West European military power, would European defences serve as the tripwire for aggression or force the European partners to determine what interests must be defended? A European definition of vital interests and determination to ensure their defence is the most promising formula, given the present American climate of opinion, to ensure prompt US participation in collective security. For these reasons, then, American commitments should remain credible and Western deterrence should hold. Such strategic concepts may increasingly appeal to West German leaders, both for domestic and international reasons. The greater initial budgetary outlay involved would result in important long-term economies, and yet would afford Bonn a proportionally larger voice in their disposition. More significant, the adoption of a more effective defence posture would provide adequate security for the Federal Republic without seeming to threaten her neighbours.

But the final appeal these strategic concepts may have for the Federal Republic is the response they could elicit from the Pact countries. To date the Soviet price for a durable solution of Central European problems has been the dismantling of the transatlantic military link. Now it is reasonable to suppose that the imaginary force of this linkage can be weakened without endangering the ultimate interests of either side of the Atlantic. The implicit aim behind the Soviet demand is that a reduced US military presence will foster greater autonomy in Western Europe and deference to Soviet interests. The former, greater regional autonomy, is probably inevitable and should not be feared by any NATO partner. The latter, the 'finlandization' of West Europe, is a possibility that must be guarded against by both Europeans and Americans.

Finally, the durability of Central Europe's problems will depend upon the interaction of the two German states and its impact on their respective allies. The political future of the GDR is more problematic than that of the Federal Republic. Yet it is possible that East Germany's form of national communism may evolve in the direction of Yugoslavia's and Hungary's, and that this might allow her to remain ideologically embattled with Bonn while exploring common grounds for political co-operation. Indeed, it is possible that by the mid-1970s the two Germanies will remain separate and the partition a grievous affront, and yet that the two entities may gradually establish a similarity of views on certain European issues. A growing German ' togetherness ' on selected foreign-policy issues would augur well for the defusing of the German question, but it would create a profound sense of alarm among both friends and foes.

Thus as the West seeks a solution to the outstanding questions in Central Europe, it must recognize the realities of West

Germany's increasing international authority and the continuing concern of her neighbours about the application of this growing power. In seeking a settlement of such problems as Berlin, the West must strive for pragmatic means of inducing East–West political co-operation, as well as legally-binding commitments. A durable arrangement should include both mutual obligations and confidence-building undertakings, such as adoption of a low-profile defensive strategy. Only a combination of this type will accommodate West German political aspirations and East European security interests in a lasting settlement of the German problem.

APPENDIX I

Principal Warsaw Pact Meetings, including the Karlovy Vary Meeting of Communist and Workers' Parties

1965

19–20 Jan.   PCC meeting, Warsaw. (Communiqué, *E-A*, 20th yr, 1965, Dokumente, pp. D 108–10.)

1966

8 July   PCC meeting, Bucharest. (Declaration on Strengthening Peace and Security in Europe ['Bucharest Declaration'], *E-A*, 21st yr, 1966, Dokumente, pp. D 414–24; *Survival*, Sept. 1966.)

1967

8–10 Feb.   Foreign Ministers' meeting, Warsaw. (*E-A*, 22nd yr, 1967, Dokumente, pp. D 123–4.)

24–26 April   Karlovy Vary meeting of Communist and Workers' Parties. (Declaration 'For Peace and Security in Europe', *E-A*, 22nd yr, 1967, Dokumente, pp. D 259–66.)

1968

26 Feb.– 5 March   Budapest consultative meeting for preparation of all-party conference.

6–7 March   PCC meeting, Sofia. (Communiqué, *E-A*, 23rd yr, 1968, Dokumente, pp. D 181–2.)

23 March   Meeting of party and government heads, Dresden (*E-A*, 23rd yr, 1968, Dokumente, pp. D 187–8.)

1969

17 March   PCC meeting, Budapest. (Address to all European Countries, *Survival*, May, 1969.)

30–31 Oct.   Foreign Ministers' meeting, Prague. (Declaration on a European Security Conference, *E-A*, 24th yr, 1969, Dokumente, pp. D 551–2.)

3–4 Dec.   PCC meeting, Moscow. (Communiqué, *E-A*, 25th yr, 1970, Dokumente, pp. D 76–7.)

1970

21–22 June   Foreign Ministers' meeting, Budapest. (Memorandum, *Survival*, Sept. 1970.)

2 Dec.   PCC meeting, East Berlin. (Statement, *Survival*, Feb. 1971.)

APPENDIX II

Draft Treaty on the Establishment of Equal Relations Between the German Democratic Republic and the Federal Republic of Germany, 17 December, 1969 [1]

The Chairman of the State Council of the German Democratic Republic and the President of the Federal Republic of Germany, guided by their endeavour to make an effective contribution to *détente* and securing of peace in Europe, to remove tension between the two German states step-by-step, to bring about good neighbourly relations as equal sovereign states, and to advance the creation of a European security system, have decided to sign a treaty establishing equal relations between the German Democratic Republic and the German Federal Republic and have appointed as their plenipotentiaries:

The Chairman of the State Council of the German Democratic Republic; Herr Willi Stoph, Chairman of the Ministerial Council; Herr Otto Winzer, Minister for Foreign Affairs.

The President of the Federal Republic of Germany; Herr Willy Brandt, Federal Chancellor; Herr Walter Scheel, West German Foreign Minister.

After exchanging their authorizations in an appropriate and seemly form, they have reached agreement on the following points:

Article I

The parties to the treaty agree to the establishment of normal equal relations between the German Democratic Republic and the Federal Republic of Germany, free of any discrimination and on the basis of generally recognized principles and norms of international law. Their mutual relations are based in particular on the principles of sovereign equality, territorial integrity, inviolability of state frontiers, non-interference in internal affairs and mutual advantage.

Article II

The parties to the treaty mutually recognize their present territorial holding within the existing borders and the inviolability thereof. They recognize the borders in Europe fixed as a result of World War II, in particular those between the German Democratic Republic and the Federal Republic of Germany as well as the frontier on the Oder and Neisse between the German Democratic Republic and the People's Republic of Poland.

---

[1] *E-A*, 25th yr, 1970, Dokumente, pp. D190–3.

Article III

The parties to the treaty undertake to renounce the threat and use of force in their mutual relationship and to solve all disputes between themselves in a peaceful way and by peaceful means.

Both sides undertake to avoid all measures contrary to the accords stated in Article I and which would discriminate against the partner of the treaty, to repeal without delay laws and regulations contrary to this treaty, and to have corresponding court decisions revised. They will also in future avoid any discrimination against the treaty partner.

Article IV

The German Democratic Republic and the Federal Republic of Germany renounce the acquisition of nuclear weapons or the disposal of the same in any way. They undertake to support the start of disarmament negotiations. No chemical or biological weapons may be produced, stationed or stocked on the soil of either German state.

Article V

The German Democratic Republic and the Federal Republic of Germany are establishing diplomatic relations. They will be mutually represented by embassies in the capitals of Berlin and Bonn. The embassies will enjoy all the immunities and privileges prescribed by the Vienna Convention on diplomatic relations of 18 April 1961.

Article VI

Relations on specific questions will be agreed upon separately.

Article VII

The German Democratic Republic and the Federal Republic of Germany pledge themselves to recognize the status of West Berlin as an independent political unit and, in accordance with this status, to regulate their relations with West Berlin.

Article VIII

The German Democratic Republic and the Federal Republic of Germany apply, without delay, in conformity with the principle of universality of the organization of the United Nations, for their admission as full members of the United Nations. They will advocate that other states support the admission of both German states to the organization of the United Nations.

Article IX

The treaty is effective for 10 years. It is subject to ratification and comes into effect one month after exchange of ratification documents. This treaty will be handed over to the Secretariat of the organization of the United Nations for registration, according to Article 102 of the Charter of the United Nations.

APPENDIX III

20-Point Memorandum of the Federal Government on the Principles and Elements of a Treaty for the Establishment of Equal Relations between the Federal Republic of Germany and the German Democratic Republic, 21 May 1970[1]

1. The Federal Republic of Germany and the German Democratic Republic, whose constitutions are oriented to the unity of the nation, conclude, in the interest of peace and of the future and coherence of the nation, a treaty regulating relations between the two States in Germany, improving contact between the populations of the two States, and thereby keep helping to eliminate existing disadvantages.

2. The agreement shall be submitted to the respective legislative bodies of both sides for approval, in the form prescribed by their constitutions.

3. Both sides shall proclaim their desire to regulate their relations on the basis of human rights, equality, peaceful coexistence, and non-discrimination as the generally valid rules of law governing relations between States.

4. Both sides abstain from using or threatening to use force against each other, and undertake to resolve all existing mutual problems by peaceful means. This includes respect for each other's territorial integrity and frontiers.

5. Both sides respect the independence and autonomy of each of the two States in matters relating to their internal sovereignty.

6. Neither of the two German States can act on behalf of or represent the other.

7. The two contracting parties declare that war must never again originate in Germany.

8. They undertake to refrain from any actions likely to disturb the peaceful coexistence of nations.

9. The two sides reaffirm their intention to support all efforts to achieve disarmament and arms control which will enhance European security.

10. The treaty must proceed from the consequences of the Second World War and the particular situation of Germany and of the Germans, who live in two States, and yet regard themselves as belonging to one nation.

---

[1] *E-A*, 25th yr, 1970, Dokumente, pp. D332–3.

11. Their respective responsibilities towards the French Republic, the United Kingdom of Great Britain and Northern Ireland, the United States of America, and the Union of Soviet Socialist Republics, which are based on the special rights and agreements of those powers with respect to Berlin and Germany as a whole, shall remain unaffected.

12. The Four-Power agreements on Berlin and Germany will be respected. The same applies to the links that have developed between West Berlin and the Federal Republic of Germany.

Both sides undertake to support the Four Powers in their efforts to bring about a normalization of the situation in and around Berlin.

13. Both sides will examine the areas where the legislation of the two States collides; they will endeavour to eliminate such collision so as to avoid creating disadvantages for the citizens of the two States in Germany. In doing so they will start from the principle that the sovereign authority of each side is limited to its respective territory.

14. The treaty shall provide for measures to increase the possibilities for travel between the two States and seek to achieve freedom of movement.

15. A solution shall be found for the problems ensuing from the separation of families.

16. The district and municipal authorities in the border areas shall be empowered to solve local problems on a good-neighbourly basis.

17. Both sides shall reaffirm their readiness to intensify and extend their co-operation in various fields, such as transport and travel, postal relations and telecommunications, the exchange of information, science, education, culture, environmental problems and sport, to their mutual advantage, and to open negotiations on the details.

18. As regards mutual trade, the existing agreements, commissions, and arrangements will continue to apply. Trade relations shall be further developed.

19. The two governments appoint plenipotentiaries with the rank of Minister and establish offices for the permanent representatives of the plenipotentiaries. The duties of the plenipotentiaries and their representatives will be specified. They will be given working facilities at the seat of the respective government and be afforded the necessary facilities and privileges.

20. On the basis of the treaty to be concluded between them the

Federal Republic of Germany and the German Democratic Republic will make the necessary arrangements for their membership of and participation in international organizations.

APPENDIX IV
The Bahr Paper, 22 May 1970[1]

1. The Federal Republic of Germany and the Union of Soviet Socialist Republics consider it an important objective of their policies to maintain international peace and achieve *détente*.

They affirm their endeavour to further the normalization of the situation in Europe on this basis, and in so doing proceed from the actual situation existing in this region, and the development of peaceful relations among all European states.

2. The Federal Republic of Germany and the Union of Soviet Socialist Republics shall in their mutual relations as well as in matters of ensuring European and international security be guided by the purposes and principles embodied in the Charter of the United Nations. Accordingly they shall settle their disputes exclusively by peaceful means and undertake to refrain from the threat or use of force, pursuant to Article 2 of the Charter of the United Nations, in any matters affecting security in Europe or international security, as well as in their bilateral relations.

3. The Federal Republic of Germany and the Union of Soviet Socialist Republics share the realization that peace can only be maintained in Europe if nobody disturbs the present frontiers.

They undertake to respect without restriction the territorial integrity of all states in Europe within their present frontiers.

They declare that they have no territorial claims against anybody nor will assert such claims in the future.

They regard today and shall in future regard the frontiers of all states in Europe as inviolable such as they are on the date of signature of the present Treaty, including the Oder–Neisse line which forms the western frontier of the People's Republic of Poland and the frontier between the Federal Republic of Germany and the German Democratic Republic.

4. The present Treaty between the Federal Republic of Germany and the Union of Soviet Socialist Republics does not affect the bilateral and multilateral treaties or arrangements previously concluded by them.

[1] *E-A*, 25th yr, 1970, Dokumente, pp. D394–5.

5. The Governments of the Federal Republic of Germany and the Union of Soviet Socialist Republics are in agreement that the Soviet–German treaty signed in Moscow on 12 August and corresponding agreements (treaties) between the Federal Republic and other socialist countries, in particular the agreements (treaties) with the German Democratic Republic (cf. Art. 6), the People's Republic of Poland and the Czechoslovakian Socialist Republic (cf. Art. 8), form a single whole.

6. The Government of the Federal Republic declares its readiness to conclude an agreement with the German Democratic Republic which will have the same binding force customary between states, as do other agreements which the Federal Republic and the GDR conclude with third countries. Accordingly the Government of the Federal Republic will shape its relations with the GDR on the basis of full equality of rights, non-discrimination and respect for the independence and autonomy of each of the two states in matters which affect their internal competence within their respective frontiers.

The Government of the Federal Republic assumes that on this basis, according to which neither of the two states can represent the other abroad or act in its name, the relations of the GDR and the FRG with third countries will be developed.

7. The Governments of the Federal Republic and the Soviet Union declare their readiness, in the course of *détente* in Europe and in the interest of improvement of relations between the countries of Europe, in particular the FRG and the GDR, to undertake steps which derive from their respective positions, to promote the entry of the Federal Republic and the German Democratic Republic into the United Nations and its Specialized Agencies.

8. The Governments of the Federal Republic and the Soviet Union are in agreement that questions connected with the invalidity of the Munich Agreement should be regulated in negotiations between the Federal Republic and the Czechoslovakian Socialist Republic in a form acceptable to both sides.

9. The Governments of the Federal Republic and the Soviet Union will further develop the economic, scientific and technical, cultural and other relations between the FRG and the USSR in the interest of both parties and the strengthening of peace in Europe.

10. The Governments of the Federal Republic and the Soviet Union welcome the plan for a conference on questions of strengthening security and co-operation in Europe, and will do everything in their power for its preparation and successful realization.

APPENDIX V

Treaty Between the Federal Republic of Germany and the Union of Soviet Socialist Republics, 12 August 1970[1]

The High Contracting Parties
ANXIOUS to contribute to strengthening peace and security in Europe and the world,
CONVINCED that peaceful co-operation among states on the basis of the purposes and principles of the Charter of the United Nations complies with the ardent desire of nations and the general interests of international peace,
APPRECIATING the fact that the agreed measures previously implemented by them, in particular the conclusion of the agreement of 13 September 1955 on the establishment of diplomatic relations, have created favourable conditions for new important steps destined to develop further and to strengthen their mutual relations,
DESIRING to lend expression, in the form of a treaty, to their determination to improve and extend co-operation between them, including economic relations as well as scientific, technical, and cultural contacts, in the interest of both states,
HAVE AGREED as follows:

Article I

The Federal Republic of Germany and the Union of Soviet Socialist Republics consider it an important objective of their policies to maintain international peace and achieve *détente*.
They affirm their endeavour to further the normalization of the situation in Europe and the development of peaceful relations among all European states, and in so doing proceed from the actual situation existing in this region.

Article II

The Federal Republic of Germany and the Union of Soviet Socialist Republics shall in their mutual relations as well as in matters of ensuring European and international security be guided by the purposes and principles embodied in the Charter of the United Nations. Accordingly they shall settle their disputes exclusively by peaceful means and undertake to refrain from the threat or use of force, pursuant to Article 2 of the Charter of the United Nations, in any matters affecting security in Europe or international security, as well as in their mutual relations.

[1] *E-A*, 25th yr, 1970, pp. D397–8.

Article III

In accordance with the foregoing purposes and principles the Federal Republic of Germany and the Union of Soviet Socialist Republics share the realization that peace can only be maintained in Europe if no one disturbs the present frontiers.

—They undertake to respect unreservedly the territorial integrity of all States in Europe within their present frontiers;

—they declare that they have no territorial claims against anyone nor will assert such claims in the future;

—they regard today and shall in future regard the frontiers of all States in Europe as inviolable such as they are on the date of signature of the present Treaty, including the Oder–Neisse line which forms the western frontier of the People's Republic of Poland, and the frontier between the Federal Republic of Germany and the German Democratic Republic.

Article IV

The present Treaty between the Federal Republic of Germany and the Union of Soviet Socialist Republics shall not affect any bilateral and multilateral treaties or agreements previously concluded by them.

Article V

The present Treaty is subject to ratification and shall enter into force on the date of exchange of the instruments of ratification which shall take place in Bonn.

Done at Moscow on 12 August 1970 in two originals, each in the German and Russian languages, both texts being equally authentic.

Notes from the Federal Government to the Governments of the Three Western Powers on the responsibility of the Four Powers with regard to Germany and Berlin, 7 August 1970[1]

The Government of the Federal Republic of Germany has the honour, in connection with the imminent signing of a Treaty between the Federal Republic of Germany and the Union of Soviet Socialist Republics, to inform it of the following:

The Federal Minister for Foreign Affairs has, in the context of the negotiations, set forth the Federal Government's position as regards the rights and responsibilities of the four powers with regard to Germany as a whole and Berlin.

[1] *E-A*, 25th yr, 1970, Dokumente, pp. 396–7.

Since a peace settlement is still outstanding both sides proceeded on the understanding that the proposed Treaty does not affect the rights and responsibilities of the French Republic, the United Kingdom of Great Britain and Northern Ireland, the Union of Soviet Socialist Republics and the United States of America.

The Federal Minister for Foreign Affairs has in this connection declared to the Soviet Foreign Minister on 6 August 1970:

' The question of the rights of the four powers is in no way connected with the Treaty which the Federal Republic of Germany and the Union of Soviet Socialist Republics intend to conclude, and will not be affected by it.'

The Foreign Minister of the Union of Soviet Socialist Republics thereupon made the following declaration:

' The question of the rights of the four powers was not the subject of negotiations with the Federal Republic of Germany.

' The Soviet Government therefore proceeded on the understanding that this question should not be discussed.

' Nor will the question of the rights of the four powers be affected by the Treaty which the USSR and the Federal Republic of Germany intend to conclude. This is the position of the Soviet Government regarding this question.'

Note from the Government of the United States to the Federal Government, 11 August 1970[1]

The Government of the United States takes full cognizance of this Note, including the declarations made by the Foreign Minister of the Federal Republic of Germany and the Foreign Minister of the Union of Soviet Socialist Republics as part of the negotiations prior to the initialling of the treaty which is to be concluded between the Federal Republic of Germany and the Soviet Union.

For its part, the Government of the United States also considers that the rights and responsibilities of the four powers with regard to Berlin and Germany as a whole which derive from the outcome of the Second World War and which are reflected in the London Agreement of 14 November 1944, and in the Quadripartite Declaration of 5 June 1945, and in other wartime and post-war agreements are not and cannot be affected by a bilateral treaty between the Federal Republic of Germany and the Union of Soviet Socialist Republics, including the present treaty.

[1] Ibid., p. 397.

Letter from the Foreign Minister of the Federal Republic, Walter Scheel, to the Soviet Foreign Minister, Andrei Gromyko, 12 August 1970[1]

In connection with today's signature of the Treaty between the Federal Republic of Germany and the Union of Soviet Socialist Republics the Government of the Federal Republic of Germany has the honour to state that this Treaty does not conflict with the political objective of the Federal Republic of Germany to work for a state of peace in Europe in which the German nation will recover its unity in free self-determination.

APPENDIX VI

Treaty Between the Federal Republic of Germany and the People's Republic of Poland[2]

The Federal Republic of Germany
and
the People's Republic of Poland

CONSIDERING that more than 25 years have passed since the end of the Second World War of which Poland became the first victim and which inflicted great suffering on the nations of Europe,
CONSCIOUS that in both countries a new generation has meanwhile grown up to whom a peaceful future should be secured,
DESIRING to establish durable foundations for peaceful coexistence and the development of normal and good relations between them,
ANXIOUS to strengthen peace and security in Europe,
AWARE that the inviolability of frontiers and respect for the territorial integrity and sovereignty of all States in Europe within their present frontiers are a basic condition for peace,
HAVE AGREED as follows:

Article I

1. The Federal Republic of Germany and the People's Republic of Poland state in mutual agreement that the existing boundary line the course of which is laid down in Chapter IX of the Decisions of the Potsdam Conference of 2 August 1945 as running from the

---

[1] Ibid., p. 399.
[2] *E-A*, 26th yr, 1971, pp. D25–6.

Baltic Sea immediately west of Swinemünde, and thence along the Oder River to the confluence of the western Neisse River and along the western Neisse to the Czechoslovak frontier, shall constitute the western State frontier of the People's Republic of Poland.

2. They reaffirm the inviolability of their existing frontiers now and in the future and undertake to respect each other's territorial integrity without restriction.

3. They declare that they have no territorial claims whatsoever against each other and that they will not assert such claims in the future.

Article II

1. The Federal Republic of Germany and the People's Republic of Poland shall in their mutual relations as well as in matters of ensuring European and international security be guided by the purposes and principles embodied in the Charter of the United Nations.

2. Accordingly they shall, pursuant to Articles 1 and 2 of the Charter of the United Nations, settle all their disputes exclusively by peaceful means and refrain from any threat or use of force in matters affecting European and international security and in their mutual relations.

Article III

1. The Federal Republic of Germany and the People's Republic of Poland shall take further steps towards full normalization and a comprehensive development of their mutual relations of which the present Treaty shall form the solid foundation.

2. They agree that a broadening of their co-operation in the sphere of economic, scientific, technological, cultural and other relations is in their mutual interest.

Article IV

The present Treaty shall not affect any bilateral or multilateral international arrangements previously concluded by either Contracting Party or concerning them.

Article V

The present Treaty is subject to ratification and shall enter into force on the date of exchange of the instruments of ratification which shall take place in Bonn.

IN WITNESS WHEREOF, the Plenipotentiaries of the Contracting Parties have signed the present Treaty.

DONE at Warsaw on . . . in two originals, each in the German and Polish languages, both texts being equally authentic.

Note Verbale transmitted to the Embassy of the United Kingdom of Great Britain and Northern Ireland, 19 November 1970[1]

... The Government of the Federal Republic of Germany has the honour to inform the Government of the United Kingdom of Great Britain and Northern Ireland of the attached text of a Treaty between the Federal Republic of Germany and the People's Republic of Poland concerning the Basis for Normalizing their Mutual Relations, which was initialled on 18 November 1970 in Warsaw.

In the course of the negotiations which took place between the Government of the Federal Republic of Germany and the Government of the People's Republic of Poland concerning this Treaty, it was made clear by the Federal Government that the Treaty between the Federal Republic of Germany and the People's Republic of Poland does not and cannot affect the rights and responsibilities of the French Republic, the United Kingdom of Great Britain and Northern Ireland, the Union of Soviet Socialist Republics, and the United States of America as reflected in the known treaties and agreements. The Federal Government further pointed out that it could only act on behalf of the Federal Republic of Germany.

The Government of the French Republic and the Government of the United States of America have received identical notes.

Reply of the United Kingdom Government to the Federal Republic's Note Verbale, 19 November 1970

... Her Majesty's Government in the United Kingdom have the honour to inform the Government of the Federal Republic of Germany that they have received the Note of the Government of the Federal Republic of Germany of 19 November 1970, enclosing the text of the Treaty between the Federal Republic of Germany and the People's Republic of Poland concerning the Basis for Normalizing their Mutual Relations, which was initialled on 18 November 1970 in Warsaw and reading as follows:

Her Majesty's Government note with approval the initialling of the Treaty. They share the position that the Treaty does not and cannot affect the rights and responsibilities of the Four Powers as reflected in the known treaties and agreements.

[1] *Survival*, Feb. 1971, pp. 69-72.

Information by the Government of the People's Republic of Poland on measures for a solution of humanitarian problems

1. In 1955 the Polish Government recommended the Polish Red Cross to conclude an agreement with the Red Cross of the Federal Republic of Germany on the reunion of families; under that agreement, roughly one quarter of a million people left Poland up to 1959. Between 1960 and 1969, an additional 150,000 people have departed from Poland under normal procedures. In carrying out measures to reunite families, the Polish Government has been guided above all by humanitarian motives. However, it could not, and still cannot, agree that its favourable attitude regarding such reunions be exploited for the emigration of Polish nationals for employment purposes.

2. To this day, there have remained in Poland for various reasons (e.g. close ties with their place of birth) a certain number of persons of indisputable ethnic German origin and persons from mixed families whose predominant feeling over the past years has been that they belong to that ethnic group. The Polish Government still holds the view that any persons who owing to their indisputable ethnic German origin wish to leave for either of the two German States may do so subject to the laws and regulations applicable in Poland.

Furthermore, consideration will be given to the situation of mixed and separated families as well as to such cases of Polish nationals who, either because of their changed family situation or because they have changed their earlier decision, express the wish to be reunited with near relatives in the Federal Republic of Germany or in the German Democratic Republic.

3. The appropriate Polish authorities have not received anything like the number of applications from persons wishing to leave the country for the FRG as is maintained in the FRG. According to the inquiries so far made by the Polish authorities some tens of thousands of people may fall under the criteria possibly entitling to leaving Poland for the FRG or the GDR. The Polish Government will therefore issue appropriate instructions for careful examination of whether the applications submitted are justified, and for their early consideration.

The Polish Government will authorize the Polish Red Cross to receive from the Red Cross of the FRG lists of the persons whose applications are held by the German Red Cross in order that they may be compared with the lists held by the appropriate Polish authorities, and carefully examined.

4. Co-operation between the Polish Red Cross and the Red Cross of the FRG will be facilitated in any way necessary. The Polish Red Cross will be authorized to receive from the German Red Cross explanatory comments on the lists, and will inform the German Red Cross of the outcome of examinations by the Polish authorities of transmitted applications. The Polish Red Cross will further be authorized to consider jointly with the Red Cross of the FRG all practical questions that might arise from this action.

5. As regards the movements of persons in connection with visits to relatives, the appropriate Polish authorities will, after the entry into force of the Treaty concerning the Basis for Normalizing Relations between the two States, apply the same principles as are customary with regard to other States of Western Europe.

SELECT BIBLIOGRAPHY

(*Note*: AP = Adelphi Papers, published by the Institute of
Strategic Studies, London.)

Albert, E. H. The Brandt doctrine of the two states in Germany. *International Affairs*, Apr. 1970.
Allemann, F. R. Berlin and the four-power talks. *German Tribune Q.*, Dec. 1970.
Ashkenasi, Abraham. Reformpartei und Aussenpolitik. *Aussenpolitik*, Dec. 1966.
Aue, Gilbert von. Der Rechtsstaatlichkeit entgegen—Dubcek betreibt Europäisierung der CSSR. *Politische Welt*, Mar. 1968.
Barzel, Rainer. *Gesichtspunkt eines Deutschen.* Düsseldorf, 1968.
Bechtoldt, Heinrich. Kiesinger und die deutsche Aussenpolitik. *Aussenpolitik*, Dec. 1966.
—— Zur Ostpolitik der neuen Bundesregierung. *Aussenpolitik*, Nov. 1969.
Bender, Peter. *Offensive Entspannung: Möglichkeit für Deutschland.* Cologne, 1964.
—— *Zehn Gründe für die Anerkennung der DDR.* Frankfurt a/M., 1968.
—— Inside the Warsaw pact. *Survey*, Winter 1970.
Bethell, N. W. *Baron Bethell, Gomulka, his Poland and his communism.* London, 1969.
Billington, James H. Force and counter force in Eastern Europe. *Foreign Affairs*, Oct. 1968.
Binder, Gerhart. *Deutschland seit 1945: eine dokumentierte gesamtdeutsche Geschichte in der Zeit der Teilung.* Stuttgart, 1969.
Bing, W. *Zum Problem der Investionsfinanzierung in der Zentralverwaltungswirtschaft; Analyse des Princips der Eigenerwirtschaftung von Investitionsmitteln in der DDR.* Stuttgart, 1970.
Birnbaum, Immanuel. *Entzweite Nachbarn: deutsche Politik in Osteuropa.* Frankfurt a/M., 1968.
Birnbaum, Karl E. *Peace in Europe.* London, 1970.
Bjøl, Erling. The USSR, détente and the future of NATO. *Orbis*, Spring 1969.
Bluhm, Georg. *Die Oder-Neisse-Linie in der deutschen Aussenpolitik.* Freiburg, 1963.
Brandt, Willy. *A peace policy for Europe.* London, 1969.
Brzezinski, Z. K. *Alternative to partition: for a broader conception of America's role in Europe.* New York, 1965.
—— *The Soviet bloc.* Rev. ed. Harvard, 1967.
—— The framework of East–West reconciliation. *Foreign Affairs*, Jan. 1968.
—— *Dilemmas of change in Soviet politics.* New York, 1969.
Buchan, Alastair, ed. *Europe's futures, Europe's choices: models of Western Europe in the 1970s.* London, 1969.
Burton, J. W. *Systems, states, diplomacy and rules.* Cambridge, 1968.

Childs, David. *East Germany.* New York, 1969.

Conquest, Robert. Stalin's successors. *Foreign Affairs,* Apr. 1970.

Conze, Werner. *Das deutsche-russische Verhältnis im Wandel der modernen Welt.* Göttingen, 1967.

Croan, Melvin. Bonn and Pankow: intra-German politics. *Survey,* Apr. 1968.

Dahrendorf, Ralf. *Society and Democracy in Germany.* London, 1968.

Dallin, Alexander & Thomas B. Larson, eds. *Soviet politics since Khrushchev.* Englewood Cliffs, NJ, 1968.

Duchêne, François. SALT, the *Ostpolitik,* and the post-cold war context. *The World Today,* Dec. 1970.

Dulles, Eleanor Lansing. *One Germany or two: the struggle in the heart of Europe.* Palo Alto, Calif., 1970.

Ersil, Wilhelm & Harold Rose. Problem of a European conference for security and cooperation (mimeo, for Bucharest Conference on European Security, 1970).

Fainsod, Merle. Some reflections on Soviet-American relations. *Am. Pol. Sci. R.,* Dec. 1968.

Falk, W. & others. *Wirtschaft, Wissenschaft, Welthöchststand; Vom Werden und Wachsen der sozialistischen Wirtschaftsmacht DDR.* Berlin, 1969.

Fedoseev, B. N. & others. *Sotsiologicheskie problemy mezhdunarodnykh otnoshenii.* Moscow, 1970.

Fijalkowski, Jürgen & others. *Berlin, Hauptstadtsanspruch und Westintegration. (Schriften des Instituts für politische Wissenschaft,* Bd. 20.) Cologne, 1967.

Förster, Wolfgang & Detlef Lorenz, eds. *Beiträge zur Theorie und Praxis von Wirtschaftssystemen; Festgabe für Karl C. Thalheim zum 70, Geburtstag.* Berlin, 1970.

German Democratic Republic, Staatliche Zentralverwaltung. *Statistisches Jahrbuch (1969) der DDR.* East Berlin, 1969.

The German Democratic Republic at the beginning of its third decade. Dresden, 1969.

Germany, Federal Republic, Auswärtiges Amt. *Die Bemühungen der deutschen Regierung und ihrer Verbündeten um die Einheit Deutschlands, 1955–66.* Bonn, 1966.

—— Bundesministerium für gesamtdeutsche Fragen. *Texte zur Deutschlandspolitik: 13 Dez. 1966–5 Okt. 1967.* Bonn, 1967.

Glaser, Hermann & Stahl, K. H. *Opposition in der Bundesrepublik.* Freiburg, 1968.

Görlich, J. W. *Geist und Macht in der DDR: die Integration der kommunistischen Ideologie.* Olten, 1968.

Grewe, Wilhelm. The effect of strategic agreements on European-American relations. AP, no. 65, Feb. 1970.

Grosser, Alfred. France and Germany: less divergent outlooks. *Foreign Affairs,* Jan. 1970.

Hacker, Jens. Konstanten in der sowjetischen Deutschland-Politik. *Osteuropa,* May–June 1968.

Hadik, Laszlo. The process of détente in Europe. *Orbis,* Winter, 1970.

Hanhardt, Arthur M. *The German Democratic Republic*. Baltimore, 1969.

Hassner, Pierre. Change and security in Europe; i & ii. ΛP, nos. 45 & 49, 1968.

—— The implications of change in Eastern Europe for the Atlantic Alliance. *Orbis*, Spring 1969.

—— The USSR since Khrushchev. *Survey*, Spring 1969.

Holst, Johann Jørgen. Parity, superiority or sufficiency? Some remarks on the nature and future of the Soviet-American strategic relationship. AP, no. 65, Feb. 1970.

Hubatsch, Walther & others. *The German question* [documents]. New York, 1967.

Jacobs, Dan. N., ed. *The new communisms*. New York, 1969.

Johnson, A. R. Poland, the end of the post-October era. *Survey*, July 1968.

Johnson, Chalmers, ed. *Change in communist systems*, Stanford, 1970.

Kaiser, Karl. *German foreign policy in transition; Bonn between east and west*. London, 1968.

—— Deutsche Aussenpolitik nach der tschechoslowakischen Krise von 1968. *Europa-Archiv*, 25 May 1969.

—— & Roger Morgan, eds. *Britain and West Germany; changing societies and the role of foreign policy*. London, 1971.

Kaysen, Carl. East and West in Europe: an American view. AP, no. 33, Mar. 1967.

Kelleher, Catherine M. The issue of German nuclear armament. *Proc. Acad. Polit. Sci.*, Nov. 1968.

Kintner, William R. & Harriet Fast Scott. *The nuclear revolution in Soviet military affairs*. Norman, Oklahoma UP, 1968.

Kissinger, Henry. Das Dilemma der Macht. *Die Zeit*, 6 Dec. 1968.

—— *American foreign policy*. London, 1969.

Klemperer, Klemenz von. *Germany's new conservatism, its history and dilemma in the twentieth century*. Princeton UP, 1968.

Kolkowicz, Roman. *The Warsaw pact*. Arlington, Va., 1967.

—— The Warsaw pact: entangling alliance. *Survey*, Winter 1969.

Korbel, Josef. German-Soviet relations: the past and prospects. *Orbis*, Winter 1967.

—— West Germany's Ostpolitik. *Orbis*, Winter & Summer, 1970.

Korbonski, Andrzei. *The Warsaw Pact*. New York, 1969.

Kovrig, Bennett. Spheres of influence: a reassessment. *Survey*, Winter 1969.

Krengel, Rolf. *Die Bedeutung des Ost-West-Handel für die Ost-West-Beziehungen*. Göttingen, 1967.

Laloy, Jean. Prospects and limits of East–West relations. AP, no. 33, Mar. 1967.

Leonhard, Wolfgang & others. The future of the Soviet Union. *Interplay*, 2/10, 1969.

Leptin, Gert. ' Das " neue ökonomische System " Mitteldeutschlands ', *in* Thalheim, Karl C. & H.-H. Hohmann, eds. *Wirtschaftsreformen in Osteuropa*. Cologne, 1968.

Levine, I. D. *Intervention: the causes and consequences of the invasion of Czechoslovakia.* New York, 1969.

Löwenthal, Richard. The sparrow in the cage. *Problems of Communism,* Nov.–Dec. 1968.

—— Changing Soviet policies and interests. AP, no. 66, Mar. 1970.

—— ed. *Ist der Osten noch ein Block?* Stuttgart, 1967.

Mackintosh, Malcolm. The evolution of the Warsaw Pact. AP, no. 58, June 1969.

Maillard, Pierre. The effect of China on Soviet-American relations. AP, no. 66, Mar. 1970.

Majonica, Ernst. *Möglichkeiten und Grenzen der deutschen Aussenpolitik.* Stuttgart, 1964.

Manescu, Corneliu. Rumania in the Concert of Nations. *International Affairs,* Jan. 1969.

Mann, Golo. *Verzicht oder Forderung? Die deutschen Ostgrenzen.* Freiburg, 1964.

Markert, Werner, ed. *Deutsch-russische Beziehungen von Bismarck bis zur Gegenwart.* Stuttgart, 1964.

Meissner, Boris. Die Breshnew-Doktrin. *Osteuropa,* Sept. 1969.

Meissner, H. *Konvergenztheorie und Realität.* East Berlin, 1969.

Morrison, J. F. *The Polish People's Republic.* Baltimore, 1969.

Noelle, Elisabeth & E. P. Neumann, eds. *The German public opinion polls 1947–66.* Allensbach, 1967.

Oschlies, Wolf. Die Tchechoslowakei nach Dubcek: der ' *verspätete* ' Januar. *Osteuropa,* Aug. 1969.

Pipes, Richard. Russia's mission, America' destiny. *Encounter,* Oct. 1970.

Planck, Charles R. *The changing status of German reunification in Western diplomacy: 1955–66.* Baltimore, 1967.

Pörzgen, Hermann. Why Moscow wanted the treaty. *Survival,* Oct. 1970.

Probleme der politischen Ökonomie, Bd. 12 (Sammelband, *Jahrbuch des Instituts für Wirtschaftswissenschafte der Deutschen Akademie der Wissenschaften*). Berlin, 1969.

Rasch, Harold. *Bonn und Moskau.* Stuttgart, 1969.

Remington, R. A. Czechoslovakia and the Warsaw pact. *East European Q.,* Sept. 1968.

—— *Winter in Prague, documents on Czechoslovak communism in crisis.* Cambridge, Mass., 1969.

Riklin, Alos. *Weltrevolution oder Koexistenz.* Zürich, 1969.

Roberts, H. L. *Eastern Europe: politics, revolution, and diplomacy.* New York, 1970.

Schapiro, Leonard. Collective lack of leadership. *Survey,* Winter–Spring 1969.

Schenk, Fritz. *Das rote Wirtschaftswunder. Die zentrale Planwirtschaft als Machtmittel der SED-Politik.*

Schick, Jack M. The Berlin crisis of 1961 and US military strategy. *Orbis,* Winter 1965.

Schmidt, Helmut. *Strategie des Gleichgewichts.* Stuttgart, 1969.

Schollwer, Wolfgang. *Deutschland- und Aussenpolitik.* Frankfurt, 1968.

Schütz, W. W. *Deutschland-Memorandum: eine Denkschrift und ihre Folgen.* Frankfurt a/M., 1968.

Shulman, Marshall D. ' Relations with the Soviet Union ', *in* Kermit Gordon, ed. *Agenda for the nation.* New York, 1968.

—— The future of the Soviet-American competition. AP, no. 66, Mar. 1970.

Skilling, G. H. *The governments of communist East Europe.* New York, 1968.

Sommer, Theo. Bonn changes course. *Foreign Affairs,* Apr. 1967.

—— A chance for Europe. *Survival,* June 1969.

—— Détente and security: the options. AP, no. 70, Nov. 1970.

Starobin, Joseph R. The prospects of evolution. *Problems of Communism,* Jan.–Feb. 1970.

Staron, Stanislaw. Political developments in Poland: the party reacts to challenge. *Orbis,* Winter 1970.

Stehle, Hansjakob. *Nachbar Polen.* Rev. ed. Frankfurt a/M., 1968.

Stern, Carola. ' East Germany ', *in* W. E. Griffith, ed., *Communism in Europe.* Cambridge, Mass., 1966.

Strauss, Franz Josef. *Challenge and response: a programme for Europe.* London, 1970.

Sugar, P. F. & I. J. Lederer. *Nationalism in Eastern Europe.* Seattle, 1969.

Szamuely, Tibor. The USSR since Khrushchev. *Survey,* Spring 1969.

Tatu, Michael. *Power in the Kremlin.* London, 1968.

—— The East: détente and confrontation. AP, no. 70, Nov. 1970.

Tigrid, Pavel. *Le printemps de Prague.* Paris, 1968.

Triska, Jan. F., ed. *Communist party-states.* Indianapolis, 1969.

Ulbricht, Walter. *On questions of socialist construction in the GDR: Speeches by Walter Ulbricht.* Dresden, 1969.

Vali, Ferenc A. *The quest for a united Germany.* Baltimore, 1967.

Wagner, Wolfgang. Aussenpolitik nach dem Regierungswechsel. *Europa-Archiv,* 22/1969.

—— Basic requirements and consequences of the government's Ostpolitik. *German Tribune Q.,* Dec. 1970.

Waterkamp, Rainer. Politische Optionen für die Europa- und Deutschland-Frage. *Aussenpolitik,* Jan. 1969.

Whetten, L. L. The legal basis for Soviet military presence in Czechoslovakia, *R. de Droit international* (Geneva), Nov.–Dec. 1969.

Windsor, Philip. *German reunification.* London, 1969.

Wolfe, Thomas W. *Soviet Power and Europe.* 2 vols. Rand Corporation, 1968–9.

Yearbook on international communist affairs, 1966–. Ed. by Richard V. Allen. Palo Alto, Calif., Hoover Inst., 1968–.

Zeman, Z. A. B. *Prague spring.* Harmondsworth, 1969.

Zimmermann, William. *Soviet perspectives on international relations: 1956–67.* Princeton UP, 1969.

INDEX

237